ONE PASSION, TWO LOVES

ONE PASSION, TWO LOVES

THE STORY OF HEINRICH AND SOPHIA SCHLIEMANN, DISCOVERERS OF TROY

BY LYNN AND GRAY POOLE

THOMAS Y. CROWELL COMPANY
NEW YORK
ESTABLISHED 1834

 DESIGNED BY JUDITH WORACEK BARRY. MANUFACTURED IN THE UNITED STATES OF AMERICA. LIBRARY OF CONGRESS CATALOG CARD NO. 66-25434

1 2 3 4 5 6 7 8 9 10

THIS BOOK IS DEDICATED TO THE MEMORY OF

HEINRICH AND SOPHIA SCHLIEMANN

Ῥητὸν γὰρ οὐδαμῶς ἐστιν ὡς ἄλλα μαθήματα, ἀλλ' ἐκ πολλῆς συνουσίας γιγνομένης περὶ τὸ πρᾶγμα αὐτὸ καὶ τοῦ συζῆν ἐξαίφνης οἷον ἀπὸ πυρὸς πηδήσαντος ἐξαφθὲν φῶς ἐν τῇ ψυχῇ γενόμενον αὐτὸ ἑαυτὸ ἤδη τρέφει.

PLATO, EPISTLES VII. 841 C.

"There is no way of putting it into words like other studies, but after much communion and constant intercourse with the thing itself suddenly, like a light kindled from a leaping fire, it is born within the soul and henceforth nourishes itself."

Alex L. Mélas, Schliemann's last living grandchild, gave invaluable assistance with long-guarded family material and newly discovered letters of his grandparents. The little-finger ring is his sole possession from the excavated treasures.

FOREWORD

BY ALEX L. MÉLAS

It is half past midnight. The air over Athens tonight is chilly, but there is a full moon. My own heart is brightened by the manuscript of the book written by Mr. Lynn and Madame Gray Poole about my grandparents, Heinrich and Sophia Schliemann.

After lunch today, I began reading what my friends wrote, and I was filled with great emotion and pride over how my grandparents come alive in this book. Night arrived and the full moon came up over the Hills of Hymettus and made the columns of the Temple of Olympian Zeus cast sharp shadows. I see the Hills and Temple from one balcony of my apartment; from the other side I see the moon shining on the Parthenon, on the Acropolis, "the Sacred Rock," as we call it.

I stood up from my armchair, where I sat watching this beautiful night. I walked to the balcony and, impulsively, I looked toward the templelike mausoleum where Heinrich, Sophia, and all the other dead members of my family are entombed. My eyes blurred and I could feel the souls of my grandparents wandering into my living room, guiding my hand to trace these lines, as I left the balcony and started to write. The night was so quiet, so beautiful and so serene. The only sound was my fast-pounding heart which said, "Thanks God, at last someone has written the truth about my grandparents who devoted their life to archaeology, created a science of this art, and brought forth, for the world to see, the ancient Trojan and Mycenaean civilization, as the great Homer wrote in his poems."

I also thanked my lucky stars for the day I met the Pooles, who have since become my dear friends. I knew at once that I had found two people to whom I could entrust memorabilia that previously I had refused to give to any other biographers.

After many talks, Lynn Poole said to me, "There is no reason merely to write another book about their archaeological excavations. The book that must be written is one about Heinrich and Sophia as two great, unique people and about the lives they lived. To accomplish this we must relive their lives if we are to understand them and tell their personal story." Truly, the Pooles have actually "lived with" Heinrich and Sophia Schliemann through these years, as they sought for every clue to their character and dug into old and newly found records to interpret what the young Greek girl, Sophia, and the German man, Heinrich, contributed to the world. The Pooles searched in seven nations for facts included in this book.

How deep and clear is the authors' thought in so many places throughout the book! Even I was startled from time to time by some of their new interpretations, based on facts never before realized. One example concerns the gold treasure of Troy. Everyone has written that the treasure was found in a copper box. The Pooles read and reread the diaries, letters, cables, articles and books. They are certain—and I am sure they are correct—that there never was a copper box, only a copper shield hiding the treasure, which had originally been placed in a wooden box.

They have told for the first time the true story of how Heinrich and Sophia met. Research and refusal to accept apochryphal accounts have shown there is no evidence to support the theory that Heinrich's major objective in excavating Troy was to find gold. My grandfather had more gold than he needed; he worked and earned it, then spent vast sums of his own money on his excavations. He did not need gold from Troy to add to his personal fortunes.

Many times we worked together in Athens for unending hours, poring over new archives, which by mere luck were found locked and forgotten in an old trunk in a basement of an Athenian house. This trunk contained twenty-nine diplomas from the most important universities, archaeological institutes and societies, museums, and governments of the time, together with letters from the most prominent men of the nineteenth century. In addition there was intimate correspondence of Heinrich and Sophia, in five different languages, according to which country they were writing from. Here we discovered letters of Heinrich's last weeks in Halle where he suffered surgical operations. I am happy that I could make these treasures, along with other data from our family records, available to the Pooles.

As my friends searched for new information throughout the world, we three worked together, communicating by letter, cable and telephone across the Atlantic, from Athens to Baltimore, Maryland.

Over these years, the Pooles and I have made our own odyssey, tracing step by step, scene by scene, motivation by motivation, the lives of my grandparents.

A little more than an hour ago, as I stood in the cemetery beside the mausoleum of my grandparents I felt sure that they know what has now been written. In the life after death, where they are joined together, they know that at last the story of their life has been set down with truth and understanding.

Who can be certain that the dead do not know what the living perform? No one can be certain. But I am sure they do know and rest better in peace. They were both somewhat superstitious. They believed their own dreams. They believed, too, in metempsychosis and transmigration. So why, as their grandson, should I not believe that Heinrich and Sophia were with us as *One Passion, Two Loves* was being written.

I was born in Iliou Mélathron and spent the most and best time of my life in that beautiful Palace in Athens, the home where for ten years Heinrich and Sophia lived, with the world of great men passing through their doors. I grew up hearing my grandmother, Sophia, and my mother, Sophia's daughter, Andromache, repeat again and again—always the same—the stories of the Schliemanns' life together. I read the many letters and diaries of my grandparents. Most of all, I saw the light of love in Sophia's eyes each time she spoke of Heinrich, until the day she died in 1932, invoking her beloved husband's name.

Because I had this privilege, I am certain that my grandparents know what has been written now and are content; as I am happy and honored being their last living grandchild.

Athens, Greece

ACKNOWLEDGMENTS

On September 28, 1963, we met Alex L. Mélas, only living grandchild of Heinrich and Sophia Schliemann. We were in Athens, participating in the Greek Heritage Symposium on Hellenic Culture, being held at the Grande Bretagne Hotel. Christopher G. Janus, publisher of *Greek Heritage Quarterly,* was eager for us to know his old friend General Mélas. The introduction made by Mr. Janus was significant for us. It concluded many years of avocational study of the lives of Dr. Schliemann and his wife, and marked the beginning of purposeful research for the writing of *One Passion, Two Loves.*

General Mélas made available to us vast amounts of family material that he had not previously shown to any author. There was also for our use the tremendous collection of Schliemann memorabilia in the Gennadius Library of the American School of Classical Studies in Athens. We sought verification and amplification of data in letters, diaries and other source material from numberless people in several countries. We did research in West Berlin, East Berlin, Paris and London. In these cities and in many villages on the Continent we found information vital to an in-depth understanding of Heinrich and Sophia Schliemann. Newspapers in Greek archives, in German, French and British repositories, shed light on facts not used by other authors; cleared up misconceptions previously written.

During extended visits to Athens we were sought out by Greeks, strangers to us, who had heard we were searching for information about Heinrich and Sophia Schliemann. An old priest brought us a well-worn book with an illustration of the church of St. Meletios as it was when Heinrich and Sophia were married there on September 23, 1869; two icons pictured are on the altar of the present church of St. Meletios. Collateral descendants of the Schliemanns had hitherto unpublished pictures of members of the family. One such remote relative presented us with an engraved calling card of

Dr. Heinrich Schliemann; a notation on it in Schliemann's own handwriting provided the missing link to an important chain of events. Many cooperative informants respectively offered tiny bits of information that proved to be invaluable to the total work. These are but a few examples of contributions made by warmhearted and wonderful Greeks.

In the fall of 1965 a locked trunk filled with 750 Schliemann letters and other memorabilia was discovered in Athens. We were privileged to have sole access to those letters, which revealed previously unknown data about the personal and professional lives of Heinrich and Sophia.

Facts used in this book have been taken from many long known documents and from original sources we used while doing intensive research. When we state in our narrative that "Sophia felt" or "Heinrich thought," we are factually reporting from letters, diaries, articles, books and other written memorabilia of both Heinrich and Sophia Schliemann, including long-missing documents stored in the trunk in Athens; we are not reporting what someone else said or thought about the Schliemanns.

Like all authors of biography, we are indebted to many more people than we can ever properly thank for assistance in seeking out source material.

Our first and deepest thanks go to Alex L. Mélas whose faith in us was confirmed by his generous sharing of the wealth of family material that he had so assiduously guarded through the years. General Mélas gave of his time and energies to help us whenever we were working in Greece and to advise us by correspondence when we were far from Athens. Through the happy years of our research on this book about his illustrious grandparents, he aided us with enthusiasm. He provided written and photographic evidence we needed to tell the personal story of the lives of Heinrich and Sophia Schliemann. The depth and scope of our book would not have been possible without the assistance and collaboration of General Mélas.

We are grateful to Christopher G. Janus, publisher of *Greek Heritage Quarterly,* for the original introduction to Alex Mélas and for continued interest and enthusiasm throughout the project.

We owe an immeasurable debt to Dr. Francis R. Walton, Librarian of the Gennadius Library in Athens, his assistant librarian

Miss Eurydice Demetracopoulou, and Miss Loukia Frangouli of the library staff. To Professor Henry Robinson, Director of the American School of Classical Studies, we pay respects and appreciation for his aid since our first meeting in 1962.

We express our thanks for valuable assistance and hospitality to D. Papaefstratiou, former Director General of the Greek National Tourist Office in Athens, and his associates, T. Frangopoulos and C. Gondikas; to George Canellos, General Manager of the Grande Bretagne Hotel, who was interested in our project and arranged interviews with many people, including the grandson of Yannakis, Schliemann's faithful overseer at Troy; to Brian Bojonell, Director of the Athens' office of Pan American World Airways, whose advice on many vital matters was ebullient and productive. With special pleasure we acknowledge the kind aid and productive assistance given by Iason Antoniades while we were in Greece.

We take pleasure in expressing our special thanks to Professor Emil Kuntze, Director of the German Archaeological Institute in Athens, and his assistant Mrs. Maria Tzannetokos, for making available rare items and specific information, as well as permission to use photographs which we selected and they provided; to Professor George E. Mylonas of Washington University in St. Louis, Missouri, currently director of excavations at Mycenae, for his enthusiastic encouragement and assistance; to Professor Oscar Broneer, who, having lived and excavated for more than forty years in Greece, gave us vital direction and provided important information about many episodes in our book; to Professor Carl Blegen whose discussions of his own excavations at Troy, long after Schliemann's death, were of incalculable help, not only with facts but in adding to our own understanding of Schliemann's work and his place in history.

We would be grossly remiss if we did not pay our respects to His Excellency Alexander Matsas, Greek Ambassador to the United States of America, for his encouragement and enthusiasm, his personal and official assistance for more than three years.

We are indebted to the late Professor Dimitri Papadimitriou, who talked with us often about Schliemann's role in the growth of archaeological investigation. While lunching beside the water at Tourcolimano at the Piraeus, Professor Papadimitriou approved our writing down his statement that, "Schliemann was the father of a totally new approach to archaeology and without him we might well still be in the dark ages of knowledge about the Mycenaen civilization." Professor George Mylonas added his belief and emphasis to Papadimitriou's conclusion. With this fact many modern archaeologists agree, in spite of the manner in which Schliemann slashed through the Hill of Hissarlik where he uncovered the cities of Troy.

Our brief thanks to the following is not commensurate with the extent of their contributions to our research:

Aileen M. Armstrong, secretary of the Royal Historical Society, London; Edward Bacon, Archaeological Editor of the *Illustrated London News;* Werner Brussau, professor at the Free University of West Berlin; Professor Heinrich Bleich, Director, Stadt. Archive, Mannheim, Germany; Sir Tranchard Cox, Director of the Victoria and Albert Museum, London; D. M. Day of the British Embassy in Washington, D.C.; Dr. Sterling Dow, Harvard University; Edward J. Dziczkowski of Frankfurt, Germany; Sir Frank Francis, Director, British Museum, London; Sir William Haley, Editor, the London *Times;* Dr. W. J. van Hoboken, Director of the City Archives, Amsterdam; Dr. Willy Gellert, Mannheim, Germany; C. H. Gibbs-Smith, Keeper of the Department of Education, Victoria and Albert Museum, London; George Kastriotes, sculptor, painter and great-grandson of Sophia Schliemann's brother, Alexandros; Dr. William G. Niederland, psychoanalyst who made a year's study of Heinrich Schliemann from records in the Gennadius Library; The Honorable Henry Richardson Labouisse, United States Ambassador to Greece, 1962–65; Dr. Roger Lyon, Cultural Counsellor of the Mission of the United States of America to West Berlin; Miss Jean K. Macdonald, secretary to the Royal Archaeological Society of Great Britain and Ireland; The Honorable Stephanos K. Galetes, Director of the Foundation of the Society of Friends of Education, Athens, Greece; Lanning MacFarland, Chicago Philhellene; Miss Nanon Manotopoulos, knowledgeable translator in Athens; Edouard Morot-Sir, Cultural Counsellor, Embassy of France, Washington, D.C.; Dr. Werner Mueller and his assistant Dr. Henrika Hesse of the Near Eastern Division, Staatliche Museum in East Germany; Professor Adrian von Mueller and Professor Wolfram Nagel of the Museum fuer Von-und Freuhgeschichte of West Berlin; Mrs. S. Riccardi,

Chief, Newspaper Section of the New York Public Library, New York City; A. M. Michael Robb, A.M. CMG, Minister, British Embassy, Washington, D.C.; Professor James Poultney, Department of Classics, The Johns Hopkins University, Baltimore, Maryland; Bruno J. Schroeder, the Henry Schroeder Company, London; Carsten Seecamp, Department of German, The Johns Hopkins University; The Honorable C. T. Rolf van Baarda, Minister, Embassy of the Netherlands, Washington, D.C.; Peter-Nick Vavalis, of Athens, Greece, who helped prepare the book *Schliemann in Indianapolis,* and who aided us whiie in Athens; Dr. John H. Young, professor of classics at The Johns Hopkins University, and his wife, also a classical scholar and archaeologist.

To Hugh Rawson, editor of *One Passion, Two Loves,* we extend our gratitude for his great contributions from manuscript to printed page.

To all who made it possible for us to prepare this book, and to all who smoothed our path and offered true Hellenic hospitality we say *Efkaristo,* a single word conveying the true depths of our affection and appreciation.

LYNN AND GRAY POOLE

Baltimore, Maryland

Appendix A, an address given by Madame Schliemann for The Royal Archaeological Institute of Great Britain and Ireland, will be found on page 285.

Appendix B, some facts and suppositions about the fate of the Schliemann Collection, will be found on page 289.

The index begins on page 291.

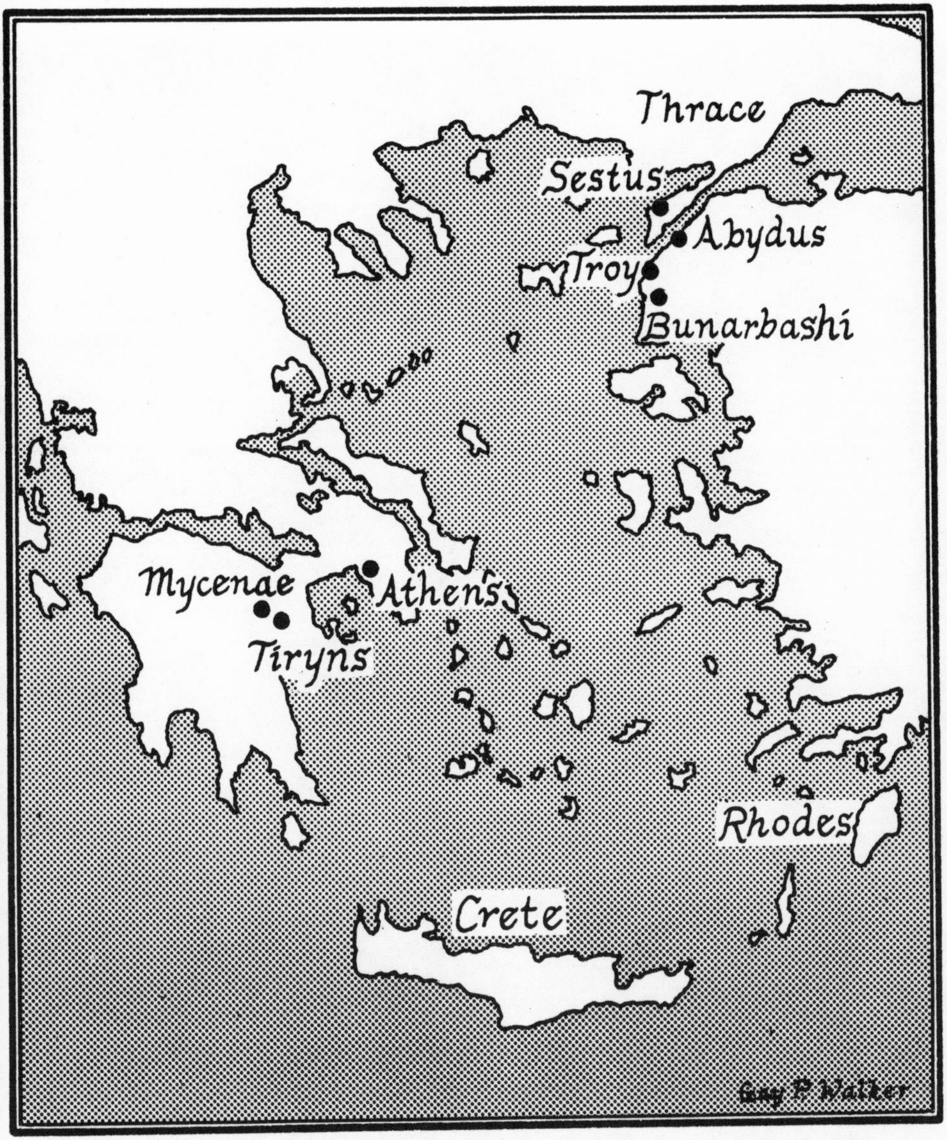

The Aegean and Asia Minor

ONE

As the S/S *Niemen*, out of Marseille, slowly approached the harbor of Piraeus, a middle-aged man, restlessly pacing the upper deck, stared at a small photograph clutched in his right hand. With the Greek port in sight on that September morning of 1869, Dr. Heinrich Schliemann was impatient to land. World citizen, self-made scholar, and international financier, he was about to start a new life as excavator searching for prehistoric Troy, and as bridegroom of a teen-age wife. It was her photograph he held; brown eyes, wide-set and with an expression as serious as his own, were the outstanding feature of the beautiful girl pictured. He peered intently at the young face, marking the conformation, the texture and the quality, all long familiar from deep study of the photograph. On the back of the frayed print, its edges torn and split by frequent handling, the name *Sophia* was scribbled.

Landing boats were close to the *Niemen* and its anchor chains clanking before Schliemann jammed the photograph into the pocket of his loose-fitting summer suit and rapidly went below. With the efficiency of an experienced traveler, he counted his luggage stacked by prearrangement for speedy removal from the ship. Schliemann's voice, reedy and high-pitched, had nonetheless a tone of authority that spurred into action the unloading crew and the captain of a small boat at the liner's side. Schliemann gave orders to deckhands in French and to the boatman in Greek, accenting the words with imperious gestures. His landing boat, shortly piled high with valises, packing cases and small trunks, reached the quay before any other; and Schliemann, the first passenger ashore, was also first at the railroad station.

A train to Athens was pulling away, and Schliemann sputtered with agitation when told that another would not leave for two hours. Moody and preoccupied, he fretted through the delay, intolerable to him. Irritation welled again when there was no carriage at the Athens station, and he had to walk to the hotel in the heat of the day. Moving with graceless gait, he entered the lobby of the Hotel d'Angleterre and signed his name on the register's page dated September 2, 1869. The staff of the hotel rallied for a cordial welcome to their returning guest, but he cut short the amenities in his haste to get on with arrangements for his marriage, the purpose of his visit to Athens.

Schliemann's compulsive drive toward the immediate realization of any project was deeply ingrained. In early life he overcame the handicaps of poverty, illness and lack of education, achieving the successful status that was to permit the pursuit of his future goal. In quest of knowledge, he traveled to many lands, everywhere attempting to separate legend and lore from history and fact. He walked the Great Wall of China and penetrated the jungles of Peru, Mexico and Chile; he crisscrossed the United States and traipsed the deserts of Arabia.

He grasped every opportunity to make the money that was essential to the financing of excavation of Troy. Leaving a flourishing business in Russia, the German-born Schliemann traveled to California, on a family matter, and made a fortune in the gold rush before returning to St. Petersburg, where he amassed enormous wealth. He was a profiteer of the Crimean War, justifying himself by saying the cash was needed to prove that Homer wrote history and Troy was a real place. Later he wrote, "I loved money, indeed, but solely as the means of realizing the one passion of my life—to find Troy." No more realistic than romantic, he wanted a Greek wife at his side while he searched for Troy.

After a miserable marriage with a physically frigid, emotionally selfish, and intellectually sterile Russian woman, he arranged to divorce her in the United States at Indianapolis. While there, he began negotiations for an Hellenic bride. Photographs of matrimonial prospects were sent to him by an Athenian friend, Archbishop Theoclitus Vimbos, who, as a theological student in St. Petersburg, had tutored Schliemann the businessman in ancient and modern Greek. Their friendship remained constant through correspondence, the most recent letters having dealt with two subjects: Schliemann's intention to excavate Troy and his hopes for betrothal to a Greek girl.

In his first letter, outlining his requirements for a wife, Schliemann stated that he wanted to marry a girl of pure Greek heritage who resembled Helen of Troy as he visualized her. He specified, too, that she should be unsophisticated as well as good-looking. Vimbos, accepting the challenge of his friend and former student, assembled a collection of photographs of prospective brides. When packing them to send to Schliemann in Indianapolis, Vimbos, as an afterthought, included one of the young Sophia, daughter of his favorite cousin. Schliemann carefully studied the photographed faces, judging one girl to be too bossy; another, obviously of Italian descent; and another, frivolous. Vacillating during his perusal of the pictures, he returned again and again to the portrait of Sophia. He had it copied and sent prints to his father and to other members of his family, with the notation: "I shall go to Athens and marry Sophia."

The morning after Schliemann's 1869 arrival in Athens, his hotel suite looked like a settled home. On his well-ordered desk were papers neatly stacked, books arranged in a graduated row, and pens lined up beside a brimful inkwell. A highly polished silver dresser set shone on the top of a bureau; its capacious drawers were filled with scarfs of silk and wool, with neckties and cravats, with piles of underwear and, by the dozens, stiff collars and shirts, labeled by his London shirtmaker. Schliemann selected a suit of linen from a huge wooden wardrobe; in it, hanging shoulder to shoulder, were other suits of tweed and twill, greatcoats in heavy weight and light, full-dress suits and cotton dusters. Schliemann, who at forty-seven possessed the accoutrements of a boulevardier, lacked the flair to make him the image of one. Before leaving his room, he glanced into a mirror that reflected not a dashing gallant but a conservatively tailored, slight man of no physical distinction.

Hat in hand, cane handle curved over his left wrist, Schliemann went down to the lobby to meet Leon Mélas, chairman of the board of The Arsakeion, the private school for daughters of prominent Athenians, where Sophia studied. Mélas knew only that Schliemann wanted to observe Sophia in her classroom, and the two men set a fast pace toward the school. The board chairman bowed to acquaintances as he and Schliemann crossed the plaza in front of the Royal Palace. They turned left into University Street and, continuing along that thoroughfare, passed a wooded acreage where Schliemann was eventually to build his own palatial home. Just beyond that site and to the right, was the University of Athens, and diagonally from it was the Arsakeion School. There the two men lingered briefly to look at the Ionic columns, supporting a pediment on which was lettered the word ΑΡΣΑΚΕΙΟΝ. Entering, Mélas and Schliemann walked down a broad hall to a classroom. A wave of nervous excitement swept through the room as the young girls surreptitiously exchanged questioning glances. What possible reason could there be for the presence of the eminent Mr. Mélas, normally seen only at the school's formal functions? And who was the unknown mustached man, as old as many of their fathers?

It was he who asked the teacher if he might hear recitations from his favorite poet, Homer. One after another, tongue-tied pupils were unable to stammer out more than a couple of lines from the *Odyssey* and the *Iliad*. Schliemann, having identified the seventeen-year-old Sophia from her photograph, eagerly waited for her to rise from her place in the second row from the front. At last, at a nod from the teacher, Sophia stood and, facing the guests, started to recite in classical Greek. Without affectation or elaborate gesture, she spoke the following lines from Homer:

"Helen rose third, leading the lament:
Oh Hector, most dear of all my stalwart brothers, and most close to my heart! Truly my husband is the royal Alexandros who fled me to Honored Troy, yet would I had died before this. Twenty years have come and gone since I left mine homeland for Troy, yet while here none among you has said an unkind and cruel word to me. If others spoke harshly of me, a sister or brother among you, or even a brother's wife, or your mother; fair indeed was your father to me as though my own; you challenged them, silenced them, with your loving spirit and loving words. For this I weep for you all and we together weep for my sorrowing self. Throughout all Troy there is no one good and kind; instead they revile me."

Sophia's rendition of the quotation from the *Iliad* so moved Schliemann that tears misted his eyes. As attentive as if he himself did not know each line of the poetry and every syllable of the words, he listened to her recitation of the concluding passage:

"Dawn on the following day showed her rosy fingers through the clouds, and Trojans circled round the funeral pyre of great Hector.

At first they quenched the flame with their wine where flames still burned. Next, Hector's brothers and dearest friends brushed together his white-ash bones, while tears of sorrow wet their cheeks. Placing his remains in a golden casket, wrapping it in fine purple cloth, they put the casket in a grave and piled heavy stones atop the grave. Swiftly they formed the marked-place as guards stood alert lest the Achaeans attack without warning. This accomplished, mourners returned to the city, and all in family and of friends partook of a great feast in the Palace of their King, Priam. That was the funeral of Hector."*

Sophia sat down to spontaneous applause. Schliemann, without showing the exultation he felt, thanked the teacher and Sophia and, with Mélas, left the school.

Jubilant, Schliemann proceeded at once to the home of Vimbos, Archbishop of Mantineia and Kynouria, who greeted Heinrich with a hug and kisses on both cheeks. The two old friends settled comfortably in the Archbishop's study, and throughout the long afternoon of September 3 Schliemann eagerly questioned Vimbos, drawing from him information about Sophia and her large family. Sophia was the youngest of seven children: the two eldest were sisters, Katingo and Marigo, and there were four brothers, Spiros, Alexandros, Yiango and Panighotes. By Greek custom, Archbishop Vimbos, as first cousin to their mother, was maternal "uncle" of the children to whom he was devoted and attentive.

Sophia was always the least lively of the children who, close in age, together competed in numerous active and sedentary games. Particularly after her matriculation at The Arsakeion, Sophia so patently preferred her books to contests of wit and athletic skill that her brothers and sisters teasingly called her Miss Philosophia, a word that could be written in Greek as a pun meaning *I kiss you, Sophia.*

Sophia's mother, a member of the Cretan family Gheladaki, was a statuesque matron, proud and formidable in appearance, inspiring everybody with awe. She was addressed and invariably referred to as Madame Victoria, never by her husband's surname. That name was confusing. Sophia's father was born George Kastromenos, whose ancestors for generations occupied a house in the Thesion section of Athens. Kastromenos, meaning house

*Translation by Lynn Poole.

nearest the castle, aptly described the patrimonial home that was the building nearest to the Acropolis. The Church of Our Lady of Vlassarou was close by, and to the west on a small hill stood the Temple of Theseus.

George Kastromenos, ebullient, jovial and talkative, had a ready laugh and a hearty appetite that, uncontrolled, produced a mammoth paunch. It earned him the nickname Engastromenos, meaning pregnant, and in the custom of the time in Greece, the nickname became the designation for others in the family. While not affluent, George owned a successful business in drapery, the importing of fine fabrics, and had, in addition to the ancestral house, a country home in the Colonos section, famous as the birthplace of Sophocles.

It was to the country place that the Archbishop and Schliemann drove in the late day. The house was tile-roofed, box-shaped, and small. Its spacious garden was adjacent to St. Meletios Church, a long low building topped with a bell tower forward, and toward the back, a small dome, centered by a cross. Flourishing cedar trees planted by George Engastromenos marked the boundary of his garden and the churchyard.

Madame Victoria and her husband welcomed Schliemann and Vimbos, who suggested they withdraw to a quiet place, away from the activity of the bustling household, for a confidential talk. Schliemann, without preamble, asked Sophia's parents for permission to marry her. Astounded, they heard him out in silence. With succinct statement he touched on his financial successes and explained that his previous marriage to the mother of his three children had failed because she refused to travel or to live with him, either in Paris or anywhere else outside her native Russia. He expressed his delight with Sophia, showing her parents the well-worn photograph that he had been carrying for more than six months, and telling them of his visit to The Arsakeion earlier in the day.

Schliemann, in a letter dated the day of his wedding, wrote to a friend, "When I asked for the approval of Sophia's parents to our wedding, I asked if there is any objection because of my recent divorce. They answered . . .: 'Thanks god we are not enemies of our daughter and it would be a wicked doing to turn down such a great happiness for which the whole of Greece must envy us.

Even if we waited ten thousand years, never a second time would it happen to us that a Schliemann should honor us (by asking) to marry our daughter. Even the Furies would punish us if we made such a sin (as refusal), so take our daughter and live with her . . .' "

Having received parental blessings for the match, Schliemann peremptorily announced that he wanted the wedding to be held within a matter of weeks. Madame Victoria demurred but Schliemann prevailed. A tentative day was decided on by the time Schliemann and Vimbos, with Sophia's parents, joined the family group. If Sophia was surprised to see the stranger of the classroom in her home, she gave no sign, but smilingly greeted "Uncle" Vimbos, who kissed her on the forehead and then said, "Sophia, this is my friend, Heinrich Schliemann." With grace she put out her hand to him.

Nothing in that casual introduction augured the misunderstandings of the ensuing days, the future clash of wills of two headstrong people, or the ultimate shared joys of a loving couple. Sophia, demure in a simple cotton frock, her unbound black hair shining across her shoulders, typified a young daughter being presented to a guest of her parents. Hardly taller than Sophia, Schliemann, slope-shouldered and balding, looked to be a most unlikely suitor for the slender girl he expected to marry, and soon.

At table Schliemann talked volubly with a sparkling wit and charm that he never evidenced outside an intimate circle of family and friends. Those acquaintances who judged him as dour and monosyllabic would not have thought it possible for him to hold companions spellbound, as he did throughout the evening. The immediate family and visiting relatives were all enthralled by the world traveler who spoke with familiarity of places known to them only as words in an atlas.

(COURTESY: ALEX L. MÉLAS)

Heinrich Schliemann was a wealthy financier, a world traveler, a scholar and linguist. At the age of forty-seven he divorced his first wife, Ekaterina, and wrote to Archbishop Vimbos in Athens to find him a new bride.

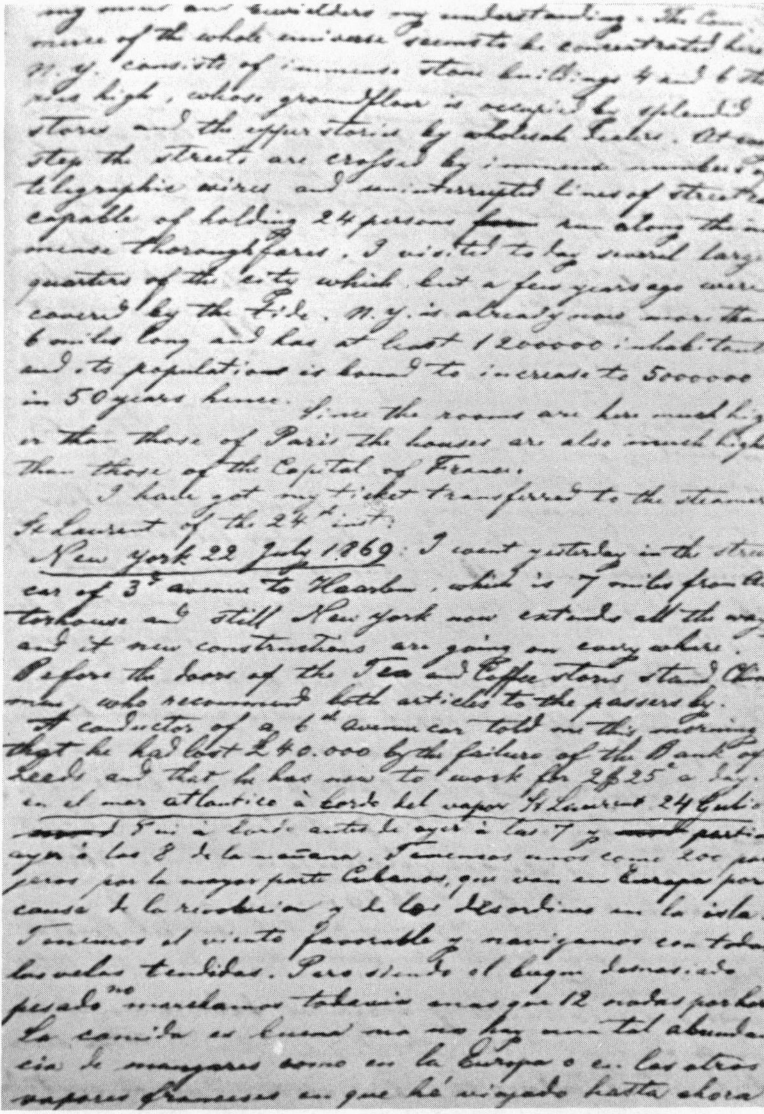

my mind and bewilders my understanding. The Com-
merce of the whole universe seems to be concentrated here.
N.Y. consists of immense stone buildings 4 and 6 stories high, whose groundfloor is occupied by splendid
stores and the upper stories by wholesale dealers. At every
step the streets are crossed by immense numbers of
telegraphic wires and uninterrupted lines of street cars
capable of holding 24 persons ~~run~~ run along the immense thoroughfares. I visited today several large
quarters of the city which but a few years ago were
covered by the tide. N.Y. is already now more than
6 miles long and has at least 1200000 inhabitants
and its population is bound to increase to 5000000
in 50 years hence. Since the rooms are here much higher than those of Paris the houses are also much higher
than those of the Capital of France.
I have got my ticket transferred to the steamer
St Laurent of the 24th inst.
New york 22 July 1869: I went yesterday in the street
car of 3d avenue to Harlem, which is 7 miles from As-
torhouse and still New york now extends all the way
and at new constructions are going on every where.
Before the doors of the Tea and Coffee stores stand Chin-
amen, who recommend both articles to the passers by.
A conductor of a 6th avenue car told me this morning
that he had lost £40.000 by the failure of the Bank of
Leeds and that he has now to work for 2$25 a day.
en el mar atlantico à bordo del vapor St Laurent 24 Julio
Fui à bordo antes de ayer à las 7 y partimos
ayer à las 8 de la mañana. Tenemos unos como 200 pas-
ageros por la mayor parte Cubanos, que van en Europa por
causa de la revolucion y de los desordines en la isla.
Tenemos el viento favorable y navigamos con todas
las velas tendidas. Pero siendo el buque demasiado
pesado no marchamos todavia mas que 12 nudas por hora
La comida es buena mas no hay una tal abundan-
cia de manjares como en la Europa o en los otros
vapores franceses en que he viajado hasta ahora

In Schliemann's diary, dated 22 July 1869, he writes of New York City, ". . . new constructions are going on every where." On July 24, once headed for France aboard the steamship St. Laurent, *Schliemann began writing in French.*

From a photo, Heinrich chose Sophia Engastromenos to be his second wife. Her parents, delighted by his offer, were happy for

Sophia; Schliemann, happy to have their permission, was delighted by Sophia. Sophia, only seventeen, obediently accepted.

A proud and formidable woman, whose appearance and manner were awe-inspiring, Sophia's mother was always addressed as "Madame Victoria," never by her husband's surname.

(PAINTING BY GEORGE KASTRIOTES)

George Engastromenos was head of a family of seven children. He enjoyed eating, talking, and life in general—qualities not evident in this severe portrait.

TWO

The Engastromenos family did not know that Schliemann's attainment of prominence was a personal triumph motivated by a boyhood dream. Heinrich Schliemann, born on January 6, 1822, at Neu-Buckow, Germany, was taken the following year to Ankershagen where his father accepted the post of clergyman. Heinrich was one of seven children, having two brothers and four sisters.

In the parsonage of the small village church, young Heinrich first heard about ancient Troy from Ernst Schliemann. Though neither scholar nor archaeologist, the pastor had a passion for ancient history and, with enthusiasm, often told of the tragic fate of Herculaneum and Pompeii. Ernst Schliemann, who related with admiration the great deeds of Homeric heroes and the events of the Trojan War, always found his son to be a defender of the Trojan cause. Heinrich grieved that Troy had disappeared without leaving any traces of its existence. The child's joy was boundless when, in 1829, he received as a Christmas gift Dr. George Ludwig Jerrer's *Universal History,* which had an illustration showing Troy in flames. Heinrich excitedly said to his father that Jerrer must have seen Troy, for otherwise he could not have represented it so well. The clergyman told the boy that the picture was merely fanciful, but Heinrich would not be convinced. He insisted that if such walls once existed they could not possibly have been completely destroyed. "Ruins must be buried by earth," he stubbornly claimed. Heinrich then and there vowed that he would one day excavate Troy, and his father agreed.

The father's concession probably was made to cut short a bootless argument and to humor a small boy who believed in legends both of faraway places and of his own neighborhood. Little Heinrich roamed in search of ghosts reputed to haunt Ankershagen and of treasure said to be buried in the local graveyard and ruins of a castle. His natural disposition for the mysterious and the marvelous was stimulated to a passion by the wonders of his locality. There was supposed to be one ghost on the grounds of the parsonage and another in the pond beyond the garden. Treasure was reputedly buried in numerous locations in and near the village, and a left leg grew out of a grave in the churchyard. In his autobiography Schliemann, affirming that "in my childish simplicity I, of course, believed in all of this," gave precise details about each tale told in the town.

On how many moonlight nights must the small Heinrich have leaned out of his bedroom window, hoping for a glimpse of the ghost of Pastor von Russdorf, his father's predecessor and haunt of the garden house of the parsonage, and of the maiden in the pond who was believed to rise each midnight, holding a silver bowl. By day, Heinrich's explorations were wide-ranging, and at various sites he optimistically dug with trowel and small shovel. There was so much to believe in: A child in a golden cradle was buried in a small hill of the German village. Treasure was concealed somewhere close to the ruins of a round tower in the garden of the town's proprietor. A long line of stones in the churchyard marked the grave of one Henning, a murderer whose left leg, covered with a black silk stocking, grew out for centuries. Local men alleged that, as boys, they had cut off the leg and used the bone for knocking fruit from orchard trees, but that in 1802 the leg had stopped growing. A footnote to this legend, written by Schliemann in his late fifties, hardly the age of "childish simplicity," indicates his continued interest. "According to tradition, when some years ago the church of Ankershagen was being repaired, a single leg-bone was found at a small depth before the altar, as my cousin, the Reverend Hans Becker, the present clergyman [1879] of Ankershagen, assures me."

Few in Heinrich's childhood shared his acceptance of legends as reality. His father, who dismissed local lore and the existence of ancient Troy, lived to see his son become famous, one of the most spectacular and controversial figures of the 19th century.

Most of the playmates of little Heinrich made fun of his constant talk about Troy and the legends of Ankershagen. But there were two sisters, Louise and Minna Meincke, who listened to Heinrich with flattering attention. Minna became his childhood sweetheart and entered into all his vast plans for the future.

The happy life of the imaginative child, who dreamed of excavating Troy, was cut short by the untimely death of his mother. The boy had little to support his ebullience for the next five years. His father, who had taken the family maid as a mistress even before the death of Mrs. Schliemann, sent Heinrich to live with an uncle, the Reverend Friederich Schliemann, pastor of a church in the town of Kalkhorst. The boy was doing well when a second disaster struck. Ernst Schliemann, accused of misguiding church funds, was relieved of his duties as pastor at Ankershagen and was not exonerated until 1838. In 1834 Heinrich left private school and entered the *Realschule* at Neu Strelitz. His formal schooling came to an end in April 1836, and at the age of fourteen, he became a grocer's apprentice at Furstenberg.

The hours, from five in the morning until eleven at night, left the apprentice not a moment's leisure for study. He sold goods at the shop, swept up, unpacked the stock, arranged it for display, and ground potatoes for the still in which his employer produced the popular potato-whisky of the region.

Heinrich's life was miserable, but he never lost his love of learning. Often he recounted a vital evening in his life. Hermann Niederhöffer, the son of a Protestant clergyman in Röebel, Mecklenburg, Germany, had almost completed his studies at the Gymnasium of Neu Ruppin, when he was expelled for bad conduct. The young Niederhöffer gave himself up to drink, which, however, had not made him forget his Homer.

One evening he entered the shop where Heinrich worked and recited about one hundred lines of the *Iliad,* observing the rhythmic cadence of the verses. "Although I did not understand a syllable, the melodious sound of the words made a deep impression on me, and I wept bitter tears over my own unhappy, uneducated fate. Three times over did I get him to repeat to me those divine verses, rewarding his trouble with three glasses of whiskey, which I bought with the few pence that made up my whole fortune. From that moment on I never ceased to pray to God that by His grace I might yet have the happiness of learning Greek."

Heinrich bore misfortune well, refusing to succumb to long work hours or illness, shipwreck or starvation. Suffering from tuberculosis while clerking at the shop, he stoically endured the stench of his own expectoration of blood and phlegm. Determined to obtain an education and to make enough money to excavate Troy, Heinrich gave up his job, realizing that financial advancement was impossible in the small community of Furstenberg. But first he must be restored to health. Thinking that a sea voyage would be good for him, he signed as cabin boy aboard the brig *Dorothea* bound for South America, a land of opportunity. The *Dorothea,* out of Hamburg, was wrecked off Texel and, after hazardous hours of exposure at sea, Heinrich reached the shores of that island of the Netherlands.

He made his way to Amsterdam, where he suffered cruelly both from the cold and at the hands of German consuls indifferent to the plight of their young fellow countryman. Finally, with the help of the consul general from Prussia, Heinrich secured a position as clerk at an annual salary of £32, some of which he spent for lessons in calligraphy. Debilitated by tuberculosis and by Spartan living, he prodded himself to stay awake when he should have slept. The zealous young clerk taught himself to read, write and speak English, devising a linguistic method that enabled him to learn nine foreign tongues in the next half-dozen years and as many more in his lifetime. By day, he observed with knowing eyes the activities of his employers and avidly investigated business procedures.

The twenty-two-year-old Schliemann, restored to good health, became correspondent and chief bookkeeper for Messrs. B. H. Schröder and Co. of Amsterdam, on March 1, 1844. By then his English and French were flawless, and he became proficient in Russian because the Schröder company maintained an office in St. Petersburg for the purpose of indigo trade. As a result of his diligence and canny planning, Schliemann was sent to Russia, as chief agent of the Schröders, in January 1846. With the approval of the Amsterdam company, he set up his own office in St. Petersburg and became an active member of the wholesale merchants' guild. Every success in business advanced Schliemann's dream of finding Troy.

In 1850 he sailed for the United States to investigate the death of a brother, Louis, in California, and to claim the estate. Heinrich, who lived through the San Francisco fire of 1851 and nearly died of yellow fever, amassed a fortune of $350,000 in the California gold rush. Returning to Russia at the end of 1852, he prospered in St. Petersburg, and set up a branch office in Moscow. He acquired fluency in Spanish, Portuguese, Swedish and Polish, while also studying Latin and reading Roman classics in the original. It was at this period that he took Greek lessons from Theoclitus Vimbos.

An ardent suitor, Schliemann had always been romantically involved with women and was much sought after as both lover and husband in St. Petersburg. Even at Ankershagen he had a precocious attachment for his childhood playmate Minna Meincke, and the affectionate children pledged their eternal love with solemnity. For years after Heinrich left Germany, Troy and Minna were the inspirations for his ambitious undertakings, and he languished when he learned that she had married just as he became successful enough to propose.

Schliemann was married in 1852 to Ekaterina Lyschin a Russian belle who bore him three children. She refused to interest herself in his passion for the excavation of Troy, and would not travel with him on business or pleasure trips. Schliemann went alone to Sweden, Denmark, Italy, and Egypt; he visited Jerusalem and Petra and, while acquiring a practical knowledge of Arabic, traversed Syria. In 1859, on his first visit to Greece, he intended to go to the Homeric island of Ithaca, but had to leave Athens for urgent business in St. Petersburg.

Schliemann's dedication to his one passion made it possible for him to endure hardship, misery and censure as he progressed from a youth of little education to a man of great learning, from an impoverished child to an international financier of immense wealth. Expanding his commercial empire, he invested in Greek olive oil, in American cotton fields and railroad lines, in Cuban sugar and tobacco plantations, and in South American hemp production. He profited from the Crimean War and from the Civil War in the United States. His business ventures provided the financial security that freed him, at forty-one, to start for his ultimate goal. By December 1863 he possessed the fortune he needed for the excavation of Troy, but wrote that ". . . before devoting myself entirely to archaeology and to the realization of my life dream, I wished to see a little more of the world."

He capsuled that world trip for the Engastromenos family at his first dinner with them in 1869. Foreign lands became real to them as Schliemann, creating excitement by dramatic detail, highlighted the experiences that began in April 1864. He retraced his route from the ruins of Carthage, near Tunis, into Egypt and on to India where he visited Calcutta, Benares, Agra, Madras, Lucknow and Delhi. From the islands of Ceylon and Java, he went to China for a two-month stay, touring seven cities including Hong Kong, Shanghai and Peking, and concluded his Oriental trip in Japan. His was no mere listing of geographic locations. Embellishing the narration for his listeners, he told of climbing in the foothills of the Himalaya Mountains and tramping along the Great Wall of China; of riding camels and elephants; of being passenger in rickshaw and sampan; of dining with dignitaries whose rich robes blazed with priceless jewels and recoiling from beggars whose tattered clothing crawled with loathsome lice.

Heinrich was urged to continue the story of his adventures whenever he paused to enjoy the food offered from serving dishes filled with tempting fare. Encouraged by the eager faces and enthusiastic comments of his intimate audience, he spun more tales of exotic travel, eating little and sipping only enough of his wine to be able to compliment George Engastromenos on its vintage. While dessert was being served, Schliemann excused himself from the table, returning with a package, which he gave to Madame Victoria. In it were gift copies of two of his books.

He explained that one of them, *La Chine et le Japon,* published in Paris in 1866, had been written during the long voyage from Japan to San Francisco aboard an English ship. The fact that crossing the Pacific Ocean had taken fifty days elicited amazement from those whose sea trips were gauged by the few hours required to reach the nearest Greek islands.

The other book, his second, was *Ithaca, the Peloponnesus and Troy,* a report of his archaeological investigations there in 1868. Pointing to it, Schliemann began to talk with intensity. The raconteur became zealot, his voice emotional, eyes aglow. He poured out his hopes for the future, looking directly at Sophia who did not understand the implication of his words. He spoke of his expectations of success in the exploration of ancient sites and his need for a partner who, with understanding and faith, would be constantly at his side. Ahead was the necessity to prove the Homeric legends to have been fact, in support of his long-held views. In preparation for his serious archaeological work, he had excavated at Ithaca, and then at Mycenae in the Peloponnesus and at two sites in Asia Minor. Certain conclusions about Mycenae and his identification of the probable site of Troy in Asia Minor were in absolute variance with those of most scholars. His two prime theories, unequivocally stated in *Ithaca, the Peloponnesus and Troy,* gained him a doctoral degree from the University of Rostock. His ambition was to attain future success with one who shared his passionate belief that Troy once existed, a flourishing city described in truth by Homer.

No one at the table—not even Schliemann himself, much less Sophia—realized that his convictions would involve him in constant controversy. In future, he was to be bitter opponent of eminent scholars, defendant at a courtroom trial, challenger of royalty, and antagonist of government officials, both petty and influential. But against such formidable obstacles, he would remain steadfast in his dedication to his one passion.

THREE

On the morning following his request to the parents for permission to marry Sophia, Schliemann arrived early at the National Bank to confer with a senior officer, Pericles Dentopoulos, with whom he had done business on previous visits to Athens. Before leaving the bank, Schliemann, unable to contain his elation over his betrothal, confided in Dentopoulos that he was engaged to marry Sophia Engastromenos. The banker, leaping from his chair, exclaimed, "What did you say? *You* are going to marry Sophaki?" Affronted by the banker's tone of incredulity no less than by the use of the diminutive for Sophia, Schliemann glared at Dentopoulos and indignantly demanded an explanation of his right to call her Sophaki. Amused by the jealousy of the offended suitor, the banker smiled disarmingly and said that he, as a close friend of Sophia's brother Alexandros, was practically a member of the Engastromenos family. Schliemann, pacified, left the bank with the congratulations of Dentopoulos and with his heartwarming assurance that "neither you yourself nor anybody else who has seen Sophaki can possibly conceive what an exceptional young woman she is and how she stands out from all the girls of her age."

In the late afternoon Schliemann, having been invited to the Engastromenos' town house, arrived there to find Sophia's brothers with several friends. He was asked to join them in the beautiful garden with its sweeping view of the Thesion and, when seated, was plied with questions about his travel experiences. The previous night he had mentioned that he had been in the great fire that destroyed San Francisco in 1851, and the young men pressed him to give a detailed account of that disaster.

Reluctantly, since the purpose of his visit was to talk with Sophia, Schliemann recounted the events of the night of June 4, eighteen years earlier. He had arrived in San Francisco after dark and was asleep in his room at the Union Hotel when shouts of *Fire! Fire!* and the clang of alarm bells had roused him. He looked out and saw flames consuming a frame building only a few feet from his window. Hastily dressing, he ran from the hotel, which itself was on fire by the time he gained safety in the city's plaza. A gale spread the blaze that immediately destroyed wooden structures, slowly caused brick homes to crumble, and turned from red-hot to white-hot the metal houses in which doomed residents mistakenly had felt themselves to be protected from fire.

Schliemann made his way from the center of the fire up steep streets, and at last reached Telegraph Hill from which he had full view of the dreadful spectacle. He heard from below the cries of human torches, victims of the fire, and the reverberations of explosions deliberately set off in unsuccessful attempts to halt the spread of flames. Through the night of tragedy and terror, Schliemann stayed in a restaurant on the Hill, descending at about six in the morning to the ruins of what only hours before had been a flourishing city.

His description of the smoldering remains of the city with no walls standing perplexed the young Athenians whose homes, truly fireproof, were made of the cheapest building materials available, stone and marble. Their homes, which might be razed by earthquake, could never be destroyed by windswept flames.

Schliemann, questioned about San Francisco after the holocaust, said that its rebuilding started the very morning following the fire. On his way down to the plaza area, he passed many foreign inhabitants of San Francisco sitting in shock and despair, numbers of them bitterly weeping. He noticed that the Americans on the other hand, seemingly undaunted, joked and laughed as they began to lay foundations for new buildings on earth still covered with hot ash.

Concluding the fire story, Schliemann brushed aside further attempts to question him when he saw Sophia sitting quietly at some distance behind the young men who ringed his chair. She returned his smile but seemed remote, her expression contemplative.

By the time Schliemann had risen from his chair and reached Sophia's side, it was too late to speak with her alone. The garden was filled with people: friends had called to offer sincere congratulations; curious gossips, to scrutinize the prospective bridegroom. These left to start mischief-making throughout the town where those envious of Sophia's good fortune publicly referred to her fiancé as "old Schliemann."

Vexed by the many visitors who prevented him from conversing with Sophia, Schliemann sent her a necklace of coral on September 6, and in the accompanying letter wrote: "Can you please ask your excellent parents and write to me if it is possible to see you without all those people around but alone with them [the parents] not once, but often, because I think we must see each other to get acquainted and to see whether our characters go along together."

The letter contained his views on marriage in general and specifics about their own. He defined marriage as the "most magnificent of all human establishments if the only bases are respect, love and virtue," but described marriage as the "heaviest bondage if it is based on material interest or sexual attraction.

"Wealth contributes to the happiness in marriage," he continued, "but cannot build it by itself, and the woman who will marry me for my money only or to become, because of it, a great lady in Paris will regret very much to have left Athens because she would make me and herself very unhappy. The woman who will marry me must do it for my value as a human being. I am not flattering myself with illusions. I know perfectly well that a young and beautiful girl cannot fall in love with a 47-year-old man for his beautiful face for the simple reason that the man does not have beauty. But I think that a woman, the character of whom completely agrees with mine and has the same love and enthusiastic inclination for the sciences, could respect me. Because we are created to respect always the person who is more learned, especially in those sciences that we are mostly interested in. And because this woman would be my student for all her life I dare to hope that she would love me, because love is born by respect, second because I would try to be a good teacher and would dedicate every free moment of my life to help the lover of science in her philological and archaeological considerations."

The letter, hardly one to arouse in a schoolgirl a desire to be alone with her fiancé or to fire her enthusiasm for marriage, served Schliemann's purpose. Sophia's parents asked him to come to their home as often as he wished, promising frequent opportunity for him to converse with Sophia. Assurance of privacy was easier to offer than to realize in their home bustling with sons and daughters, with relatives and friends by the dozens. Moreover, Sophia was required to spend hours with fittings for trousseau clothes. Even Heinrich was drawn into conferences about the wedding reception. There was more chaos than calm whenever he and Sophia met, whether at the city house or in the country, where the wedding was to be held at St. Meletios Church.

Schliemann himself found it difficult to get away to be with Sophia, because he was besieged at his hotel by fathers and brothers importuning him to consider their daughters and sisters as prospective brides. With lack of tact, insistent Athenians extolled their female relatives as more suitable in age and sophistication for a man of Schliemann's years and experience. "Old Schliemann" though he might be, he was, in Athens, the matrimonial catch of the century. He gave short interviews and curt dismissals to the blatant solicitors, but they, by their very numbers, kept him engaged for hours of every day.

By September 12 he was so frustrated by the obstacles that kept him from private talks with Sophia that he decided to escape from Athens, taking her with him. Early that morning he sent her a note asking her and her "honorable mother" to join him at two in the afternoon at the railway station. "You will find there Mr. Lamprides and his excellent wife and we will all go to the Piraeus together. There we will take a boat and go sailing a little, which you will maybe do for the first time in your life. Hoping that you will not deprive us of the joy to have you with us I beg you to receive the expression of my respect. Please answer me with one or two words. H.S."

By return messenger Sophia explained in a note that, before accepting, she had to ask the permission of her "venerable and beloved father," who was not at home. Schliemann, impatient at the delay, sent her another letter saying that he must have an answer, and to this she replied, "This very moment my father arrived home and saw fit to extend me the permisison for us to go to the Piraeus." In spite of her innate fear of the water, Sophia, with Madame Victoria, met Schliemann and his friends at the train station in Athens.

The group traveled in holiday mood to the Piraeus and embarked on an ill-fated sail. Heinrich, at last free to talk with Sophia alone, asked her why she had consented to be his bride.

Artless and incapable of subterfuge, she gave him an honest and straightforward answer: her parents wanted her to accept him. The ingenuous reply infuriated Heinrich. Having searched for a bride who was unsophisticated, he was deeply hurt by irrefutable proof that he had found one. At a time and in a country where marriages of arrangement were common and love matches rare, he was unreasonably angered by a dutiful daughter's acquiescence. Leaving Sophia's side, he huffily ordered the sailing captain to return the little boat to port, and on the train trip back to Athens was withdrawn and hardly civil.

He seethed over Sophia's forthright answer for several days, then wrote her a farewell that created consternation in the Engastromenos family. Urged by her parents to try to placate Heinrich, Sophia wrote him that, after reading his letter, she "prayed to God to bring back to you the feelings that have fled." She asked that he visit her before he left Athens and hoped that his "gentle soul" would not decline the request.

Schliemann did not at once capitulate, but sternly taxed Sophia with having acted as a slave to her parents in consenting to marry him at their request. He described her answer to him on the boat as having been so "unworthy of an educated human being" that he had been unable to converse with her longer that day and had decided not to "think on you any more." Referring to a ring sent to remind her of the "love I have had for you," Schliemann then gave a probable date for his sailing and a tentative itinerary for Europe. After a lively exchange of notes carried by busy messengers, steadily shuttling between his hotel and Sophia's home, Heinrich finally initiated a reconciliation.

Correspondence was ever a thread of life to Schliemann, and in letters written during the days of his courtship in Athens, he dashed off random thoughts, penned fanciful interpretations of much that transpired, and contradicted himself on decisions, opinions and dates. These letters show him to have been as muddled and flustered as any young lover. The one constant was his reiteration to distant friends that Sophia would be his student for her lifetime. He regretted that she spoke only ancient and modern Greek, but pledged to do "my best that she learns four languages in two years." That she might have some difficulty in keeping to his imposed schedule never crossed the mind of Schliemann, a linguistic genius, who already spoke and wrote seventeen languages. He had no qualms about Sophia's ability to acquire such graces as piano playing and the fine manners of the fashionables of Paris, and was hopeful of making a scholar of her although she lacked "any profound scientific education." Sophia, a "docile and obedient plant, clever and intelligent," was to have her chance to prove herself while he educated her "according to my will."

Without realizing to what extent she was to be involuntary pupil as well as wife, the young Sophia busily prepared for her wedding. It took place on September 23 at the close of a breathlessly hot day. The tiny church was jammed with guests long before the hour set for the ceremony. Light from hundreds of flickering candles enhanced the glitter of silver and gold threads and semiprecious stones that decorated the colorful regional costumes of Sophia's relatives from Crete and from distant communities on the mainland. Patriarchs wearing jackets of embroidered velvet and voluminous kilts, tightly pleated, stood elbow to elbow with dignitaries in full-dress suits.

Sophia, with serene dignity, passed through the congregation, the long train of her simple bridal gown broadening behind her. A short veil of white tulle was attached to a floral cap that lay flat on her black hair, which was parted in the middle and braided into a slight coronet. She held a dainty bouquet from which a flowering vine showered. Around her neck she wore the necklace of coral strands that was Heinrich's first gift to her.

They stood before the *iconastisis,* dominated by a life-sized icon of St. Meletios painted in rich colors accented by gold-leaf wristlets, halo and cross. In a smaller icon only the face of the saint was painted; all else within the frame was hammered silver.

Archbishop Vimbos, resplendent in his robe weighted with gems and embroidery, officiated at the ceremony with the parish priest assisting. The solemn service was long, following the published Liturgies of the Orthodox Church prepared by Symeon of Thessalonika. The deep voices of the archbishop and the attending priest reverberated throughout the small church, but few could catch the responses of Sophia and Heinrich made during the high nuptial Mass. The bride and groom received communion during that rite; and at the actual marriage ceremony they again sipped wine from a chalice, the formal and traditional Orthodox plighting of the troth.

The wedding party and guests, moving out of the church, walked the short distance to the Engastromenos' garden where the wedding banquet was served to the accompaniment of music and laughter. Heinrich was constantly at the side of his smiling bride. Beaming with pride and joy, he for once looked younger than his years.

The feasting and dancing and singing continued even after Sophia went into the house to dress for the journey ahead. When she and Heinrich, with her family, were ready to leave for the Piraeus, Sophia asked to be left alone for a few minutes in her own room. There she had played children's games, studied school lessons, read for pleasure, and indulged in daydreams. These could not have been fanciful enough to approach the reality of her future as professional partner to her husband and, as skilled diplomatist, his invaluable aide.

Whatever Sophia's thoughts in her room, she emerged from it dry-eyed and controlled. Immediately the members of the family, calling goodbye to the guests still celebrating, stepped into waiting carriages and, in cavalcade, started for the harbor from which the bride and groom were to sail at 1 A.M. At the Piraeus, Sophia, in tearful farewell, kissed her parents and sisters and brothers. They remained on the quay calling "Kalos taxidi! Good trip!" until Heinrich and Sophia stepped from the little harbor boat onto the anchored ship. It was typical of Heinrich to have booked passage on that specific vessel with its name significant for a honeymoon: *Aphrodite.*

Sophia, uneasy throughout the short sea voyage, was happy with the landfall off the boot-tip of Italy that was her first view of a foreign shore. The Schliemanns landed at Messina and stayed for two days on Sicily before crossing to the mainland for a week at Naples.

Naples, site of the ancient Greek colony Neapolis, and its surrounding countryside pleased Sophia more than Sicily with its rugged hills and valleys. The Neapolitans—gay, noisy, lively—seemed carefree and created a bustling activity day and night. Like the vendors of Athens, those in Naples crowded the streets, calling their wares, chiefly amulets and edibles. In a letter to her parents, Sophia wrote that the Neapolitans were more swarthy than Greeks, but were happy and "do much as our own people."

She evidently pondered at length about whether the Greek origin of the city accounted for its atmosphere, for in every letter written from Naples she mentioned the heritage of the Neapolitans, questioning their relationship to the Greeks.

The honeymoon travels of the Schliemanns were well documented because Sophia proved to be as persistent a letter-writer as her husband. In daily correspondence she gave detailed accounts of their activities, along with her opinions and impressions of what she saw and experienced. Heinrich, in letters and his diary, wrote in similar vein, frequently adding his perceptive comments on Sophia's conduct and reactions.

Nothing in Naples delighted Sophia more than La Villa (Villa Nazionale), the public garden enlivened by strolling musicians, ambling couples, and gamboling children. Like fashionable Neapolitans, she and Heinrich drove along the Via Carácciolo, enjoying views of the sea and the park. In La Villa she was amazed to see temple-memorials to Virgil and Tasso, poets whose work she had studied at school.

San Domenico Maggiore depressed Sophia. The family chapels of prominent Neapolitans seemed dark and gloomy to her, and she was repulsed by the velvet-covered coffins in the sacristy. The architecture of San Gennáro was so foreign to her that she was unable to appreciate the original French Gothic construction, somewhat obscured by a succession of hodgepodge alterations made after the mid-15th century.

Their tour of the Palazzo Reale, the former royal palace, was complete and exhausting. Heinrich pointed out its wonders: the great staircases of white marble, the carved bas-reliefs, the floors of mosaic, the exquisitely painted walls, the huge collection of statues. While resting on the terrace of the palace garden, with its breathtaking view of the sea, Heinrich told Sophia that he would one day build her such a palace with a view of the Aegean. She reported in a letter that she was about to question his statement but then, on second thought, remained silent. Already she was beginning to learn how to live with Heinrich.

On another day, at the national museum, she listened to his expansive projection of excavations at Troy with her at his side, digging and searching for artifacts that would irrefutably establish Homer as the author of fact, not fiction. Heinrich led Sophia from gallery to gallery, explaining the significance of the treasures excavated from Herculaneum, Pompeii, Stabiae, and Cummae, and pointing out many forms of antiquities from numerous countries. Suddenly weary beyond endurance, Sophia surprised Heinrich by interrupting his definitive description of an encased object and insisting that they leave at once for the hotel. There, although footsore and bone-tired, Sophia allowed Heinrich to inveigle her into going out for dinner and to the theater.

Early the following morning they took the electric train for the hour's ride to Pompeii. Sophia, having studied Pliny at The Arsakeion, knew well the tragic story of the ancient city buried when Vesuvius erupted A.D. 79. Setting a rapid pace, the eager Heinrich took Sophia on a tour of the excavated ruins. She was shocked by the murals depicting Actaeon peeking at Diana bathing and then being torn to death by his own dogs. The paintings of nudes in sexual positions made Sophia blush, and she turned away in girlish confusion and embarrassment. Heinrich, sensibly, did not insist that they linger.

They drove by carriage from Pompeii to Sorrento. Heinrich did not want Sophia to miss the spectacular setting of the little town, enclosed by mysterious deep ravines on the land side and, on the seacoast, perched high on a cliff against which dramatic waves crashed nearly two hundred feet below. Toward the end of that particularly taxing day of sightseeing, Sophia was in no mood for views, and the natural beauty of Sorrento escaped her. In the fading light of late afternoon, she found the ravines not haunting but forbidding. Ever fearful of water, she was repulsed by the violence of the white surf pounding at the base of the cliff. Sorrento's orange and lemon trees, growing from tufa rock, instead of pleasantly reminding her of the citrus groves of Greece gave her an acute attack of homesickness.

After she and Heinrich were back at the hotel in Naples, Sophia demanded that she be allowed to have an entire day to rest and just to be alone. The tireless Heinrich, accustomed to being active every waking minute, was both puzzled and hurt by her request, to which he acceded with reluctance. The evening of her solitary day, they went to the theater, where Sophia was as delighted as a child by a gay operetta. Heinrich was so "stimulated by the joy of my Sophithion's reaction to the pretty music and colorful costumes, I applauded much more than the spectacle was worth."

The next week was spent in Rome. Although Heinrich as cicerone was relentless, Sophia began to appreciate the facts and the quotations he recited at museums and historic sites. In a letter to her mother, Sophia wrote that she had confessed to Heinrich the extent of her ignorance, begging him to share his vast knowledge with her and promising, in return, to be a good wife.

Captivated by the wonders of a world previously unknown to her, Sophia began slowly to place things in perspective. St. Peter's, which thrilled her, "is the most great and splendid church I have ever seen," she wrote her family, adding how wrong it had been to think of the Metropolitan Church in Athens as the biggest in the world. Receptive as she was to the new experiences, Sophia found all things "so big that they cannot enter fully into my small head."

In Rome, as in Naples, Heinrich and Sophia went to the theater every evening. The performances, being in a language she did not understand, often bewildered her, although Heinrich patiently explained the substance of what they were seeing. At the opera *Traviata,* the story as he told it so moved Sophia that she leaned her head on his shoulder, shuddering and softly weeping. But even Heinrich's résumés could not lessen the tedium of wordy plays without music that she endured with eyelids heavy from lack of sleep.

Only remarkable stamina sustained Sophia through the mental, physical and emotional strain of her honeymoon. She was "so confused by the splendors that I am most certain I can never put them in place or good order." The strenuous days gave her no time for relaxation, and she was constantly fatigued, in part because of the late hours to which she was unaccustomed. Heinrich, determined to educate her mind, was not one to make easy her adjustment to the intimate relationships of marriage. It was not in his nature to be a restrained lover. But even had he been disposed to be a tender tutor in the art of love-making, the frenetic schedule permitted no time for dalliance.

The last week of the honeymoon was the most hectic of all. The Schliemanns spent two days in Florence, two in Venice, and two in Munich. At Florence, after again insisting on a day to herself, Sophia so pleased Heinrich with her intelligent questions about architecture that he described her as "remarkably quick to learn." She liked Venice in spite of its waterways and wrote, more in astonishment than aversion, that travel was in small boats through canals and "there are no carriages at all." In Munich the Schliemanns did a whirlwind tour of museums, and Heinrich bought for Sophia a collection of luxurious lingerie that she felt was too beautiful and expensive for underwear.

Boarding a train for France, they were both in high spirits at the prospect of being settled in their home. Heinrich looked forward to the resumption of his archaeological planning, and Sophia yearned for rest and the comforts of a normal routine in Paris. The name Paris conjured up an enchanted city, but it did not materialize as magic for the child bride.

Now in ruins, Engastromenos' country home at Colonos stands in Meletios Square surrounded by bus stand and kiosk, vegetable carts, stores, and cafés. Large trees were planted by Sophia's father a few years before her marriage.

(LYNN POOLE)

(PHOTOCOPY BY LYNN POOLE)

(LYNN POOLE)

Two icons of Saint Meletios—a life-size painting and a small portrait of hammered silver—decorated the old church during the Schliemann wedding and are now in the new church.

St. Meletios Church as it was on September 23, 1869, the day Sophia and Heinrich were married. The church, which adjoined the Engastromenos' country home, has since been demolished and a new one erected in its place.

General Mélas photographed in the excavated Agora in Athens, with the site of his grandmother's ancestral home in immediate background. The Temple of Theseus on the hill could be seen from the garden of the family's town house.

(LYNN POOLE)

(COURTESY: ALEX L. MÉLAS)

Immediately after the ceremony the Schliemanns posed for a typical wedding picture, then joined guests for reception. Sophia's large family accompanied bride and groom to the Piraeus, where they boarded S.S. Aphrodite *for Sicily, first stop of a three-week honeymoon trip.*

After an exhausting honeymoon of sightseeing, Heinrich installed his bride at 6, Place St. Michel, his elaborate Paris home. Here young Sophia, as hostess, charmed both her husband's scholar friends and the city's haut monde *with her wit and beauty.*

(LYNN POOLE)

(COURTESY: ALEX L. MÉLAS)

FOUR

Home was hours away for Sophia when she reached Paris because Heinrich, not content to permit her a fleeting first impression of the city, guided her on an immediate tour of instruction. At his order, two carriages filled with their luggage were dispatched from the station to the Schliemann house. A third carriage in which Heinrich and Sophia rode followed a circuitous route, leading from one historic site to another. Heinrich was determined to provide Sophia "with learning and required graces" as quickly as possible.

The carriage clattered along the Rue de la Paix and stopped in the Place Vendôme, where Heinrich stepped down and restrained Sophia from jumping out. Speaking softly, he told her how a Parisian lady should descend from that type of carriage, with the left foot placed on the first metal step, then the right foot on the second. Demonstrating, Heinrich explained how her hand should be extended to the person assisting her, and in what position she should gather up her cloak and skirt. When Sophia performed the maneuver with elegance, he nodded in approval. Side by side they promenaded in the imposing octagonal area named for the palace of the Duc de Vendôme, son of Henri IV of France. Heinrich, rapidly recounting the history of the column at the center of the Place Vendôme, left out no detail from its erection in 1708 on plans of the architect Mansart, through alterations made by Louis XIV, Napoleon I, and later by rabid Royalists Louis Philippe and Napoleon III, who even then was considering the replacement of the column with another.

Returning to the carriage, the Schliemanns rode down the Rue de Castiglione, turning left onto the Rue de Rivoli; and Heinrich, after outlining changes made through the years in the Tuileries Garden to their right, had the driver halt at the mediocre bronze statue of Joan of Arc in the tiny Place de Rivoli. Without leaving the carriage, Heinrich jabbed his cane toward the equestrian Joan, reciting passages from Homer that seemed to link the girl saint with Helen of Troy, a tenuous association that defied elaboration. The carriage moved on toward the River Seine and stopped, the front of the Louvre to its left and the Carrousel Arch to its right. The Schliemanns descended from the carriage, and Heinrich expounded on the Arc de Triomphe du Carrousel.

The arch, erected by Napoleon I, was modeled on the Roman Arch of Severus "which you now remember well, my beloved Sophithion." The structure of Corinthian columns had three arches topped by bronze capitals supporting marble statues of Napoleon's soldiers, and Heinrich pointed out which achievements of the Little Emperor and his armies were commemorated in the marble reliefs. Repeatedly stressing the small size of Napoleon I, Heinrich noted how much a little man could accomplish through intelligence and a driving passion.

Walking backward as he talked, he gestured up at a bronze quadriga and reminded the dazed Sophia of the four-horse chariot they had seen atop St. Mark's in Venice. That one had once crowned the Carrousel, but was returned to Venice in 1814 by Emperor Francis. By order of Louis XVIII, the quadriga they were looking at had been designed by Bosio.

Reeling from the spate of dates and data, Sophia nonetheless retained what she heard, because every detail was included in a letter to her family. The nightmare of her first tour of Paris was unforgettable since she "wanted merely to reach my unknown future home and rest."

That rest was to be further delayed by Heinrich's discourse on the Louvre, its name originating from the Louverie, an ancient hunting château situated in a forest filled with wolves. Heinrich gave the Louvre's history, decade by decade, commenting on additions made by successive rulers until the single museum, a composite of many, had become the most famous edifice in all Paris.

They continued their slow-paced ride, and Heinrich, with the unceasing volubility of a tour guide, pointed out even the minor sights along the right bank of the Seine. Then apparently eager to reach home, he merely touched on the history of the Place du Châtelet and instructed the driver to turn right across the Île de la Cité.

Sophia brightened when she recognized the Cathedral of Notre

Dame, which she knew about from pictures and textbooks. Softly she asked Heinrich if they might go into the holy place but he, intent on reaching their destination, apparently did not hear her. The carriage, moving faster, shortly swept into Place St. Michel, opening in curving splendor from the left bank of the Seine.

The carriage slowed and stopped. Heinrich, with agility, jumped out; but Sophia sat staring with wonderment at the great houses, their walls touching, standing side by side. She scanned the house numbered "6" with its massive double doors of fine-grained oak heavily carved, a large bronze knocker centered on the right panel. Above the fanlight there was a cameo face that might be Zeus or Dionysos. The façade was hung with elaborate marble balconies, the kind seen in Athens only on the homes of royalty and the very rich.

Gently nudged by Heinrich, Sophia slowly rose and stepped from the carriage in the manner she had just been taught was proper in Paris. The giant doors of 6, Place St. Michel opened wide, and Dr. and Mrs. Heinrich Schliemann were welcomed home by smiling servants. Crossing the threshold, Sophia entered a new world for which she was ill prepared.

She, who had been impressed by the handsome exterior of the house, was overwhelmed by the elegance of its interior. The entrance-hall floor, a stark pattern of black and white marble, shone from recent polishing. White walls were shadowed by carved pilasters, and the ceiling beams and cornices were decorated with pseudo-Hellenic designs. Heinrich and Sophia mounted a curving staircase leading to the upper stories. On the third level they reached their own spacious suite of sleeping quarters, dressing rooms, and Heinrich's study.

He led Sophia through her bedroom and flung open French doors onto a balcony. Carriages rattled below and wagons rumbled. Sunset was reflecting on buildings across Place St. Michel. With sensitivity Heinrich, the man of dichotomous nature, held Sophia tight and, voice emotional, told her of the glories they would share, of the dream that together they would make come true. Briefly she clung to him and then, pulling back, looked deep into his eyes, as if to penetrate his very soul. She wrote to her family that at that moment she realized for the first time the strength, the power and the inherent tenderness of the man who was her husband.

Stepping back into the room, Heinrich closed the glass doors against the chill of evening and said, "My beloved, you must dress. Renan will be here soon, and you shall meet one of the greatest philosophers and authors of our age." He looked at Sophia and, slowly rising on the balls of his feet, kissed her on the forehead. Fervently he whispered, "My own Sophithion. *Gnothi sauton!*" And turning abruptly, he left the room.

Gnothi sauton, the inscription on Apollo's Temple in Delphi in faraway Hellas—Know Thyself. How could she? Would she . . . ever? Sophia undressed and, exhausted, stretched out on the huge bed, sinking into the sleep of Endymion that mercifully offered release from reality.

Ernst Renan, the man Sophia was to meet, was as much a maverick as Heinrich. Renan, disinherited by devout parents when he decided against being a priest, turned to letters as a career. He and Schliemann became epistolary friends in 1852 after Schliemann had read Renan's illuminating treatise on Averroës, the renowned Spanish–Arabian philosopher of the 12th century. On a business trip to Paris, Schliemann called on Renan, who was then being supported by his wise and worldly sister—the subject of one her brother's most famous literary works, *My Sister Henriette.* Renan, historian and critic, and Schliemann, financier and scholar, were mutually attracted and their friendship flourished.

Both men were individualists and intellectuals, original thinkers attacked by critics among their contemporaries. Schliemann defied established scholars by contending that Homer wrote history, that Troy was a real place and the Trojan War an actual conflict, with heroes who were human, not mythical beings. Renan outraged religious autocrats by questioning the Christian Trinity and suggesting in *The Life of Christ* (published in 1863) that Christ was merely one inspired leader among many in numerous religions. For that audacity Renan was dismissed from his professorship at the University of Paris.

Schliemann insisted that "we gave no thought to those we aroused, nor for their ill regard of us," and Renan concurred. Actually, being human, they unwittingly revealed from time to time how much they were affected by vituperation, frequently speaking of each other as being disturbed, upset and unhappy.

In a letter to a close mutual friend, Émile Egger, professor of classics and philology at the University of Paris, Schliemann wrote: "Renan says little but I know he is deeply hurt by the calumny aimed at him, a reaction with which I sympathize and understand." Neither Renan nor Schliemann ever revealed his innermost feelings to the world, although both sometimes erupted so volcanically against detractors that the latter regretted their criticism.

In the drawing room at 6, Place St. Michel, Heinrich warmly welcomed the elegantly tailored Renan. The two old friends, sipping sherry, were oblivious to their surroundings as they discussed Renan's latest work on the history and philosophy of religion.

Sophia approached the open door and stood watching the two men, her eyes half closed. With perception she recognized the quality of their relationship. "I stood alone, neither part of the room, the two men, nor their bond. Will I break through the barrier and one day become part of it? I wonder." Then she entered and the drawing room soon was enlivened by the conversation of an animated threesome. With Greek as their common language, they talked of Paris, Italy, and Greece, a country much admired by Renan. Sophia, dark eyes flashing and smile sparkling, told Renan about being a mail-order bride after a courtship bizarre even in those days.

Renan chuckled at her wit with anecdotes and roared with laughter about a prank of Heinrich's in Venice. Fully clothed, he had intentionally slipped over the side of the gondola in which they were passengers, swimming under it and coming up on the other side. Sophia, "always having the fear of water," was no less stunned than the speechless gondolier. The staff and guests of the hotel were astounded when the eminent Dr. Schliemann, soaked to the skin, entered the lobby. To Renan the tale revealed a Schliemann he had never known, a carefree and lighthearted man. Heinrich really was different after his marriage to Sophia, often indulging in tricks and jokes as he never had in his earlier years.

To Schliemann and Sophia the story about his Venice escapade recalled an ecstatic experience. In their hotel room they had laughed like children while Heinrich peeled off his sopping suit, stripping to dry off his body. Their mood had swiftly changed to one of passion, and for the first time they had experienced together a physical union that was amatory, not perfunctory. The memory was fresh as they looked at each other in their Paris drawing room.

At table that evening, Schliemann and Renan delved into the subject of comparative religion. They traced the Hellenic godhead Zeus back to Dan, an even earlier all-embracing divinity, relating both to deities of the religions of Indo-China, and sketching how all were synthesized and unified in the Christian faith. Each man tried to cap the other with passages from Hellenic literature found verbatim in the Bible. Schliemann completed the exchange with references to Acts XVII.28: *In Him we live and move and have our being* and *For we also are Thine offspring.* In Hellenic hymns the deity referred to by those lines was Zeus; in the Bible, Christ.

Sophia, excluded from the discussion felt herself to be an outsider at her own dinner table. As course followed course with the serving of proper wines, she consciously concentrated on what was being said. Listening intently, she learned more about the two men than their subject.

Besides Renan, who was Heinrich's most intimate friend in Paris, other scholars dined with the Schliemanns and spent long evenings discussing subjects about which Sophia knew nothing, and often in French, which she did not yet understand. She was forlorn "when Henry is surrounded by his learned friends and I sit endlessly by like an untutored child." Daytime hours, which she spent alone when Henry was taking care of his many business affairs, were lonely.

There were many servants in the huge mansion, but Sophia did not speak their language, nor they hers. She and her personal maid, a pleasant girl about her own age, communicated by sign language until Sophia tried her first faltering words of French. The housekeeper, a tall unsmiling woman who received her orders directly from Schliemann, efficiently managed the rest of the staff, moving about with a great ring of jangling keys suspended from the belt of her stiff uniform. Little bright-eyed girls, carrying dusters, skittered through the house and twittered to one another when the housekeeper was not near. The cook stayed within the kitchen area, which Sophia never entered, and the solemn butler seemed to appear out of nowhere only when he was needed. The whole atmosphere was repugnant to Sophia, accustomed to the warmth and liveliness of a home occupied by her large and endearing family.

She was in every sense a full-time student. When she and Heinrich were at home without guests, they read aloud poetry and from philosophical and scientific literature. They quoted from Homer, each picking up exactly where the other stopped, an exercise that was wearing to a mind already overburdened. Sophia was being tutored in French and English and, after her lessons with the two teachers, spent hours studying grammar and vocabulary "until I trip over words, speaking three languages at once, using whatever familiar word first comes to my mind." On shopping expeditions she was instructed by Heinrich, who, being intrigued by the world of fashion, did not doubt his own judgment of the accessories and costumes suitable for a young matron.

Sophia complained, justifiably, that "Henry's insistent demands on me to learn more leaves me with headaches and illness in my stomach." He took her to museums where he methodically passed from painting to painting, from sculpture to sculpture, explaining the meaning and aesthetic importance of each. They went from the Jardin des Plantes to the Louvre, from the Archaeological Institute to meetings of the Society of Architects. Sophia was forced to study the architecture of Notre Dame and Sacré Coeur, of St. Sulpice and St. Germain des Prés, of the Madeleine and Sainte-Chapelle. She had to learn how each architectural style, born of its own specific time, owed its origin to classical Greece. Heinrich, pondering over the ecclesiastical significance of the many styles of architecture, expounded on their relationship to temples that he might find "when I complete my excavations at Troy."

Wherever Sophia and Heinrich went, he was personally recognized by some people and unfailingly attracted the attention of others because of his commanding manner. He invaded rather than entered a room; asked no favors but demanded concessions. Never one to amble, Heinrich charged through shops and museums, streets and passageways. His energy was immeasurable; his mind, brilliant. Sophia often was more than a pace behind him, physically and mentally.

In Schliemann's sincere desire to spread all knowledge before his bride, offering her only things of lasting quality, he failed to sense her increasing exhaustion. The gloom and dampness of one of the coldest autumns in Paris depressed and chilled Sophia, who was used to the bright sun and sky of Greece with its crystal-clear air. Tours of museums sometimes delighted Sophia, whose youthful emotions responded to beauty. On other days she moved like an automaton through dark galleries, apathetic to exhibits. Small wonder that she often despaired of becoming the true partner of her scholarly husband.

Constant turmoil induced a physical condition that persisted for Sophia throughout her life. Nervous tension with complications of gastro-intestinal upsets resulted from the actions of the capricious Heinrich, who was alternately tender and tyrannical, calm and excitable.

Within a month Heinrich finally accepted the evident fact that Sophia was not well and showered her with attention, devoting his complete energy to her care. When the best doctors in Paris agreed that her condition was due to homesickness, exhaustion, and rich food, Heinrich himself set up the regimen for her recovery. He retained yet another teacher, a gymnastics instructor who put Sophia through a course of regular exercises. The number and length of her daily rest periods were prescribed by Heinrich, who also supervised her diet, hiring a special cook skilled in the preparation of Greek dishes. Even familiar food did not tempt Sophia during listless spells when she ate little or nothing. Her slow progress was marked by setbacks.

One of these occurred on an evening when the Schliemanns were going to the opera. As they were about to leave the house Sophia suddenly became ill and retired to her room, faint and pale. Heinrich, all sympathy, soothed and comforted her, saying that he would remain at home to read to her. Relaxed in his arms, Sophia began to revive and the color returned to her face. Heinrich, pleased by the sign of improvement, suggested that they could proceed to the opera together as planned. Sophia leaped to her feet and, with rage, ordered him to leave her where she was and to go alone to the opera. Astounded by her outburst, Heinrich was for once not in command, and Sophia literally pushed him out of the room, slamming the door behind him. Lingering outside, he tentatively turned the knob only to find that the door was locked against him.

Frustrated and annoyed, he went down to the waiting carriage, a figure of dejection even in his handsomely tailored full-dress clothes. He entered his first-tier box, but looked neither to right nor to left, nor at the decorations of the opera house that normally amused and delighted him: the ceiling frescoes with allegorized classical scenes and the caryatid figures. Nervous and fidgety, he sat inattentively through the first act, and during intermission remained seated, bowing absent-mindedly to acquaintances and friends. As the house lights were dimming for the second act he hurried from his box and dashed down the staircase, trailing his opera cloak and sliding a white glove along the handrail of Algerian onyx. He ran across the vestibule, went out through the gilded doors, and shouted for his carriage. Reaching his home, he rushed up the staircase, discarding hat, gloves and cloak on the way. At Sophia's door he stopped, breathless. The door knob responded to the pressure of his hand, and he entered the room where Sophia, in pale blue peignoir, was stretched out on a chaise longue. Heinrich stood, unmoving. Sophia held out a hand to him, and with an anguished cry he knelt, burying his face in her bosom as she gathered him to her.

Following that quarrel, Sophia and Heinrich both recorded some of its details. But its crucial import was not manifest until later years when, in his diary, Heinrich referred to "my fretful first act alone at the opera when Sophia's docile nature was cast off." A note of even later date contained the parenthetical passage "and after the opera, so paralyzing and frightening, I knew I loved and needed a woman of her grandeur."

Sophia's spontaneous revolt, which had long-range effects, did not immediately establish stability. The relationship of the Schliemanns swung like a pendulum. Her ability to absorb amazing amounts of knowledge delighted the teacher in Heinrich. Her use of the French language increased her ease as hostess. His latent sense of humor burgeoned. Frolicsome, they capped each other's pranks and jokes. All would be serene for a day or two; then the pleasant tenor of living would be upset by mounting tensions that caused Sophia's recurrent headaches and abdominal pains.

One night, following a day complicated by several vexing business letters, Heinrich was particularly annoyed when Sophia failed to be prompt for dinner. After a reasonable time had passed, he went to Sophia's room and found her missing. He searched the house with mounting agitation; then not stopping to put on a greatcoat, he went out into the cold night. Calling his wife's name, he strode along Place St. Michel where fog rose in eddies around the street lamps. Half sick with fear, he hesitated, wondering which direction to go in search of Sophia. On instinct, he went to the bridge over the Seine where she often lingered to enjoy the view of her favorite building in Paris, the Cathedral of Notre Dame. Heinrich was almost beside her huddled figure before he made it out through the fog. He slipped close to her, whispering "Sophithion." There was no answer, no reaction from the slender form hunched against the clammy buttress. Sophia stared straight ahead, as if trying to penetrate the eerie mist for a sight of the Cathedral.

Gently Heinrich slipped his arm around her body that trembled with cold and was soon wracked by gasping sobs as Sophia was overwhelmed by emotion. Homesick and in deep need of understanding, she clung to Heinrich, who took off his suit coat, put it around her shoulders, and tenderly led her home and to bed.

Sophia's spirits and health fluctuated with her own daily struggle for maturity and with Heinrich's unpredictable moods that reflected his conflicts with both governments and individuals. He fretted continually over delays in his plans for excavating at Troy and about rebuffs from fashionable Parisians who had once been his friends.

The Turkish government was recalcitrant about granting Schliemann a *firman* that would allow him to dig at the Hill of Hissarlik, the mound in Asia Minor where he knew he would find the ancient city of Troy. Major efforts in Schliemann's behalf were being made by Frank Calvert, United States vice-consul at the Dardanelles, who owned one part of the Hill. Calvert had to cope with captious Turkish officials, who would promise to sign Schliemann's *firman* one day and refuse the next. Calvert's letters were alternately disheartening and encouraging, and Heinrich's moods matched their tone.

Schliemann's main concern was to be free to dig at Troy, but while in Paris, he wanted to be accepted by the social set in which he had moved before his marriage to Sophia. He was irked that hostesses who had entertained him in the past neither called at once on Sophia nor sent invitations to their dinners and balls.

Their husbands, members of an influential group, acknowledged only with frigid bows Schliemann's greetings to them at the opera, the theater, and in other public places. From gossip that reached him in bits and pieces, Heinrich learned within a fortnight after his return to Paris with Sophia that many ultraconservative Parisians of his acquaintance did not consider his American divorce to be legal. Aware at last why he and Sophia were being ostracized, Schliemann consulted with leading attorneys in Paris and wrote posthaste to his lawyers in the United States. He soon possessed papers proving that his divorce decreed in Indianapolis was honorable and binding, and he shrewdly disseminated the information throughout Paris.

Socially prominent Parisians, assured of the sanctity of the Schliemann marriage, promptly accepted Heinrich and Sophia into their circle, overwhelming them with invitations. Sophia's shy charm and quick wit captivated hostesses and boulevardiers. Heinrich, noted for his business acumen and erudition, was deferred to during after-dinner conversations over brandy and coffee.

FIVE

Schliemann schemed to have the season's most brilliant ball mark Sophia's debut as hostess in Paris and set December 10, 1869, as its date. Renan, Egger, and one or two other close friends, informed early about the event, offered assistance that Heinrich hardly needed. Under his direction the guest list was meticulously compiled in time for the elegant invitations to be issued in late November. In full control he consulted with caterers and florists, engaged musicians, supervised the regular staff, and arranged for the extra waiters, footmen, and maids needed for the ball.

Although Sophia enjoyed the bustle and noise that animated the house, she was only on the periphery of the activities. She was not even permitted to have her own way about her ball gown. Heinrich had decided to have it made by an obscure little dressmaker, Madame Claire Monteux, because the couturiers of the famous houses, where Sophia's other Paris clothes had been ordered, were patronized by the ladies invited to the ball. He wanted Sophia's gown to be unique, and a secret until the night of the party.

On the day of the first consultation about the gown, Sophia had to go alone to Madame Monteux. Heinrich was detained by an emergency business meeting, and arrived at the dressmaker's establishment to find himself faced with another crisis. Strained silence pervaded the room where Schliemann was greeted by Sophia, her expression stern, her jaw firmly set. Madame Monteux, a look of despair in her eyes, bowed to him and shrugged her shoulders, as if in defeat. It took Heinrich only a few seconds to find out that Madame Monteux's design for a sleek gown displeased Sophia, who wanted a frock trimmed with furbelows. With the skill of a diplomat, Heinrich made Sophia examine her own face, figure and carriage in the full-length mirror of the salon, and stressed how perfect for her the ball gown sketched by Madame Monteux would be. In a matter of minutes Sophia was convinced that it was her idea to have the very design she had scorned, accepting it as one that would be totally unlike any other at the ball. When finished, the ball gown was a tribute to Heinrich's judgment, Madame Monteux's artistry, and Sophia's beauty. White satin, skillfully molded for the bodice and luxuriously draped in stiffened skirt folds, highlighted her olive complexion; and black velvet, entwined in the white lace edging the demure neckline, accented her black hair.

At precisely 8:30 on the night of the ball, Heinrich entered Sophia's dressing room just as her maid was attaching a ringlet of white flowers to her coiffure. Overcome by his bride's loveliness, he drew in his breath sharply and gazed at her with adoration. Radiant and seemingly calm, Sophia slowly pivoted, like any child showing off her party dress. She confessed to Heinrich that inside she was shaking, unsure of her ability to carry off her role as hostess; but he allayed her fears, assuring her that their ball was to be an occasion for shared joy, not an ordeal through which to suffer.

Kissing her lightly on the cheek, he led her to the drawing room's foyer, where they received at the top of the sweeping staircase. Head high, Sophia greeted her guests in French, carefully phrased, while Heinrich, proud at her side, seemed to increase in stature. For some time couples in steady flow moved up the steps, the ladies, magnificently garbed, attended by distinguished escorts, some titled, many wearing decorations signifying honors bestowed for valor in battle or for achievement in scholarship. Sophia's ball gown was appreciatively appraised by the women guests, all much older, who, themselves wearing priceless gems set in necklaces, bracelets and brooches, did not fail to notice that her youthfulness was dramatized by no other ornamentation than tiny earrings of diamonds and pearls. Gallants of Paris showered Sophia with compliments and she, slowly gaining inner security, began to enjoy herself, responding to the stimulus of soft music, discreet laughter, and the lively conversation that filled the house.

When the last arrival had been announced, Heinrich led Sophia into the drawing room where guests sipped champagne of rare vintage that bubbled in priceless crystal. No flûte was ever refilled, each empty one being replaced with another freshly filled, a refinement which so impressed Sophia she included that minor detail of service in her letter describing the ball to her family. Guests, who as hostesses were knowledgeable about the foods à la mode that season, raised speculative eyebrows when they glanced at the hors d'oeuvres on silver platters passed by liveried servants. The unusual bite-sized delicacies, unrecognized as the *mezés* of Greece, the little foods traditionally served before dinner, were tentatively tasted and unanimously enjoyed.

Sophia and Heinrich waltzed together for a few minutes, and then he wandered as attentive host among the guests, occasionally stepping to the ballroom door. From there he quickly located Sophia whose white gown stood out in the whirl of richly colored fabrics: satin, velvet, brocade. Sophia swung from partner to partner until supper was served at the stroke of midnight. The opening of the dining-room doors was accomplished by the faint echo of bells pealing outside in the frosty air.

The dining room was aglow with candlelight and the gilt of chairs ringed around small tables covered with heavy damask. Buffet tables, lavishly laden with flowers, held elaborately garnished meats, salads, pâtés, mousses in various forms, and pastries abloom with candied blossoms, buds and leaves. What was offered appeared to be typical fare, but Heinrich had seen to it that his guests would be surprised by exotic dishes made from food supplies shipped from the Orient, the United States, England, Scandinavia, the Caribbean islands and Hawaii. The taste buds of gourmets were titillated by the flavors of herbs and spices subtly blended in concoctions of varied textures. Palates accustomed to the vintages of France and Germany were pleased by the unfamiliar wines of Greece. The menu, skillfully arranged by Heinrich to be impressive in the city renowned for its cuisine, fittingly climaxed the party. Dawn was not far off when guests took reluctant leave of the Schliemanns. And the host and hostess retired to Sophia's room, fully confident that Heinrich's dream of social triumph had been realized.

The excitement of the ball was almost at once eclipsed by Heinrich's preoccupation with plans for their excavations in Asia Minor and by Sophia's return to a rigorous and exhausting daily schedule. Heinrich, like many men of consequence, concentrated on one project at a time. Having brought off the ball to his complete satisfaction, he turned his full attention to the major passion ever seething within him. Archaeology and excavations were the subjects of correspondence written in seven languages to friends, acquaintances and colleagues; of carefully phrased letters to London, Paris and New York newspapers, which published his refutation of scholarly opinion that Homer and Troy, the city he wrote about, were as much fiction as Oedipus and the Sphinx. Voluminous mail, prepared without secretarial assistance, was sent from 6, Place St. Michel, as from every place Heinrich stopped, whether for a brief stay or long.

Sophia resumed her strenuous language lessons, continuing French, starting German, and dropping formal instruction in English, practicing it by herself. The return to an enforced routine of museum-going failed to revive her interest in art, architecture or archaeology. She was wearied by long performances of plays and operas foreign to her, and suffered from the strain of a social life that was formal and demanding. Existing alternately in a whirl of activity and in the tedium of loneliness, Sophia again deteriorated physically.

Doctors called into consultation suggested to Heinrich that Sophia needed to spend more time with friends her own age. One of these, a confidante to whom Sophia was affectionately attached, was Renan's daughter Naomi, who was also married to a dynamic man. He, known by the single name Psycharis, was a young Greek of Chiote descent, who had been born in Odessa. Already embarked on a literary career, he was the leader of a controversial group involved in a crusade to reform the Greek language, both written and spoken. Psycharis and his friends held that change and growth vitalize language. They campaigned against the current usage and pronunciation of the Greek language, and were opponents of traditionalists, both professors and literary men, whose encyclical pronouncements against the new group were couched in scathing terms.

It was inevitable that Schliemann and Psycharis should be at odds, ranting at each other whenever they met. The two young wives deliberately instigated arguments between Heinrich, the fanatical Homerist who was already evolving his own classic form of Hellenic language, and Psycharis, the avant-garde spokesman who philosophized about a revised language, modern and lucid.

Even the companionship of young friends did not release Sophia from conflict. Struggling to extricate herself from the cocoon of youth, she was neither totally committed to Heinrich's serious world of scholarship nor completely reconciled to her life with him. On her own, she asked to be taken to performances offering congenial amusement. Released from the pressure of weighty matters, she was delighted by the magic tricks performed at the theater of Houdin, and Heinrich beamed with pleasure at hers. Eager to see his Sophithion happy, he enjoyed their first visit to the circus, where she laughed at the clowns and screamed at the feats of the daring aerialists. When she wanted to return to the circus again and again, Heinrich's own interest in it flagged, and he turned morose. He was jealous of the magician Houdin and of the clowns, freaks, and other circus performers, who could make Sophia react as he, with blandishments, could not.

He was being irritable and increasingly unpredictable in his behavior, when a letter mailed from the Dardanelles by Frank Calvert conveyed the long-awaited information that the *firman* would soon be granted, signed and officially sealed. That assurance was what Heinrich needed to lift his spirits. The Christmas holidays were brightened for him and for Sophia by plans for a return to Athens, to be followed by a trip to the site of Troy.

SIX

Paris was bathed in sun on the morning of January 3, 1870, the depressing fog of past weeks gone, overnight. Heinrich and Sophia, in high good humor, sat in his study completing arrangements for their departure to Greece and sorting through the mail. They were chuckling over an amusing letter from his sister in Germany when a servant entered bearing a silver tray, from which Heinrich took a telegram. He put it aside and finished reading aloud his sister's account of the antics of one of her grandsons. Still laughing, Heinrich picked up the telegram, slit open the envelope, and scanned the short message.

Natalya was dead. His adored Natalya, daughter by his first wife, Ekaterina, had died in St. Petersburg. And "when the horrible telegram arrived, Henry looked himself to be dead," Sophia wrote to her parents.

Dazed by the blow, Heinrich hunched in his chair, overcome by emotion and bitter memories. Russia, source of the major part of his immense fortune, was fountainhead of the personal misfortune that separated him from his three children, one now forever gone from his life.

Arriving in Russia as a businessman in 1846, Schliemann from the first was sought out as eligible bachelor by wealthy merchants with marriageable daughters and by royalty intent on pleasure. A succession of women of the court willingly accepted him as paramour, and his prowess as lover was common gossip. One young lady to whom he was affianced so displeased him by her frivolous flirtations that he broke their engagement. Again in love, he asked for the hand of Ekaterina Lyschin, but she confounded him by refusing his offer. On his return to Russia from his first trip to the United States, Schliemann, misjudging Ekaterina as a woman with all the virtues he wanted in a wife, repeated his proposal. She accepted him, and they were married at St. Petersburg on October 12, 1852—the year Sophia was born in Athens.

The union with Ekaterina was a mismatch from the first. Shortly after the wedding, Heinrich wanted Ekaterina to accompany him to France. She refused then and ever after to go with him on essential business trips to foreign countries. During the Crimean War he increased his fortune by traffic in arms, a circumstance that disturbed him, as his friends and family in Germany knew. He wrote his father that he hated being a war profiteer, but that the money gained would serve to finance the search for Troy. Schliemann talked incessantly to Ekaterina about Troy and his passion for excavation there, but she, bored, only half listened. She viewed with cold contempt his obsession with foreign languages and his dedication to scholarship. He, hot-blooded and sexually demanding, found himself rejected by a frigid and resistant wife.

The birth of their son Serge in 1855 overjoyed Heinrich, but the child did not draw the parents closer together, nor did the daughters, Natalya and Nadehsda, born later. Schliemann said that he stole the two youngest children by forcing himself on their mother.

Heinrich came to the realization that Ekaterina had married him only for his wealth, but he continued to beg her, for the sake of their children, to make a home with him. Although secure and living extravagantly in St. Petersburg, Ekaterina complained of Heinrich's miserliness and treated him with disdain. He promised her fine homes in whatever cities she chose, and she reiterated that she would live nowhere but in St. Petersburg.

Retiring from business in 1858, Heinrich traveled restlessly and was in Athens in the summer of 1859, when his plans for excavation at Ithaca were disrupted by a lawsuit in Russia. While awaiting the favorable settlement of the suit, he re-established himself in business and made tremendous sums, dealing in indigo, cotton, olive oil and tea. In possession of a fortune greater than he had ever "ventured to aspire to," Schliemann once more liquidated his business and for the last time forsook Russia as homeland.

In 1866 Schliemann settled in Paris, investing in real estate, studying with university scholars, and participating in social activities. Following his first archaeological expedition to Greece in 1868, he decided that he should be free of the woman who refused to share his life. For the purpose of divorce, he sailed for the United States and obtained his final citizenship papers at New York, where he had applied for the first on February 17, 1851.

In the brief autobiography in his *Ilios, City and Country* Schliemann stated, with more enthusiasm than accuracy, that "happening, therefore, to be in California when, on the 4th of July, 1850, it was made a State, and all those there resident in the country became by that very fact naturalized Americans, I joyfully embraced the opportunity of becoming a citizen of the United States." California became a state on September 9, 1850, two months later than Schliemann said, and he first visited it in the spring of 1851, after his New York application for first papers.

Although he later seemed to be confused about his American citizenship, it was legal and served him in the matter of divorce. He could have obtained a New York divorce by the use of "false certificates and perjury," but would "have nothing to do with such horrors." Carrying a letter of introduction to a lawyer in Indianapolis, Schliemann went there to take advantage of Indiana's flexible divorce law. He established residence and, with a team of attorneys, became involved in political machinations surrounding a proposed revision of the divorce law which threatened to delay his decree.

He offered as grounds for divorce Ekaterina's refusal to live with him, and for proof submitted to the court a sheaf of letters written by her during the preceding twelve months. In those letters Ekaterina monotonously repeated that she would neither leave Russia nor live with him any place else. He received his final divorce papers in July 1869, several months after he began correspondence with Archbishop Vimbos about a Greek bride. As early as May, Schliemann sent a photograph of Sophia to his aged father in Germany, explaining that happiness was possible only with a Greek wife.

That happiness was not yet assured on the morning when Heinrich received the news of Natalya's death at 6, Place St. Michel in Paris. Sophia, dismayed by his stricken expression, made no move to detain him when he rose from his chair and tottered toward his bedroom. He locked himself in and refused admittance to Sophia who, shuddering, stood outside, listening to his tortured sobs. He paced the floor, overwhelmed by an unreasoned sense of guilt, blaming himself for the death that might have been prevented had he not divorced the child's mother. Crying and moaning, he mourned for the daughter lying in a coffin in St. Petersburg, when she could well have been alive and happy if he had been a proper father.

In desperation Sophia sent for Ernst Renan and Émile Egger, who tried to mollify Heinrich through his locked door. For three days he refused to leave his room, and when he did, Psycharis tried to reason with him practically and philosophically, and Renan attempted to exorcise the sense of guilt. Weeping had not released Heinrich's pent-up emotions, and he remained unconsoled and morbid. Sophia, in anguish for her husband, broke under the strain and went into uncontrolled hysteria. In Renan's presence Heinrich vocally castigated himself for reducing Sophia to such a state of misery, and wondered aloud whether he should not release her by divorce and at the same time abandon his own dream of excavation.

Sophia recovered her composure, and taking Heinrich's head in her hands, held him close and rocked him like a child. Her intuitive action comforted him, and another conflict in his stormy life was resolved. Husband and wife, in need of each other, merged again as two loves.

Uneventful days passed with Heinrich and Sophia reading, visiting museums, and leading a quiet life. Disheartening letters from Frank Calvert reporting that the Turkish officials had not signed the *firman* were followed by a cheering, short message: "The *firman* will be signed."

SEVEN

Aboard the S/S *Niemen,* out of Marseille, as it slowly approached the harbor of Piraeus on February 9, 1870, a young girl and a middle-aged man leaned against the rail of an upper deck. Sophia, eager for the ship to anchor, could hardly wait to embrace her family and to place her feet on Greek soil. She peered toward the horizon, trying to make out the outline of the Acropolis rising above her ancestral home. Heinrich was as oblivious to his surroundings as he had been on the day of his arrival on the same ship five months earlier. Again concerned about a matter of future consequence, he was anxious to know whether confirmation of the signing of the *firman* awaited him in Athens.

In joyous reunion, Sophia was welcomed home by her family waiting on the quay. She was squeezed and hugged by her sisters and brothers, tenderly kissed by her mother, and held at arm's length in admiration by her father, in whose eyes tears welled. The repetition of the phrase "How you have changed!" was no idle parroting of a cliché, old as time. Their Sophaki, the little sister and youngest child who had left as a bewildered girl bride, was returned to them a composed young matron, dressed in Continental high fashion from the top of her fur hat to the tips of her exquisite leather shoes.

Chatting and laughing, questioning and reminiscing, the group reached the Hotel d'Angleterre, where Heinrich, after registering, hurried them all to the spacious suite reserved for him and Sophia. Without delay he hastily leafed through a great stack of mail, carelessly scattering envelopes as he searched for a letter addressed in the handwriting of Frank Calvert. Finally Schliemann jerked from the pile an envelope that he all but pulled apart in his eagerness to get at its enclosure. He quickly read the brief note and, face ashen, let the letter drop to the floor.

Sophia knew from Heinrich's expression that the *firman* was not yet signed, and without hesitation she turned to her family, saying,

"Heinrich must be alone." Dazed, they put on wraps removed only minutes before and, subdued, one by one left the suite, Sophia shepherding them toward the public hall. Turning back into the sitting room, she motioned to Heinrich that he should sit down and, facing him, dispassionately began to talk about the *firman*. She urged him not to give up hope of getting a permit to dig from the Turkish government, but to accept the latest disappointment as routine for negotiations with bureaucracy. She reminded him of the challenge to be met when they eventually reached Hissarlik, paraphrasing the plans he had so often detailed for her. Assuring Heinrich of ultimate success through his efforts and those of Frank Calvert, Sophia suggested that the inevitable wait should be endured with patience. She asked whether Heinrich's anxiety throughout the trip to Greece had not indicated that he was uncertain about good news on arrival. He admitted that the possibility of another delay had been in his mind, and agreed to relax until he received the message that would signal his departure for Asia Minor.

But relaxation was impossible for Schliemann. For the next few days he kept to a frantic schedule of business meetings, consultations with officials, and participation in archaeological disputes with friends and other scholars. Futilely engaged in unnecessary activities, he took no part in the festivities celebrating Sophia's homecoming. On the sixth day after their return to Athens, he moved Sophia from the d'Angleterre to her family's home and, on the seventh, sailed alone on a tour of the Greek islands.

His was no aimless jaunt to fill time. He planned to visit ancient places he had not previously seen, to study archaeological sites and objects of antiquity that he might be better prepared when he began his own excavation. His first destination was the island of Syra, in the Cyclades, to which he traveled on the Austrian ship *Schild* that anchored at Hermopolis, the city of Hermes. That seaport, its shipping tonnage greater even than that of the Piraeus, mushroomed in population in 1821 through the influx of refugees from the islands of Chios and Psara, both occupied by the Turks. The city's prosperity was due to its location on the trade route between the Mediterranean and the Black Sea.

Schliemann registered at the Hotel d'Amerique, which he described as one of the most miserable and unpleasant hostelries in which he had ever stayed. Finding a live object swimming in soup served him at the evening meal, he got up from the table in disgust and, without dining, retired to his room. Its rickety bed was infested with lice that made his night wakeful. Loud in his complaints about conditions at the hotel, he nonetheless decided against changing to another with higher rates.

In spite of the physical discomforts endured, Schliemann thoroughly explored Syra, delving into the archaeology of its ancient sites and, as he did everywhere, taking an interest in contemporary life as well. Syra lent itself to such study because it was the See of a Roman Catholic bishop, whose seat on a high hill picturesquely contrasted with that of a Greek Orthodox Archbishop on an opposite hill. Since the two Sees were separated culturally, as well as geographically, Schliemann lingered in long discussions with people sharply divided by religious conflict. As an outsider he evaluated the situation, drawing conclusions along generally the same lines followed more than half a century later by social psychologists.

At the small museum in New Town, Schliemann scrutinized the exhibit of Hellenistic statuary, pottery and artifacts. In the ruins of the Theater of Apollo, he let his fancy take him back through the centuries to classical times when the latest plays from Athens were performed for an audience made up of islanders. Strolling along the waterfront, Schliemann watched workers in the shipyards and at dye plants. He admired the mosaics and murals of the island's Byzantine churches. With vigor he walked up 590 feet to the Church of St. George, and climbed to the top of Pyrgos, a hill where marble, mottled with veins of mica, was quarried. At the pinnacle of Pyrgos, 1,360 feet high, Schliemann, enjoying a sweeping view of Syra, the Aegean and surrounding islands, recited aloud from the Fifteenth book of Homer's *Odyssey*:

> A certain island, Syra by name—
> you may have heard of it—rests off Ortygia
> straight west, and gathers the sunsets of the year.
> Not overpopulated, but fine for grazing
> sheep and cattle; rich also in wine and grain.
> No lack is ever known there, no disease,
> wars on its people, or ills that plague all men;
> but finally when its people reach old age, Apollo,

with his silvered great bow arrives, and Artemis,
shooting arrows of kind death.
Two towns divide the lands of that entire domain,
both ruled by Ctesios, my father,
heir of Ormenos, truly a gentle godlike man.

There on the very spot described by Homer, Schliemann characteristically felt himself close to historical roots, his imagination and emotions evoking within him an empathy from which he derived stimulation for the exploration of Troy. As often at such solitary moments, Schliemann's knowledge and inner sensitivity fused so that he became the hero of an ancient era. It might have been of him that Henry James in the *Art of Fiction,* 1888, wrote: "The power to guess the unseen from the seen, to trace the implication of things, to judge the whole piece by the pattern, the condition of feeling life in general so completely that you are well on your way to know any particular corner of it—this cluster of gifts may almost be said to constitute experience. . . . If experience consists of impressions, it may be said that impressions *are* experience."

At interludes Schliemann honed impressions to a sharp edge, experiencing the seen and conjuring the unseen as he prepared for the realization of his life's ambition. The brief exploration of islands was such an interlude. Having finished at Syra, Schliemann inquired about passage aboard a regular vessel that would visit the islands of the Aegean, and was told that the "only boat available to take me to those islands I wish to explore would cost me ninety-six French francs. Furthermore, the agent said that I would have to follow the schedule of the boat, arriving at each island and leaving that island at the pleasure of the captain. All of these people are robbers, and I shall not allow them to take all my money."

Schliemann, who turned penurious whenever he thought that he was being exploited, searched until he found better terms for the expedition ahead. Ever one to weigh cost against return, he engaged a boat for only 52 francs, which price included the service of a five-man crew—captain and four seamen—willing to conform to Schliemann's individual schedule. He used as guide for the island trip some works of Pausanias, the observant traveler of the second century, to whom not only Schliemann but generations of sightseers and scholars owed a great debt. The small boat put out from

Hermopolis just after midnight, March 1, and late that same day reached the island of Delos.

In ancient times the Greek world was commercially ruled by Delians. Their island, the mythical birthplace of Apollo and his twin, the goddess Artemis, was also a great religious center. On Delos, Ionian Greeks worshipped their gods at ritual ceremonies and, in honor of the deities, celebrated at opulent festivals and in exciting athletic contests. In the sixth century B.C. the Athenian ruler Peisistratos ordained the purification of Delos by removal of all tombs. Subsequently the purification was extended by a decree against burial on Delos. At a later date, to prevent death from occurring on the island, seriously ill people were removed to nearby Rheneia. With passing centuries the status of Delos as a great Aegean power fluctuated. Devastation by the generals of Mithradates put an end to the island's prosperity in 88 B.C., and complete destruction was effected by pirates in 69 B.C. Slowly the silted earth of land and sifted sand of sea covered the island.

Schliemann traversing Delos saw some landmarks described by Pausanias, but wrote in his diary that "others seen by Pausanias are most certainly covered with the soil of time." The middle-aged romantic, ignoring the crew of five accompanying him, waxed lyrical about being alone on the totally uninhabited island. In imagination he became a citizen of ancient times, striding from one sacred spot to another "amidst such grandeur and beauty." He actually saw some unburied evidence of early glories of architecture, but in his mind's eye he viewed temples, treasures, palaces, stadia, amphitheaters, sculpture of pure Parian marble, columns of bluish marble, and figures carved in porous limestone or Naxian granite.

Sitting alone on Mount Cynthos, he gazed across the dead island and pondered on the fates of civilizations. Why did a civilization rise, fade, and fall into oblivion until man, uncovering its remains, released the essence of its greatness? Schliemann dwelt on the misconception of many people that their civilization will forever survive in spite of historical evidence that every culture eventually fades and is superseded by another. Verities of the past and present in conflict coursed through his mind. *Why* and *how,* two questions firmly rooted in the philosophy of ancient Greece, fired in Schliemann the maelstrom that would never let him achieve the inner peace he thought he sought. He wondered what answers were to be found beneath the layers of earth and sand that blanketed ancient Delos. For one brief moment he entertained the idea of restoring the island to its original glory by digging below the surface, putting into the project his full power of wealth, imagination, and physical effort. That notion was short-lived because he knew that he could never be false to his early dream of excavating for Priam's Troy.

Leaving Delos, Schliemann's little boat set out for Paros, where he once again was impressed by the reliability of Pausanias. Thrilled by the discovery of inscriptions not mentioned by that observant traveler, Schliemann decided that the stones had been uncovered in later centuries, by man or the forces of nature. Schliemann proceeded to Naxos, Nio and Santorini, then doubled back to Paros and Syra, the starting point of his expedition. Each island had its special attraction for him, every object its unique value. The joy of the solitary journey into the past and the opportunity offered for time to think were tempered for Schliemann by his inability to communicate with others. He missed his "adored Sophithion without whom my days are but nothing," and was eager to report on the trip "to you, my beloved wife, who has come to know and understand me, who gives me strength and will."

He joined her in Athens on March 20 and wrote in his diary ". . . together we shall wait most patiently until the *firman* is granted, and only then shall we leave this glorious city." Undoubtedly, when he wrote those words he did mean them. But four days after his return to Athens, an entry in his diary stated: "My wife and I made today an excursion to Phyle."

Schliemann was warned that on rural jaunts he was exposed to risk of attack from brigands who terrorized the countryside up to the very outskirts of Athens. Some of the outlaw bands were in league with government officials whose constituents were kept in line by threat of outlaw reprisal for disloyalty. The collaboration of brigandage with officialdom was at its height in 1863 when the teen-age Prince William of Denmark was proclaimed King George I of Greece. He, blinking at the liaison, which was a political scandal, made little attempt either to curb official participation in banditry or to control the maurauders. In 1876 outlaws continued to swoop down on settlements of peasants and estates of landowners, demanding money, livestock, foodstuffs and household effects in return for the promise of protection from other brigands. The bands attacked defenseless travelers on the highways, taking jewelry, money, and even clothes off the backs of unfortunate victims, ruthlessly killing those who resisted.

A government official friendly to Schliemann, after unsuccessfully trying to dissuade him from setting out for Phyle, offered him two horsemen as bodyguards. Under most circumstances two men were not sufficient for protection, but those recommended to Schliemann were described as being well known in the region to be traveled. It was implicit that they, being either related to or associated with brigands of the area, would not be molested, nor would any group with which they rode.

In an open carriage flanked by the outriders, Sophia and Heinrich left for Phyle at 6:45 A.M. on a day sunny and warm in Athens. But as they progressed along the ancient road into the snow-covered hills Sophia became chilled, and Heinrich, taking off his greatcoat, ". . . used it to cover and warm this beautiful creature to whom I am so fortunately married." Marveling at the superb scenery, they crossed the Kephisos River, continued through the villages of Kamatero, Ano Liosia and Menidi. A primitive trail, rutted by cartwheels, that led down into the Potami Gorge disappeared, and the carriage rolled on across untracked ground. Outcrops of rock separated stands of pine trees with bark slashed at intervals along their trunks; from the slashes, in warm weather, sap ran down into crude earthenware or natural stone bowls, to be collected for making *retsina,* the resinated wine of Greece. Heinrich described the trees as "shining magnificently as they cast their shadows on the virginal snow lying on the ground."

He and Sophia had to climb a distance from their carriage to the summit of Phyle, in the heart of the mountains. From its 2,255-foot height, "the view was so spectacular that we near lost our appetite for food." But they did eat their picinic lunch, and Sophia was warmed by the soup heated over an open fire by the carriage driver. She and Heinrich spent two afternoon hours examining the famous fortress of Phyle, headquarters of the gallant Thrasyboulos after the Thirty Tyrants expelled him from Athens in 404 B.C. Construction of the massive fort was a feat accomplished by his devoted followers. "The castle sits like a nest of birds on a high rock. Big stones are joined together without cement," Heinrich observed. With tactile appreciation he ran his hand over the barely visible joints as he and Sophia walked around the walls surrounding the stronghold. The outer wall was 8 feet thick and 12 feet high, with a door only 4 feet high. An inner wall, also 8 feet thick, had an even smaller opening, easier to defend from within.

Heinrich and Sophia, fired by his enthusiasm, imagined what life must have been like for the daring men who made sorties from this aerie against the Thirty Tyrants of Athens. "My Sophithion applauded with pleasure my explanation of how Thrasyboulos' band captured the Piraeus and delivered Athens from the hated yoke of the tyrannical oligarchy in 403 B.C." Hand in hand Sophia and Heinrich stood beside the outer wall and looked at nature's *vue sauvage* of harsh land, deep gorges, small valleys, and peaks jutting upward as if tossed by the gods. "One can see the plain of Athens and the tip of the Acropolis, and because the weather is so sparkling one can see clear out to sea. Visible too is the Saronic Gulf with Aegina and the coast of the Peloponnesus. All opens as through a window."

For Sophia there was a figurative opening of a window through which she had an expanded view of her native land and its history. Sensing Heinrich's deep attachment for and appreciation of the past that was her heritage, she understood his dream as never before. He wrote that from Phyle they "returned to Athens after this most stimulating day." She returned with an understanding of her husband that deepened with subsequent excursions.

The next was to Marathon, the seaside battlefield where a small force of Athenians beat off a massive invasion of Persians in 490 B.C. The Schliemanns, again protected by bodyguards on horseback, were accompanied by a professor from the University of Zurich and by Mrs. George Markly, an American from Philadelphia. Their carriage, as it proceeded toward Kaphissia, passed Mt. Lycabettus etched against the Greek-blue sky, as were the honeyed hills of Hymettus and, ahead, Penteli. Much farther along the dirt road, the villages of Chalandri and Maroussi nestled amid vineyards and olive groves; and here and there, according to Schliemann, early-growing beans turned colorless rocks green. After the carriage and the outriders swung north from the summit of the castle-shaped Ettos, the party overlooked a magnificent view of pine-clad hills close by, a tip of the Plain of Marathon below, the azure Aegean beyond, and the island of Euboea in the distance.

The carriage stopped at the base of Soros, the isolated knoll that supposedly marked the mound grave of the 192 Athenians who fell at the Battle of Marathon on September 10, 490 B.C. The Schliemanns and their friends, pushing through brush and weeds, climbed the 40 feet to the top of the knoll, which at its base was 200 yards in circumference. They viewed the Plain of Marathon from Soros, and then descended to the battlefield stretched out along the sea. While they picnicked, Heinrich talked knowledgeably of the battle that raged around the very spot where they were, and discussed the historical account of the conflict in Herodotus' work on the Persian wars.

On the way back to Athens, the carriage stopped on the banks of the River Valanaris, where Heinrich was told by an old man that skeletal bones of Athenians who died at Marathon were to be found in the vicinity. At the spot indicated by the peasant, the coachman and Heinrich picked up bones that he carried back to Athens ". . . to have them examined on the implausible chance that the old man was correct." As it developed, he was not. Professors at the University of Athens informed Schliemann that the bones were fossilized specimens from the last Tertiary period.

Every time Heinrich and Sophia returned safely from a one-day excursion, their friends and her family were relieved, having been tense and worried about bandit attacks. Sophia was no more apprehensive of highway robbers than Heinrich and did not even worry about him when he rode alone each morning for his daily swim at Old Phaleron, a bathing place on the sea between Athens and the Piraeus. He was addicted to sea baths for keeping physically fit. It was not only the exercise of swimming that Schliemann considered to be health-giving, but also the contact with sea water filled with minerals that had healing and invigorating properties.

On March 29 the Schliemanns set out together for New Corinth, refusing to be bothered with safe-conduct guards. At New Corinth they strolled over ground where Heinrich had earlier made a few test excavations. He explained to Sophia why, after unearthing a few funeral vases, he had abandoned hope of finding the tomb of Pericles in the area. He came to the conclusion that ". . . my work at New Corinth was fruitless and I could tell at once that this site would provide no antiquities or historical information of importance, so I ceased work there forever." Later excavations by others proved he was correct. After enjoying a leisurely day of sightseeing, they returned to Athens.

The next morning Heinrich went alone to the Piraeus where he had his sea bath before embarking on the *Panallinion* bound for the Peloponnesus. He landed and took a cart to Old Corinth, where he inspected a cave, the ancient amphitheater, the Bath of Venus, and the "splendid seven columns of the Temple of Apollo." The *Panallinion* crossed the Bay of Corinth to Itea, and from that tiny town Heinrich went by small carriage up the winding mountain road through Skala and Solano to Delphi, site of the shrine of Apollo. He had once thought of excavating at Delphi, but the French school of archaeologists were already negotiating for rights to dig. Schliemann carefully studied the terrain and the remains visible without excavation, ". . . learning all I could to be useful when I go soon to Troy to begin my work."

The short expedition to Delphi took Schliemann to the brink of a major decision on which he concentrated during the trip back to Athens. When he joined Sophia there on Monday, April 4, a plan for immediate action was full blown in his mind.

Late on the afternoon of April 5, Heinrich, without preamble, calmly announced to Sophia that they were leaving for Troy the following day. Momentarily taken aback, she quickly recovered her composure and reminded Heinrich that he had not been notified of the signing of the *firman,* for which he had said he would wait. Brushing off her remark, he answered that he was willing to wait no longer. She logically pointed out that he had made no preparations for excavation and asked how he expected to dig without equipment or a crew of men. Irritated by her opposition to his headlong decision, he said that they would obtain tools and workmen after reaching Asia Minor. Then he peremptorily ordered Sophia to begin her packing at once. She looked straight at him and refused, saying that she intended to remain in Athens, and if he insisted on carrying out his helter-skelter plan, he should do it alone.

Neither of the strong-minded couple gave in and, still smarting over Sophia's show of independence, Heinrich sailed for Constantinople on April 6. The first proof that Sophia had been correct about lack of preparations for the trip came when he was forced to accept second-class passage on the S/S *Menzaheh* on which he traveled uncomfortably to the Dardanelles.

EIGHT

Upon his arrival at the Dardanelles in early April 1870, Schliemann went by horseback to the village of Renkoï for a talk with Frank Calvert, Heinrich's intermediary with Turkish officials and part owner of the Hill of Hissarlik. It was the place that Schliemann, without question in his own mind, identified as the site of ancient Troy.

Although Calvert was sick in bed and unable to go to Hissarlik, he arranged for a bodyguard to ride on with Schliemann to Chiplak. At that tiny community not far from the Hill, Schliemann placed his few personal possessions in a dingy room rented from the occupants of a miserable hut. He and two hired workmen from the village started toward Hissarlik on the morning of April 9. They were an incongruous trio on burros. The two men from Chiplak, dressed in rough work clothes, tattered and filthy, rested sturdy shovels on the backs of their animals. Schliemann, wearing a London-tailored suit, a bowler, and fresh, white linens, grasped a pickaxe in gloved hands.

At Hissarlik, Schliemann, tense with an excitement that pervaded his whole being, looked out across the Trojan plain. Standing alone on the Hill, he was isolated theoretically as well as physically from most scholars of literature and archaeology. These contended that the *Iliad* and the *Odyssey* were collections of songs composed in different ages by various bards, each celebrating the deeds of some mythical hero. It was generally thought that the songs, being inconsistent in their artistry, were not the works of a single poet. Most professors of ancient literature were convinced that the subjects of the collected songs were fictional, not factual. Nevertheless, the so-called collections of songs were the only source of knowledge about prehistoric Greece.

Schliemann, having accepted Troy as a real place in his early childhood, amassed evidence to defend his theory against scholars of opposite view. He was as certain that Troy had existed as he was of its location at Hissarlik, a site controversial even among the few who agreed with Schliemann that Homer's tales were based on real events. Some thought that the ancient site of Troy, called Ilium, would be found at Bunarbashi, a mound several miles south of Hissarlik. One of these was General Helmuth Karl Bernhard von Moltke, hero of the Austro–Prussian War and favorite of Wilhelm I of Germany. General von Moltke, a dilettante in archaeology, based his opinion that Bunarbashi was a likely site for Troy on its military potential, not on classical evidence.

Schliemann's conviction, in part intuitive, was primarily based on facts as he interpreted them from Homer's *Iliad*. Intuition affected all of Schliemann's archaeological explorations, but he bolstered that innate sense with precise information extracted from Homeric and other ancient writings. On a previous visit to Hissarlik and to Bunarbashi, he had made geographic comparisons of the two locations, dismissing the possibility that the latter could have been the site of Homer's Troy.

At 162 feet above sea level, Hissarlik was the crown of a continuous ridge, 12 miles long, that angled east from the Plain of Troy. That expanse, about a two-hour ride in breadth, was consistent with Homer's placement of the battles of the Trojan War. The spectacular panorama encompassed the Hellespont to the north and the Aegean to the west, with high mountains of the island of Samothrace towering over the low-lying Imbros just offshore. Schliemann remembered from his earlier expedition that from Hissarlik, the cone of Mt. Athos, 119 miles away on the mainland's Chalcidian peninsula, was visible at sunset on clear days. He had clearly seen Asia Minor's Mt. Ida, the seat of Zeus, from which the god watched the battles of the Trojan War.

The Aegean Sea was three and one-quarter miles west from Hissarlik, and the Hellespont, three and three-quarter miles north, distances compatible with those from ancient Troy. Bunarbashi, an inland mound, was eight miles from the Hellespont. Homer had his heroes going back and forth from the Hellespont to Troy between "awakening light and sunrise," a passage possible to and from Hissarlik but not from Bunarbashi. Priam left Troy at sundown, according to Homer, spent the night feasting at the Grecian camp at the Hellespont, and was back home before sunrise. That and other Homeric incidents indicated that the distance from Troy to the Hellespont was short.

Homer described the Greek camp and the citadel of Troy as

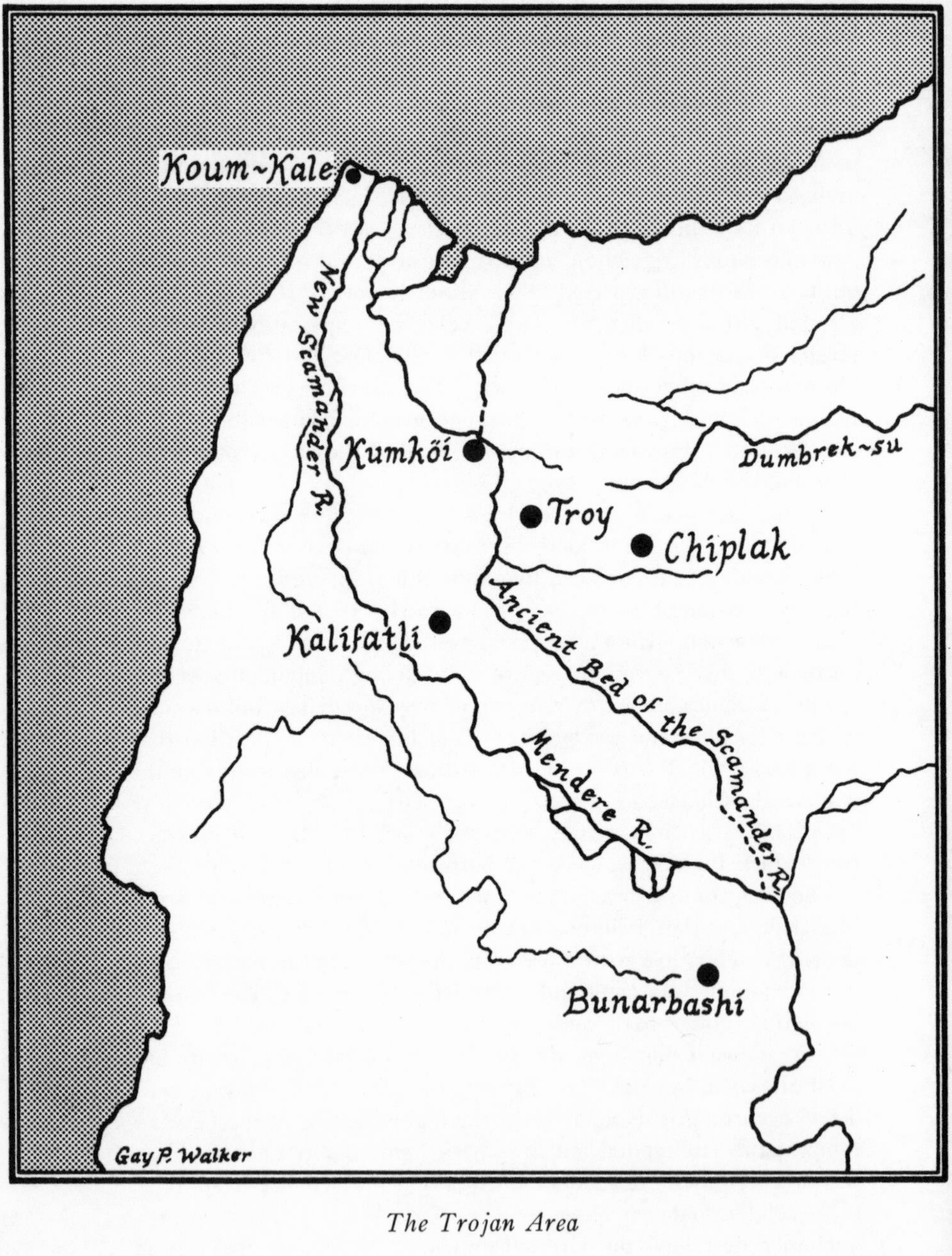

The Trojan Area

being separated by the chief river of the region, the Scamander, which, rising on Mt. Ida, flowed with such force that it could be forded at only one place. The Scamander of the *Iliad* marked the boundary of the warring forces who often skirmished along its banks during the ten-year war. A smaller river, the Simoes, flowed from the northern base of the citadel, and emptied into the Scamander, which ran north to form a delta at the Hellespont. When Schliemann was at Hissarlik, the ancient Scamander had long since changed course, and the Simoes (Dumbrek-su) joined with the new Scamander to form the Kalifatli-Asmak, the river emptying into the modern delta.

Homer placed the Greek flotilla at the point where the Scamander emptied into the Hellespont from which a river road led by the most direct route to Troy. Greek ships sailed right up to the gates of Troy, as Homer told it, and in spring that would have been possible when melting snows on Mt. Ida produced flash floods that widened and deepened the ancient Scamander at Troy or Hissarlik, not at Bunarbashi.

An episode from the *Iliad* that seemed to prove beyond all doubt that Bunarbashi could not have been Troy was the one in which Achilles pursued Hector three times around the wall of the city. The position of Bunarbashi on a steep and rugged height precluded any such feat, even by supermen; at Hissarlik the chase by foot would have been within the bounds of reasonable accomplishment.

Prominent in the Homeric tale were two springs flowing from the base of the citadel, one hot, one cold. Those who favored Bunarbashi as the site of Ilium offered as evidence two springs issuing from the mound at the place the Turks called Kirk-gios, meaning forty eyes. Schliemann asserted that there were actually forty springs, not just two, and he "found in all the springs a uniform temperature of 17° Centigrade equal to 62° Fahrenheit." He could not prove that two springs of different temperatures existed at Hissarlik, but wrote that "one day while digging I know I shall find the two springs."

Schliemann staked everything on his judgment that the Hill of Hissarlik was that described by Homer, that Bunarbashi could not possibly fit Homer's epic. There was much changing of sides in the debate. Some who decided Hissarlik was the site of ancient Ilium had originally favored Bunarbashi; others had held with

Hissarlik from the beginning. Among those who agreed with Schliemann about Troy's location were an Austrian consul at the Dardanelles, G. von Hahn; the astronomer A. Schmidt of Athens; M. Émile Bournouf, honorary director of the French School of Archaeology at Athens; F. A. Wolf, E. D. Clarke, and P. Barker Webb of England; the Germans George Grote, Julius Braun, and Gustav von Eckenbrecher; Ireland's classical scholar Professor J. P. Mahaffy; Charles MacLaren of Edinburgh, who announced for Hissarlik as early as 1822; and, of course, Frank Calvert. Only Schliemann, firm in his conviction, was willing to put the theory to test by hiring diggers to start excavation.

On April 9, 1870, Schliemann, alone with two workmen from Chiplak, showed them where to dig, by sinking the first pickaxe into the ground. He then climbed to the top of the Hill of Hissarlik and gave himself up to a play of imagination that brought to life scenes from the *Iliad,* which he knew by heart. He wrote in his diary that he "could fair see the handsome Paris and fair Helen landing at this spot in their flight from Sparta." Lines of the epic poured forth as he recited highlights of its story: Paris, debonair son of Priam, king of Troy, hospitably received by Menelaus, king of Sparta, was irresistibly attracted to the beautiful queen, Helen. Having seduced her, Paris abducted Helen, returning with her to his father's realm where they lived luxuriously within the citadel at Troy. Heinrich, certain that Troy's remains existed below the ground on which he stood, transported himself back through the centuries to the departure of Menelaus for Mycenae, ruled by his brother King Agamemnon. Together the brothers planned a flotilla that would sail to avenge the honor of Menelaus and to rescue the fair Helen. The sibling kings were joined by Achilles and his blood-brother Patroclus; by Odysseus, ruler of the island of Ithaca; and by the man Homer called "the Telamonian Ajax," who was Ajax, son of Telamon, chief of the island of Salamis.

Two years were spent in gathering the forces of army and navy before the ships sailed across the Aegean, into the Hellespont, and reached at last the broad delta where the fresh-water river Scamander emptied into the salt-water strait. The Greeks landed on the shore of Asia Minor, and for ten years their war with the subjects of Priam raged across the Trojan plain. Battles were won and lost; heroes of both sides were wounded and many were killed.

The Olympian gods, some favoring the defenders and some the aggressors, aided and abetted their respective favorites in the decade-long war.

Schliemann, standing on the overlook of that ancient battle, was entranced by his own recitation and, "with my flesh creeping with bit-bumps covering my skin," could see a massive wooden horse pulled to the great Scaean Gate of Troy. He felt the dust close in around the scene, the gates swinging wide as the horse, gift of the Greeks to the Trojans, was drawn into the citadel. He imagined the Greek soldiers, concealed within the horse, leaping out when the full dark of night had fallen, and setting fire to the city before opening the gate to their cohorts, who entered and sacked the city of Priam. "Although it was morning, with the sun rising high, to me it was night and I saw flames leap into the sky, as they did in Jerrer's book read at age seven. I was filled with intense desire to begin my digging and lay bare, for the world to see, the city of Priam and the war recorded by Homer."

Unable to break the spell in which he was held by Homer's lines, Schliemann recited part of the poet's second epic, the *Odyssey,* story of the adventures of Odysseus, who spent the ten years following the Trojan War searching for his home island, Ithaca.

More than ever convinced that he was at Troy, Schliemann walked down from the top of the Hill to where his workmen were cutting a trench from north to south. Rolling up his sleeves, he helped the two men to make ". . . a preliminary excavation in order to test the depth to which the artificial soil extended. I made it at the northwestern corner, in a place where the hill had increased considerably in size, and where, consequently, the accumulation of debris of the Hellenic period was very great." In three days they had sunk a shaft to a depth of 16 feet below the surface and laid bare a wall of huge stones, 6½ feet thick, which, "as my later excavations have shown, belonged to a tower of the Macedonian epoch."

Schliemann, no longer able to restrain his urge to dig, was excavating at Hissarlik without a Turkish permit. From experience he knew that every application for permit had to pass through a maze of political intrigue, not only in Turkey but also in Greece. Such machinations beset him throughout his archaeological work. Representatives of both countries suspected that all foreigners requesting rights to digs had ulterior motives. Some officials simply put off the consideration of matters unimportant to them, and others expected bribes for their cooperation. Schliemann from the first was unwilling to conduct archaeological research under threat of bribery, because he felt that his scientific exploration would benefit the country where it was conducted. In 1870, he boldly bypassed officials in Constantinople.

By April 12 Schliemann had managed to obtain four workmen, who rode with him from Chiplak and began their day by starting a trench running from east to west across Hissarlik. Midmorning he was repulsed by a snake that slithered in front of him "but with instinct I swung my shovel and cut the serpent in half." Later that day he had an encounter with another unpleasant intruder, a Turk who demanded 300 gold francs in return for permission to dig on his land. Schliemann explained dramatically that he was digging to find the famous city of the Turk's ancestors, but the man, unimpressed, insisted on payment. Schliemann turned out his pockets to prove that he had but 40 francs. The suspicious Turk took the money but refused to leave until he had searched through Schliemann's greatcoat and hat, thrown to one side of the trench. While the Turk pawed through the clothing, Schliemann returned to his digging.

Word of his firm handling of the irate landowner spread overnight, and in homage to the intrepid foreigner who was digging, nineteen men signed up for work at the excavation. That day the diggers removed from the east-west trench two coins, two clay pots, a funeral urn containing the ashes of a human body, a silver cup, a leather ring, three terra-cotta statuettes, and fragments of a broken cup ". . . which I have put together in full except for one piece that is missing."

Standing in the deepening trench, Schliemann dug down into the soil ". . . which lay on top of Priam's palace in the area where I shall uncover the Ilium of Homer. My only regret and sadness as repeatedly I sink my spade is that my cherished wife is not beside me at the moment." He stopped often to examine some object uncovered by a workman, putting it with the pile of other artifacts to be examined on his return to Chiplak that evening. Although small in stature, Schliemann had great strength and agility and seemed to be everywhere at once in the digs, directing, cajoling, examining, digging. ". . . my muscles as they respond to the efforts so physical are able to function because I have kept my body strong with swimming. Muscles are matched with the channels of my mind and rivers of my soul. I am at work at last!"

His spade was midair in a wide swing when he saw the Turk from Koum-Kale who, only the day before, had been paid off with 40 francs. Malevolent and greedy, the Turk leaned over the side of the trench and, spewing forth a barrage of Arabic, demanded more money. As the volley of words continued, Schliemann laid down his spade, slowly climbed out of the trench, stared the Turk in the eye, and "then spat a splash of spittle" at his feet. Jumping down into the pit, Schliemann calmly continued his digging, and in final insult turned his back on the hulking Turk. Although Schliemann appeared unafraid of his well-armed adversary, several workmen protectively closed in around their employer. Enraged, the Turk screamed obscenities describing Schliemann's ancestors and actions, and, shouting that he would return the following day, stormed away.

The next day passed and then a second without a sign of the man from Koum-Kale. But on the third day he returned with his brother and a dragoman, all three creeping up on Schliemann before workmen were alerted. Towering above him, the first Turk said that he and his brother must be paid £3,000 for their section of the Hill of Hissarlik. It was true that part of the Hill belonged to them—Frank Calvert owned the other part—but Schliemann had no idea of submitting to extortion. Asking for the return of his 40 francs, he went through the digs telling his workmen to fill in the exposed trenches. As they began to shovel back the earth Schliemann returned to where the brothers were standing and firmly repeated that he wanted his money back.

When the landowners saw what was being done they became agitated and begged Schliemann to please stop his men. He shrugged, and the devious brothers, explaining that they were really after the great, newly exposed stones for use in the construction of houses and bridges, implored Schliemann to go on with the digging. Satisfied that he had brought off a coup for the small price of 40 francs, Schliemann gave orders for continued excavation. That night when he wrote in his diary, "my audacity was too much for the Turk," he was unaware that the purchase of the land was far from settled.

Every evening when Schliemann returned to Chiplak he carried with him the day's finds and, in his squalid room, spent as many hours as required for his paper work. That April he established the pattern that continued throughout his years as excavator and archaeologist. He wrote voluminous notes about each object collected, giving its position and depth in the digs and a comparison with other objects found at the same spot, often adding a detailed drawing. In his eagerness to share the news of his finds with the outside world, he expressed his ideas about them in hasty letters to friends and scholars and in articles for publication in journals. He frankly admitted that he often jumped to conclusions, allowing his imagination to override his sounder judgment. By his rashness Schliemann exposed himself to criticism while, as egotist, he hoped to be praised for his daring work. If his interpretations of his finds were sometimes faulty, his records of them were not. He returned to the digs each new day secure in the knowledge that the previous day's work was meticulously recorded.

His work crew varied from the minimum of two to the maximum of nineteen, and he had obtained the services of an outstanding overseer, Nicholas Saphiros Yannakis, a Greek living in Asia Minor. The tall and powerfully muscled Yannakis was a wanderer ". . . who the gods of Olympus and the Fates of time have caused to cross my path." At a chance meeting the two men—one elegantly dressed if looking somewhat like a scarecrow; the other, regal of bearing, although shabbily clothed—were immediately attracted to each other. It is not clear from Schliemann's diaries and letters whether he actually hired Yannakis or Yannakis simply attached himself to the archaeologist. It is unlikely that there was ever a formal agreement or contract between them, but through the years their personal bond strengthened and the responsibilities of Yannakis increased. Until his untimely death in the summer of 1883, Yannakis was Schliemann's factotum, bodyguard, foreman, and blood brother in the best Greek tradition.

After the middle of April, 1870, it became clear to Schliemann that the success of the excavation for Troy would depend on official sanction and on more thorough preparation—as Sophia had told him. On romantic impulse he had rushed to Asia Minor to dig and to explore without plan. Faced with his first trench, 16 feet deep, he shrewdly evaluated the situation, concluding that more men and matériel were needed for the formidable job ahead. Leaving Yannakis, his friend and *skopós*—sentinel, not servant—to guard the excavation, Schliemann packed up and prepared to leave Hissarlik.

NINE

Schliemann's resolve to concentrate his efforts on a straightforward and steadfast pattern for achieving success at the excavation in Asia Minor was dissipated during the ensuing months. The tribulations ahead were only in part due to his own vacillations and precipitate actions. Even before he reached Greece, he was shaken by the death of three people in a collision at sea of his ship, the *Menzaheh,* with two others. Landing on April 22, he was horrified to learn that only the day before, brigands had murdered four men whose ransom Schliemann had offered to pay.

Ten days earlier a gay party in two carriages had left the Hotel d'Angleterre for Marathon. On the return trip brigands had attacked the sightseers half a mile from the village of Pikermi. Four of the captives, three Englishmen and an Italian nobleman, were hustled to the mountain hideout of the marauders; three were returned to Athens with messengers carrying demands for ransom. Because of the prominence of the men captured, the kidnapping had made news that reached even remote Hissarlik. Schliemann, a realist who knew when payoff was necessary, sent word to Athens that he would give whatever amount was required to free the four prisoners, whose lives he knew to be in danger. Both his warning and his offer had been ignored by Greek authorities and the British minister in Athens. The latter, less alarmed, had engaged in delaying tactics that were inexcusable. While the authorities resorted to subterfuge in the hope of outwitting the brigands and paying no ransom, the men were removed from the first hideout. But when rescue forces from Athens closed in, the bandits killed the four captives in the countryside near Dilessi.

The bungling that led to the Dilessi murders had violent repercussions in England where an aroused public pressed for punitive action against Greece and her people. The British government nearly toppled when Prime Minister Gladstone, by his refusal to sanction reprisal, displeased Her Majesty Queen Victoria, defied the members of Parliament, and dismissed popular opinion. William Gladstone—statesman, classics scholar and philhellene—was powerful enough to survive the British crisis over the Dilessi murders which could have been prevented had not Schliemann, as private citizen, been powerless to influence Greek and British officials in Athens.

This experience confirmed his convictions about the shortsightedness, incompetence, and chicanery of bureaucrats. Even while he brooded over the kidnapping's tragic climax, Schliemann was in daily communication with Turkish officials to whom he cabled requests for permission to dig in their country. Their answers, though prompt, were evasive and noncommittal, further examples of devious scheming. In addition to his efforts to obtain the Turkish *firman,* Schliemann attempted to obtain permits for digging in Greece from Mr. F. Eustratiades, Minister of Public Education, who, as in previous encounters, was curt and uncooperative. Irked by the stumbling blocks set up in Greece and Turkey, Schliemann vowed that thereafter he intended to lead a life of contemplation, never again "offering my services to countries controlled by stupid and grasping officials."

In peevish mood, he booked passage for himself and Sophia aboard the *Nile,* which sailed on April 27 for Constantinople. Throughout the trip Schliemann was difficult about petty matters. It pleased him to have dickered successfully for a 10 percent discount on their steamship fare, and annoyed him that the bill for a five-day stay in Constantinople's Hotel d'Angleterre was 176 francs. "This, in spite of the fact that my darling Sophithion has eaten practically nothing during the past few days. Again her illness of the stomach is upon her and we shall leave, never to stay here again." It was no wonder that her nervous tension increased during the round of sightseeing for her continued education and of parties for influential Englishmen and Americans.

The time that Heinrich spent exploring the city with Sophia might better have been spent in personal application for the permit he was so eager to obtain. But he wrote that he would "not talk with any officials because I refuse to be used as an object of scheming and grasping politicians." Although he should have realized from past experience that no Turk would initiate talks about rights to dig at Hissarlik, Schliemann apparently hoped to be approached with a proposition for settling the "thorn of the matter of my rightful *firman*." When the Turks continued to ignore him, and British and American representatives at Constantinople expressed discouragement about the granting of the permit, he huffily sailed away on a ship called the *Sophie*.

Sophia and Heinrich spent the month of May on a bootless peregrination spurred by his restlessness. Mind inactive and imagination dormant, he lapsed into a dull period almost unique in his life. No drama enlivened his written account of the journey that from start to finish was commonplace. His report of a few days spent on the Danube was dreary. The river boat had clean baths, wide deck promenades and a magnificent dining room; but he wrote that the vessel was without staterooms, the beds being separated only by curtains. For diversion he and Sophia, taking advantage of the frequent stops of the slow boat, examined the shrubbery, trees, and flowers growing along the banks. On board they spent many hours in the company of a Madame de Belgarrie, who was very deaf and "talked altogether too much" in a high voice. Although Madame's voice worked "like a windmill," Heinrich listened as the chatterbox spun historical tales of the region and described the customs of the people living on the land through which they passed "at the pace of a sluggish water animal."

At Vienna, Schliemann was annoyed at himself for having forgotten to make hotel reservations at the height of the spring season in Austria. He was forced to take inferior accommodations at a rooming house. Sophia was soon exhausted from tours of museums and bored with night life, enjoying of all the things she saw only a performance of the opera *L'Africaine*. From Vienna the Schliemanns went to Dresden, Stuttgart, Lake Constance, Zurich, Lake Lucerne, Geneva, and Lyons, arriving at Marseille on May 27. There Heinrich "bought many new clothes for the wardrobe of my beautiful and darling wife" during the sort of shopping spree that he always enjoyed, spending money with abandon and expending time with patience. But once the purchases were complete he was eager to get away, and bullied a clerk at the hotel into getting the best accommodations on the *Nile* sailing for the Piraeus.

Sophia, relieved to be back in Athens, was looking forward to the enjoyment of a long period of relaxation that was not to be realized. She mistakenly thought that Heinrich would be involved for weeks in negotiations for permits to dig in both Greece and

Turkey. Instead he was informed immediately by spokesmen for both countries that he must agree to hand over to the respective governments all objects excavated on their land. That he refused to do. Forced into a quick stalemate and furious at his failure to get his own way, the impatient Schliemann decided to leave Athens only five days after their return.

Still weary from the tour through Europe, Sophia reluctantly repacked her luggage and set out with Heinrich for Paris. Settling there for an indefinite stay, she visited back and forth with her young friends, shopped, stood for fittings of more new clothes and, assuming increased responsibility for the management of the large ménage at their home, planned parties with the housekeeper. By day, Heinrich attended to his financial affairs and inspected his real estate with his French agent. Convinced that by perseverance permission to excavate at Hissarlik would soon be obtained, Heinrich optimistically inspected equipment of the types needed at the digs, placed his orders, and arranged for shipments to Yannakis. Sophia and Heinrich were guests at balls and banquets, went to the theater and the opera, but gaiety everywhere was restrained because of the insistent rumors of war between France and Prussia. After only two weeks in Paris, Heinrich, disturbed by the acute political situation, overnight decided to leave. In one chaotic day Sophia canceled engagements, recalled invitations, and packed in great haste for the return to Greece. Again as passengers on the *Niemen,* she and Heinrich sailed for the Piraeus just five days before the start of the Franco-Prussian War.

Summer had settled a pall over Greece. Its people were in a state of torpor, and its land was parched. The tempo of life, slowed almost to a standstill, bothered Schliemann no more than the monotony of the climate that surrounded him "like a blanket of dead boughs covering the casket in which a living person lay drugged." He had ample opportunity to observe the desolate landscape and to suffer from the heat, because he took Sophia on numerous excursions into the country, driving in a carriage always protected by guards.

While others sought protection from the hot weather in the shelter of their homes, Heinrich tried to escape the oppressive present by journeying into the past. He and Sophia spent one Sunday exploring and picnicking at Eleusis, site of the ancient

Eleusinian Mysteries. There King Celeos sheltered the goddess Demeter while she was seeking her daughter Persephone, who had been abducted by Pluto, ruler of the Underworld. Demeter, Mother Earth, in gratitude for the hospitality of Celeos, gave to Triptolemos, his son, a kernel of grain and instructions for tilling the soil. The King-Priest Eumolpos was ordered by Demeter to hold fall ceremonies commemorating her gifts. According to historians, the main ceremony was held from September 12 to September 23, when the harvest had been gathered and after Demeter's earth was at rest, gathering strength for another year.

With passing time a cult centered about the ceremonies, which came to be known as the Mysteries of Eleusis. All who participated in the secret rites were reborn each year, like the land, and were assured of a better life after death. Initiation into the Mysteries was available to every Greek. When eventually the god of revelry, Dionysos, became associated with the rites, an orgiastic element was added to them. Initiates swore never to reveal what happened during the ceremonies, and their secrets were so well kept that no hint of them survived in legend, nor did the revelations experienced or the prophecies foretold. "He who says he knows what happened here is a liar, or an outcast who reports what never occurred," Schliemann wrote with conviction. "Fiction forms stories of any who says he knows the rites. No man would dare, in fear of immediate death or living hell, repeat that experienced during the Mysteries."

Drenched by midday sun, Heinrich and Sophia wandered among the ruins which were mere outlines in stone of ancient buildings. Lizards darted across the dry, pebbled ground as he described the great Temple of Demeter, the even greater Propylaea, the Sanctuary of Pluto, and the most sacred edifice of all, the Telesterion, where the devout were intiated into the Mysteries. Heinrich did acknowledge that ". . . although bound to secrecy, writers gave hints and it is well known that the vortex of the culture was fertility, rebirth. We know also that the performance of the Mysteries was accompanied by orgiastic dances, by what to us today would be obscene hymns, and a spectacular torchlight procession to the temple of Demeter and her sad-eyed daughter, Persephone. This can be deduced."

Heinrich asked Sophia if she recalled his discussions about

Eleusis with Renan, who had written in his treatise on the Mysteries, "The revelations of the Mysteries seem to have been the truly serious part of the ancient religion." Renan had studied the religions of the many lands where he had traveled, and none held more fascination for him than the central core centered in Eleusis ". . . where the life-giving hope found in fertility is the central theme. Would that we knew more about the Mysteries so we could understand more about ourselves."

Sophia not only remembered the talks with Renan, who had become her devoted friend, but she wrote him a letter saying that while Heinrich was at Eleusis he seemed to become an initiate, and the "beyond look in his eye told that he was for the moment living then, not now." Heinrich afterward referred repeatedly to that day at Eleusis, and when seasons had changed and months passed, he went back there—alone. He returned from his solitary pilgrimage in changed mood. His pace quickened. His mind charged. His emotions soared. "I myself have been initiated, purified and given strength to wend my way toward a newer and fuller life."

He was circuitously headed for that life when shortly he set out for Troy, again alone but not forlorn. Sophia was pregnant. He rejoiced when her condition was confirmed by a doctor, and shared the glad news with everyone. Heinrich publicly announced that sometime in May was "when my son who shall be called Odysseus will be born!" It was as much Heinrich's decision as Sophia's that she should not accompany him to Hissarlik where the rigorous weather of winter would not be good for her. A tender father-to-be, Heinrich gently advised Sophia about prenatal care, and bade her an affectionate farewell.

On December 3, 1870, Heinrich left for Chiplak, where he was met by Yannakis, who managed to recruit a skeleton crew for digging. The weather was unsuitable for excavation, but Schliemann was determined to work as long as possible. Winds that swept across the Plain of Troy bombarded the Hill of Hissarlik with icy blasts, chilling the workmen and Schliemann, who dug at their side, muscles tired and back aching.

Schliemann, in spite of the low temperatures, rode out early every morning to take a swim in the frigid waters of the Hellespont. At night in his unheated room, he sat at his desk wearing heavy coats and woolen scarfs that did not properly warm him. He wrote daily letters to his "most darling wife who is behind me in Athens," admonishing her variously to rest, to control her diet, to walk slowly, to bathe daily in the sea, and never to hit against any object, sharp or blunt, for fear the "precious thing you bear may be troubled or hurt."

After a fortnight of battling the cold at the digs, Schliemann was forced to concede that the excavation should be closed down for the winter. He proceeded from Chiplak to the Dardanelles, where he had the "pleasure of meeting Frederick Calvert, Counsil (sic) of England, the brother of Frank Calvert." After a long talk about Troy with the British consul, Schliemann went to Constantinople on the *Schibin,* enjoying the short run because the captain "stocked a good cabinet and an excellent closet," and was, in addition, an amusing companion. Schliemann approved the captain's maxim that "during months which had an *R* in them, one should not put water in wine; and during the months without an *R* in them, one should not mix wine with water."

In Constantinople, presenting himself to Safvet Pasha, Minister of Public Instruction, Schliemann immediately stated the purpose of his visit forthrightly, saying that he was there to obtain the *firman.* While at Hissarlik he had at last arranged for the purchase of the principal site of Troy for 1,000 francs, Schliemann said, and the deal with the two landowners would be concluded as soon as the Minister granted the permission to excavate. Later Schliemann wrote: "He knew nothing of Troy or Homer, but I explained the matter to him briefly, and said that I hoped to find there antiquities of immense value to science." The crafty Safvet Pasha, thinking that gold in quantity might be found, asked for more information, and then suggested that Schliemann call again several days later.

The delay meant that Heinrich was not going to be able to reach Athens in time to celebrate Christmas with his wife, but nothing took precedence over obtaining the *firman.* He remained in Constantinople and, with Mr. Wayne McVeagh, United States Minister Resident, returned on the appointed day to the luxurious office of Safvet Pasha. From him Schliemann "heard to my horror that he had already compelled the two proprietors to sell him the field for 600 francs, and I might make my excavations there if I wished but that everything I found must be given to him personally."

Schliemann exploded with a rage that seemed certain to lead to physical violence which was prevented only by the prompt intervention of McVeagh. He wedged himself between Safvet Pasha and Schliemann, who shouted obscenities in Turkish interspersed with every vile word he knew in at least a dozen other languages, as he was led protesting from the Minister's office.

Previously Heinrich had informed Sophia that he had learned "Turkish during my stay here," which was not quite true because he had begun to work on the language some days before he reached Constantinople. It was correct that in eighteen days he had mastered Turkish and could ". . . assure you, my darling wife, I speak and write it fluently, and already have a vocabulary of six thousand words." His six thousand words failed to sway the scheming Safvet Pasha. In Athens on New Year's Eve, Schliemann wrote: "Will my rightful *firman* be mine? Or, must I succeed without it?"

Six days later he entered his forty-eighth year, and a period of emotional conflict that jeopardized his future.

TEN

In the early days of January 1871 Schliemann, eager to escape from Athens, rationalized his plans for a return to France by an expressed concern for his friends in that war-torn country. Though he was worried about them and about the condition of his various Paris properties, his prime reasons for wanting to get away were more personal. Some members of the Engastromenos family were being increasingly troublesome, and Sophia was unforgiving about his failure to return home for the celebration of their second Christmas.

He reasoned that his presence at Constantinople had been of prime importance to their future, but she, not yet nineteen, held to the girlish view that her husband should have been with her for the important church and family holiday, especially when she was carrying his child. Sophia was neither swayed by Heinrich's explanation of his absence nor understanding about his point of view. He was annoyed at her and by the solidarity of the Engastromenos family, which sided with Sophia. Vexed by the discord at home and preoccupied about the effect of the war on his friends and his business, Heinrich, irritable and distracted, decided to go to Europe. With a farewell that was strained and far from loving, he took leave of Sophia, and departed for Munich to obtain a permit for safe conduct into France.

The war that had started six months earlier was well advanced, and Prussian armies, led by Helmuth Karl Bernhard von Moltke, were besieging Paris. Famine threatened the city, and Schliemann's compassion for those in it was repeatedly stressed in his letters and diaries. As scholar, he wondered what was happening to the members of the great societies devoted to science and to those ". . . teaching the young of the coming generation who will carry on the French tradition of investigation in all realms of knowledge." As businessman, he was anxious about his Paris real estate which "must continue to be the source of funds to carry on my excavations." Through the years he had made substantial investments in rental properties: warehouses, factories and residences.

Confident that he would be able to pass through the lines tightly drawn around Paris, Schliemann applied at Munich for the permit. When his request was summarily refused, he moved on to Bismarck's headquarters at Strasbourg, expecting to be cordially dealt with by Europe's man of iron, who was a nodding acquaintance. Bismarck not only denied the permit but brusquely dismissed Schliemann by ordering him out of the territory. He persisted, but in a sharp exchange of words was bested by Bismarck.

Thwarted at Strasbourg, the defiant Schliemann forged a safe-conduct permit and set out for Paris, reaching it by way of repeated acts of bribery. Having sneaked through the Prussian lines, he crossed the city on foot, becoming more anguished with each step. The mark of starvation was on every face. Gaunt old men shuffled along sidewalks strewn with litter, and emaciated children listlessly pawed through debris in the gutters. The façades of once-beautiful buildings were mutilated by gaping holes opened by the direct hits of heavy bombardment; walls, cornices and exterior woodwork were chipped, broken and splintered by the spatter of shellfire.

Heartsick for Paris and her people, and weary from trudging miles with his heavy valise, Schliemann turned into Place St. Michel, bracing himself for a shock. The Place had escaped the shelling that had laid waste to streets and avenues close by; Schliemann's home was intact, and the house at Number 5, which he also owned, had only a small "scar on its exterior." A subsequent check of his other properties revealed that, with incredible luck, only one of his buildings had been demolished during the siege.

Schliemann, ever fastidious, was appalled by the destitution of Parisians, living in filth and existing without the common necessities of food and heat. It revolted him that exorbitant prices were paid for dogs, cats, and even for rats by people desperate for meat of any kind. Tenderhearted, he mourned for the children suffering and dying from malnutrition. Appreciative of fortitude, he reported with pride that friends and acquaintances bore their misfortune with gallantry.

Scholars, shivering and hungry, carried on with their research in freezing studies; students, their clothes tattered, filled bleak classrooms; and academicians, wits keen and stomachs empty, held meetings on regular schedules. Schliemann reported on a surprisingly spirited and lively session of the *Société Géographique,* and told of serving tasteless tea to scholar friends who met informally at his house where "we huddled together in the hope that an exchange of body heat might sustain us and add fuel to our minds."

Rumors in the city were matched with counter tidings. The war would soon end in victory for France, or the war was all but lost by France. The French were mustering reserves to beat off the Prussians, or the Prussians were mustering reserves to take over Paris. Schliemann changed his mind with the rumors. One day he was going to stay in Paris for the duration; the next, after collecting what rents he could, he would return to Greece.

Living alone in the great house at 6, Place St. Michel, he had time to think seriously about his problems with Sophia's family and about their marriage. From its start, Sophia's sister Katingo and Madame Victoria had asked for money, and for more money that Sophia, being young and inexperienced, had given as she could. Loyal to her family, she had unwittingly aided and abetted the greedy ones who thought that money from her exceedingly rich husband was their due. Heinrich ignored the false claim of the redoubtable Madame Victoria that he had promised her a diamond necklace and 150,000 gold francs, and she retaliated by playing on Sophia's sympathy. In the role of poor dear mother, she made a pathetic case for herself as unrewarded by a daughter on whom she had showered devotion, and as mistreated by a neglectful son-in-law. In the role of loving mother, she repeated in letters to and in talks with Sophia how cruel Heinrich was to his bride, forcing her to study, making her travel endlessly, and leaving her at home when it suited his pleasure.

Heinrich, mentally listing the faults of Madame Victoria, should have realized that the pressures from that indomitable woman were in some measure responsible for Sophia's nervous tension manifested by abdominal pains, headaches and fainting spells. But he, distant from Sophia, thought only of her limitations as perfect wife. He had hoped she would become linguistically fluent, but her German and English remained faulty. Her enthusiasm for museum tours and scholarly symposiums was sporadic. She said that she loved him for himself and expressed an overwhelming interest in his plans for excavation, yet when she might have gone to Troy with him, she had refused.

Physically uncomfortable and mentally perturbed, Schliemann brooded in his loneliness and arrived at an unreasoned conclusion. In depressed mood he decided that, having made a second bad marriage, he would divorce Sophia, giving her a financial settlement large enough to satisfy even her acquisitive mother. On impulse he dismantled his Paris home and put its furniture and other household effects in storage. After settling on a rental fee for the house, he arranged for the collection of rents on his other real estate and prepared to leave Paris. Making do with a single iron bed, three dishes, one glass, a fork and a knife, Schliemann spent the night of February 22, 1871, at 6, Place St. Michel. The next day, leaving behind bittersweet memories, Schliemann headed for Greece and for what he expected to be the unhappy conclusion of another segment of his life.

Divorce was dismissed as unthinkable by Heinrich when, at home again, he was entranced by the beauty, warmth and loveliness of Sophia, who was "carrying my very own Odysseus." As if by telepathy, she too had suffered over their marriage while he was in Paris. She was tortured by fear for his safety, and missed as never before his tender solicitude and affectionate embraces. She found family chatter dull in comparison with Heinrich's conversation, and was provoked by her mother's constant complaints, mostly criticism of the absent Heinrich. Facing up to her family, Sophia concluded that "in vows of marriage you give yourself to your husband to stand by his side and follow where he goes." Her allegiance, given wholeheartedly to Heinrich, was never to waver; and she did stand ever by his side, ready to defend him against detractors and to fight for his rights with womanly wiles.

Their love—deep, abiding, and fervent—survived occasional personal differences that were inevitable for two such strong-willed people. After Heinrich's return from Paris in 1871, he renewed plans for the future, with Sophia as his committed partner at last. The Schliemanns, physically, emotionally and intellectually interdependent ever after, were truly happy only when together. In separation, their relationship was apt to be marred by strain and by misunderstanding that often led to recrimination and dissension. She accused him of neglect if he was too long absent from home, and he chided her for petty transgressions; but together they faced the world, united in their aims and ambitions and in their passionate dedication to Homeric verities.

When, in the fateful winter of 1871, Sophia took a stand against her family, Madame Victoria intelligently accepted the inevitable. She saw to it that unreasonable requests of largess from Heinrich ceased, and that Sophia be permitted to live her own life. Madame Victoria's begging and carping stopped as soon as she recognized that her daughter, finally matured as a woman, had gone over to the side of the enemy Heinrich. To Sophia she became the doting mother, supplanting cajolery with affection, incessant demands with constant attentions. With Heinrich, Madame Victoria remained remote but grudgingly respectful. He, forced to travel on business that spring, left Sophia, without any qualms about being undermined by Madame Victoria.

Early in May Heinrich rushed away from London, reaching Athens just in time for Sophia's delivery of a healthy, beautiful baby. Heinrich took the child in his arms and smiled down at Sophia, eyes twinkling with amusement. It was no Odysseus that he held but a girl, Andromache, a name on which Heinrich and Sophia had previously agreed in the event that the baby was not a boy. Andromache, wife of Hector, was one of the Trojan women of the *Iliad* and the titular heroine of plays by Euripides and Racine.

Another hot and dry summer settled a pall on Greece that went unnoticed by Sophia and Heinrich. She cared for the infant, and he gave his unswerving attention to the major assault on Troy that they would make together in early autumn. Every detail of planning made by Heinrich was shared with Sophia that she might be as prepared as he for the operation at the Hill of Hissarlik. In mid-September, leaving Andromache with Madame Victoria, the Schliemanns left for Constantinople.

They called on Achmed Pasha, Governor of the Dardanelles and the Archipelago, who, though gracious, informed them that Safvet Pasha's personal purchase of part of the Hill of Hissarlik having been set aside, the site had been acquired by the Turkish government for 3,000 piastres. Sophia and Heinrich listened in consternation while the Governor explained that his government was in the process of acquiring ancient art objects for the recently established museum in Constantinople, and the Sultan was routinely withholding legal rights to excavate from all but Turks.

Schliemann, pertinacious as always, bowed out of the office of Achmed Pasha and marshaled his forces for a double flank move. With Sophia, he planned lunch parties and dinners at which they lavishly entertained Turkish ministers, several of whom were captivated by the conversation and sparkling personality of their hostess. Heinrich enlisted the help of the Americans John P. Brown and Wayne McVeagh, who used their considerable influence with Turkish officials eager to be in the good graces of representatives of the United States. By social and diplomatic courting, the Turks were persuaded to issue a *firman* with the restraining stipulation that all objects excavated would belong to the Turkish government. Signed *firman* in hand at last, Schliemann voiced no objection to its restricting conditions, but gave tacit agreement to the terms of the permit.

At the Dardanelles the Schliemanns encountered further difficulties, "this time on the part of the before named Achmed Pasha, who imagined that the position of the field which I was to excavate was not accurately enough indicated in the document, and therefore would not give me his permission for the excavations until he should receive a more definite explanation from the Grand Vizier. Owing to the recent change in ministry, a long time no doubt would have elapsed before the matter was settled, had it not occurred to Mr. Brown to apply to His Excellency Kiamil-Pasha, the new Minister of Public Instruction, who takes a lively interest in science, and at whose intercession the Grand Vizier immediately gave to Achmed Pasha the desired explanation. This, however, again occupied 13 days, and it was only on the evening of the 10th of October that I started with my wife from the Dardanelles for the Plain of Troy, a journey of eight hours. As, according to the *firman,* I was to be watched by a Turkish official whose salary I have to pay during the time of my excavations, Achmed Pasha assigned to me the second secretary of his chancellery of justice, an Armenian, by name Georgios Sarkis whom I pay 23 piastres daily."

Heinrich and Sophia occupied a hovel at Chiplak, getting up before dawn each morning, traveling the couple of miles to Hissarlik, and working side by side with the men from sunup to sundown. Sophia had a crew of her own, a group of Greeks from the village of Renkoï, who on the first morning refused to take orders from her. Woman's place, as they well knew, was at home, cooking, washing, cleaning, bearing and rearing children, or in the open, hoeing the fields for crop planting and gathering firewood that, like a beast of burden, she carried to her house. Men of Renkoï sullenly stared at Sophia when, according to instructions given to her by Heinrich, she told them where to cut into the Hill and how to proceed with their work. Leaning on their shovels, unmoving, they glared at the young woman who wore a fancy hat and a fine dress with a bulging bustle.

Sophia knew that if she were ever to be of assistance to Heinrich she must win over the Renkoïts, all afraid of losing face by taking orders from a woman. Tiers of petticoats rustling under the skirt of her dress, she stepped forward and took a shovel from one of the workmen. Digging it into the ground, she demonstrated how the earth should be lifted up and thrown into a basket. As she worked, she talked in glowing words about the purpose of the excavation, emphasizing the vital part that each man would play in the drama of uncovering a world long lost. She recited passages from Homer and, in conclusion, flashed a dazzling smile at her crew, saying, "Without you I am nothing. With your leadership, we shall set an example for other work crews here, outshining them by our success at the day's end."

Her appeal to the masculine ego had an immediate result. The man from whom she had borrowed the shovel walked slowly toward her and took it back, nodding to the others, who, calling out "We'll show them," began to dig with vigor.

That night in the hut at Chiplak, Sophia told Heinrich about the success of her histrionics with the crew. She acted out the scene, in turn standing stiff and unbending like a grim-faced Renkoït and simpering like the helpless female she had pretended to be. Heinrich laughed heartily at her antics and affectionately patted her cheeks, praising her for her cleverness.

At the digs Heinrich worked with various crews, checking on each section of the wide trench being cut in the steep northern slope of Hissarlik. The difficulties of excavation in such a wilderness increased daily. The problem of disposal of debris mounted in proportion to the length and depth of the trench. Rubbish thrown directly down the outside slope eventually would have to be removed, which would make double work, so Schliemann insisted that earth and rock be disposed of at some distance to the right and left of the mouth of the trench.

Boulders had to be dragged from the trench to the top of the slope and rolled down the steep hill, a procedure that consumed time and stopped work. "The numbers of immense blocks of stone which we continually come upon cause great trouble and have to be got out and removed . . . when a large block of this kind is rolled to the edge of the slope, all of my workmen leave their own work and hurry off to see the enormous weight roll down its steep path with a thundering noise and settle itself some distance in the Plain." Schliemann, who personally made every minute at the digs count, would not let the men stop work just to enjoy the rock-rolling. They grumbled about his decision that no man should leave his work to watch a boulder crash down the slope, but he would not rescind the order. And daring them to strike, as they threatened, he went from crew to crew shouting orders like a slave driver.

Heinrich suffered through every delay at the excavation. He fumed to Sophia about the refusal of Renkoïts to report to work either on Sunday or on any of the many feast days of the Orthodox Church. They could not be swayed by offers of money or by appeal to their loyalty, so Schliemann told Yannakis to recruit crews of Turks for work on holy days. But Renkoït and Turk alike ran for cover whenever a sudden shower drenched the Hill. Rainy weather caused work loss that Schliemann could not prevent, but he made the most of every series of wet days by drawing skillful sketches of his finds, by writing articles for publication, and by padding the notations in his diary in whatever language appealed to him at the moment. Whim alone seems to have been the basis for the entries, which were variously in Greek, Arabic, Persian, French, Italian, German, and English.

ELEVEN

Under Schliemann's direction the crews dug through the top debris of Hissarlik's soil and, at 13 feet below the surface, came on foundation walls of a building, nearly square. Inscriptions indicated that the structure had been a city hall, built probably in the 4th century B.C. when Lysimachus, King of Thrace and ruler of both sides of the Hellespont, held the region in protectorate for the young Alexander the Great. Schliemann, impatient to get down to the level of Homer's Troy, tore down the walls that were in his way, an act for which he was later castigated by archaeologists.

Undamaged pottery objects were carefully catalogued each night by Heinrich and Sophia. They also laboriously pieced together such broken segments as could be matched from the hundreds of sherds found, painstaking work rewarded by the excitement of accomplishment. Every new object discovered or produced from fragments thrilled Heinrich, who was prone to interpret the find by romantic deduction, not always a guide to accuracy. He repeatedly expressed his willingness to revise his first thoughts, and later wrote, "If my memoirs now and then contain contradictions, I hope that these may be pardoned when it is considered that I have here [at Hissarlik] revealed a new world of archaeology, that the objects which I have brought to light by the thousands are of a kind hitherto never or but very rarely found, and that consequently everything appeared strange and mysterious to me. Hence I frequently ventured upon conjectures which I was obliged to give up on mature consideration, till I at last acquired a thorough insight, and could draw well-founded conclusions for many actual proofs."

Unforgiving, many scholars in France and Germany, as well as a few in England, constantly attacked announcements precipitously issued by Schliemann from Hissarlik. They criticized him for not asking for advice from those considered to be more scholarly than the "romantic financier with the destructive manner of a grave robber." Such invective angered Schliemann, who gratefully accepted constructive criticism. In a letter to the *Times* of London, he was circumstantial about the advice he had sought from scholars whose knowledge he respected, and offered proof that his reading on the subject of archaeology embraced the whole literature of the science, including the latest articles published in obscure journals.

But he continued to make impetuous judgments with resultant errors. Recovering stone objects from the earth, he wrote that he undoubtedly had reached the level of the Stone Age, describing in detail the amazing workmanship and marveling that people "so many centuries past could produce stone objects of such perfection with the primitive tools they had." He found no implements in the layer with the man-made objects of stone, but within the month discovered in the same strata metals and other evidence that made him recant. "Hence I must not only recall my conjecture that I had reached the stone period, but I cannot even admit that I have reached the bronze period, for the implements and weapons which I find are too well finished." He concluded that he had reached a level showing a higher degree of civilization than the one under the first soil layer. Objects of copper, bronze, and other substances were fashioned with the same precise skill as those of stone. The Schliemanns were in a constant state of suspense as they wrested from the entombing earth weapons of hard stone, black and green; hammers and knives of flint; and needles, bodkins and spoons of bone.

Heinrich's total experience of living contributed to his thinking about what was excavated. Sociologist, archaeologist, and romantic, he fused the past with the present in his mind, ever attempting to envision the whole civilization of any one period exemplified in his finds. That he was often wrong in his conclusions he did not deny, but he arrived at certain truths by intuition that sometimes seemed just short of clairvoyance, and by dependence on his aesthetic instincts and broad knowledge, gleaned from study and world travel.

Primitive miniature canoes excavated at Hissarlik reminded him of those formed from hollowed tree trunks that he often had seen in Ceylon. "Again to my surprise, I frequently find the Priapus, sometimes represented quite true to nature in stone or terra cotta, sometimes in the form of a pillar rounded off at the top (just as I have seen in Indian temples, but there only about four inches in length). I once also found the symbol in the form of a little pillar only about 1 inch in length, made of splendid black marble topped with white and beautifully polished." Schliemann correctly supposed that the Trojans of the period worshipped Priapus and, as members of the Indo–Germanic race, brought their religion from Bactria, India, where the god of reproduction (Priapus) was represented in forms similar to those found at Hissarlik.

He did not always have a basis for comparison of objects, and he was confused by many "round articles with a hole in the center, which have sometimes the form of humming tops or whorls." These were carved in marble or made of baked clay, with decorative lines scratched into the surface; some were in the shapes of temples or of animal and human figures. After long discussions with Sophia about the whorls, Heinrich questioned: *"For what were these objects made?* They cannot have been employed in spinning or weaving, or as weights for fishing-nets, for they are too fine and too elegant for such purposes; neither have I as yet been able to discover any indication that they could have been used for any handicraft. When, therefore, I consider the perfect likeness of most of these objects to the form of the heroic sepulchral mounds, I am forced to believe that they, as well as those with two holes which occurred only at a depth of 6½ feet, were used as *Ex Votos*." The following day, obviously still wondering about the objects, he wrote in his diary, "The mystery of these innumerable and fascinating whorls—their use and production—must remain unsolved until I can further study into the history of such items and discuss them with colleagues throughout the world."

Correspondence and discussion with scholars confirmed that the whorls were *ex votos,* votive symbols placed in temples and homes and worn on chains as good luck charms. Almost identical whorls had been found by archaeologists studying the ancient civilizations in many countries.

While seeking proof of his deductions and interpretations of his finds, Heinrich surmounted daily challenges at Hissarlik. A recurrent problem was created by workmen who refused to dig on religious holidays. On rare occasions when it was impossible to round up substitutes for Greek Orthodox workmen absent because of a feast day, Heinrich, Sophia and Yannakis labored as a crew of three at the Hill. When rains turned the great trench at Hissarlik into a silt-filled river where no one could work, Heinrich, fretting, was forced to remain at Chiplak with Sophia; she measured and numbered objects, and he did his paper work. With the efficiency of a bookkeeper, which he once was, he not only recorded his finds in his diaries, but also noted them on separate sheets. These were used by him when writing books about his excavations, as well as by succeeding generations of archaeologists to whom the detailed material was invaluable as reference.

The recurrent damp weather that delayed spade work also caused absenteeism among workmen wracked with fever. Sophia and Heinrich took daily doses of quinine as fever preventive; and he treated sick men with the same drug, which he had in large supply, along with other medicines. In New York, when he had nearly died from a fever contracted weeks earlier in the marshes of Nicaragua, his physician, Dr. Hans Tellkampf, had prescribed 64 grains of quinine in one dose. Schliemann took that amount as his control in the Troad and administered whatever grains he thought were needed, based on each patient's degree of fever. The method was so successful that Schliemann was able to say, "I have this far cured all the fever patients who have applied to me for help." The number of his patients increased daily as workmen brought their wives and children, relatives and friends to Schliemann for various treatment. Within a short time he was operating a free medical clinic for bedraggled men, women and children, who reached the Hill on foot or sagged across the backs of burros.

Schliemann was a health faddist who freely gave out information on diet, exercise and routines for sensible living. His cure-all for "almost all diseases" was sea-bathing, a prescription resisted particularly by most female patients, who thought that cold water on their bodies would bring death. However, some took the plunge and Heinrich wrote that many women "now go joyfully into the water and take their dip."

With his fame as physician established, Schliemann was sought out by peasants and landowners who had ailing animals: camels, donkeys, horses, and dogs. As veterinarian, he attempted medical and surgical treatment with which he had had no previous experience. Tincture of arnica cleared up many of the contusions and joint swellings of animals. But he often had to use a knife for slicing fistulas or for cleaning out infected cuts, and once was midwife to an overdue mare from which he forced a colt that had resisted being born.

His duties as doctor and veterinarian began to take up so much of Schliemann's time that he, grumbling, became short-tempered at the digs. He had gladly performed medical services, but complained that he had received no proper thanks from human sufferers or from owners of sick animals. Since not one of his patients had ever expressed their gratitude for his help, he concluded that it was "not one of the virtues of the present Trojans." Finally one night, Heinrich, pacing up and down in the tiny house at Chiplak, told Sophia firmly that he would no longer treat either people or animals, but would turn all away with a curt refusal of further help.

The very next morning he and Sophia reached Hissarlik to find a pitiful girl from the miserable village of Chutzpa waiting for Effendi Schliemann. The seventeen-year-old patient had a disgusting festered sore around her blinded left eye and seemed too emaciated to have managed the three-hour walk from her home. Heinrich glared at the girl and then at Sophia, who could only laugh. She knew that he would not refuse help to someone so obviously in need of attention. There being no shelter for privacy at Hissarlik, Heinrich stripped the girl of her ragged clothes right out in the open, arousing mixed reactions from workmen watching. Some stared lecherously at the bare body; others who muttered about the exposure of a young virgin were placated by Sophia. She moved among the workmen explaining why the Effendi had to examine the girl's body, revoltingly covered with running ulcers.

The young patient was too weak to answer the questions put to her by Schliemann, who turned to her mother for information. He found out that her daughter, whose chest was alarmingly caved in, coughed constantly and had no appetite. She had been bled seven times in four weeks by the parish priest. Schliemann disapproved of debilitating bleeding, but knew that it was the usual panacea of the priests, who were the only doctors available to villagers of the Troad.

He gave the girl a spoonful of castor oil, as Sophia winced.

Heinrich explained to the mother that her daughter should bathe nude three times a day in salt water, so it might "enter the pores, act against the poison and heal the ulcers." Then he said that after the girl had gained strength her father should "put her through some passive gymnastic exercises" to expand her chest and develop her lungs. Just before the mother and daughter were about to leave Hissarlik, Yannakis rode up with a dress that Sophia had sent him to fetch from Chiplak for the girl. She, animated for the first time, looked at the new dress with a radiance that was mirrored as envy in her mother's eyes.

Ten days later Heinrich was moved to tears when the girl appeared at the platform where he was working, threw herself to the ground, and kissed his dirty shoes. The sea baths had healed her sores, cured the cough, and restored her appetite. The grateful mother gave Heinrich a package of food which, though it reeked of rancid oil and herbs, he accepted with profuse thanks. Sophia, in turn, received a package containing a threadworn piece of crude, yellowed lace. Touched literally to tears by the sacrifice of what she knew must be a prized possession, Sophia leaned forward and kissed the girl's mother on the brow. There was not a dry eye at the digs as workmen and the principals of the scene wept.

Schliemann, having received his first appreciation for medical advice, was nonetheless skeptical about the reason for the return of the patient and her mother. The girl was still blind in her left eye, and he surmised that the three-hour trek had been made in hopes of having him cure her eyesight. It was his opinion that the skin-covering of the eyeball might easily be removed by an oculist, but daring as Schliemann was in his surgical treatment of animals, he would not attempt a delicate dissection on a human.

Illness in the Schliemanns' own family was responsible for the departure of Sophia, who heard from Madame Victoria that little Andromache, nearly six months old, had contracted a cold. Leaving to Heinrich the responsibility of closing up the digs for the winter, Sophia returned home. Weather, increasingly severe, was obstructing excavation, which was further delayed by feast days that were proliferating with the approach of Christmas. Two weeks after Sophia sailed for Athens, Heinrich joined her there. Looking down at the tiny Andromache, he said that he would remain with his "beloved wife and divine daughter" until he returned to Troy for the spring excavations.

He stayed through the holiday but, typically, soon after was off to Paris, London, Munich and Berlin for conferences with friends and confrontations with his detractors. At Paris he spent long evenings talking about the work at Troy with Egger and Renan. In London, Schliemann met for the first time "the Honorable Mr. Gladstone, himself a classical scholar of great capacity. I found to my astonishment and delight that he has followed my work with keen interest. Although we disagreed on many points of view, in general he seems certain that my major premise is sound. My darling Sophithion, how much I wish you were here with me instead of in faraway Athens with our cherished daughter, Andromache."

Sophia again was suffering from the stomach trouble that had not bothered her at all while she was in Turkey. Andromache was creeping, crawling, and haltingly trying to walk, and Heinrich was much amused by reports of those antics in Sophia's letters, which often had to be forwarded to him as he moved about rapidly.

Living out of a suitcase and traveling by rail and ship, Heinrich wrote papers for scholarly journals and letters to leading newspapers on two continents. He addressed the members of learned societies, and sought ever more explicit information about objects that he had excavated at Troy in the autumn of 1871. In various capitals of Europe, he shivered through endless hours in unheated libraries, delving into books written in more than a dozen languages. He flipped pages in feverish search for clues that might solve mysteries of the Trojan finds, and fluently translated passages of interest to him, often copying whole pages for his files.

His research led to correspondence with distinguished authors and with authorities on special subjects. Answers to Schliemann's inquiries were stored in his brain for ready reference when he needed to correlate information about some disputed point or new find. One of his bitter opponents was Ernst Boetticher, a German army captain turned scholar, who admitted that "Schliemann's brain is like one of the sponges brought up by naked divers from the islands of his adopted country. Even I am at pains never to contest a *fact* he may suddenly fling at me without first checking its source. Maddeningly, the man is pedantically accurate in this realm, although in scholarship and deduction he is a mere romantic."

Boetticher had reason to regret that statement when he and

Schliemann met face to face at a conference in Berlin. With deceptive charm, Schliemann led into a discussion of Homer by first quoting passages that he asked Boetticher to finish. This the former army captain was not consistently able to do. Then, entwining Boetticher in a tight-spun web, Schliemann answered his own rapid-fire questions every time Boetticher faltered. Boetticher became so enraged that he obviously could not think clearly. Most of those present at the exchange between the two men disagreed with Schliemann's point of view, but they listened with veiled amusement, which turned to uproarious laughter as Boetticher's fury reached such a peak that he was unable to control his quivering jaw. Schliemann then clearly, for all to hear, said, "Pedantic I may be, but I can state facts and be certain of my ground. You, sir, have allowed your vaunted scholarship and powers of deduction, if they exist, to be buried under your uncontrollable temper. A word of advice, sir. He who permits emotion to supersede logic is no match for a lowly pedant." Schliemann, outwardly humble, turned on his heel, leaving Boetticher to the mercy of his peers.

(GERMAN ARCHAEOLOGICAL INSTITUTE, ATHENS)

(GERMAN ARCHAEOLOGICAL INSTITUTE, ATHENS)

Left: First photo of Schliemann at Hissarlik shows him looking down into a portion of the excavation that reveals rubble of walls of one of the later cities of Troy. Above: Wide trench cut through Hill. Three workmen can be seen at top right.

(ILLUSTRATED LONDON NEWS)

In a painting of 1871 excavation at Hissarlik, the Schliemanns are at the far right with their trusted factotum Nicholas Yannakis. Though many scholars disagreed with him about Troy's site—and even its existence—Heinrich proved he'd been right all along.

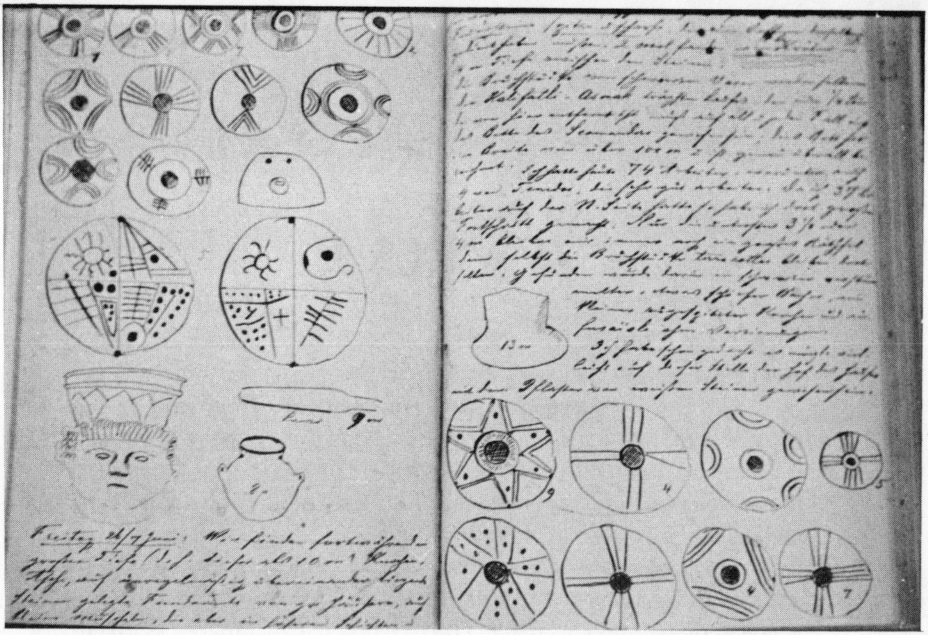

(GENNADIUS LIBRARY, ATHENS)

Two pages of Schliemann's diary containing sketches and notes of objects found on June 7, 1872. After digging all day, Heinrich and Sophia catalogued and described daily finds at night.

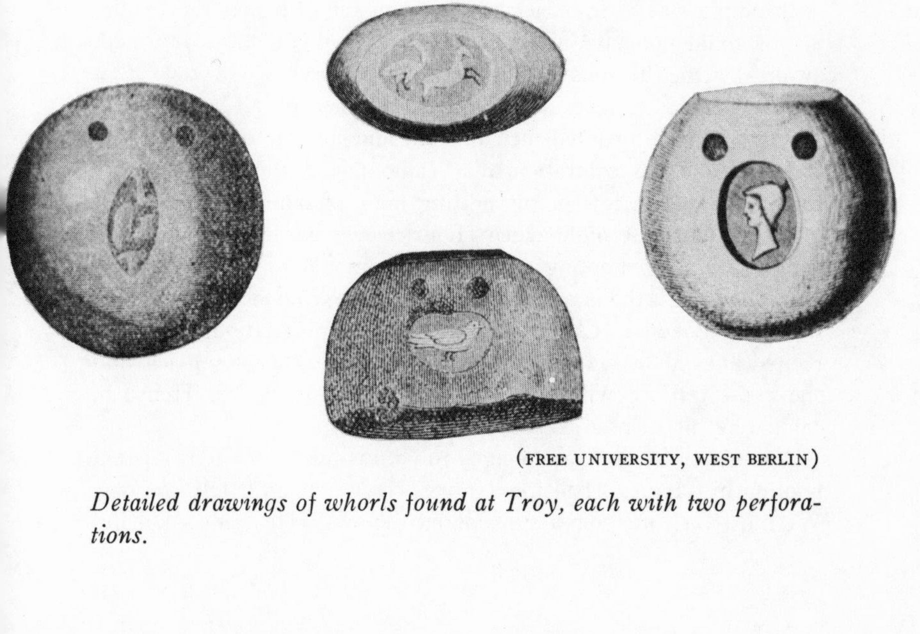

(FREE UNIVERSITY, WEST BERLIN)

Detailed drawings of whorls found at Troy, each with two perforations.

TWELVE

Sophia and Heinrich left for Hissarlik in late February 1872 and resumed digging at the excavation on March 1. Activity was accelerated, and a successful season anticipated. Heinrich, having obtained essential materials for the digs, was assisted by an engineer-adviser and by two experienced foremen, who supervised the complement of workers engaged by Yannakis. Sophia, energetic and ebullient, was a diverting helpmeet to Heinrich and an industrious member of her work crew.

Even daily living was easier for the Schliemanns, who now had a house of their own on the Hill. Heinrich had ordered the construction of a complex of three small frame buildings, all roofed with waterproof paper for protection from heavy rains. There was a tiny magazine, a three-room structure for Heinrich and Sophia and, across from it, a cookhouse built on the rim of the great trench that bisected the Hill from north to south.

Insomnia was a drawback to living on the Hill that the Schliemanns could not have foreseen. Night after night, they were kept awake by the hideous and penetrating screeching of owls that roosted in the excavations. After a number of all-but-sleepless nights, Heinrich ordered men to hunt and kill the owls; but they had a protective coloration that camouflaged them against the earth, and only a few of the nesting flock of hundreds were ever exterminated. One night when Heinrich was working himself into a fury about the hooting pests, Sophia quoted to him a classical passage about Athena and the owl that was symbolically identified with the goddess. Challenged by Sophia's quotation, Heinrich recited lines about owls from the literature of other countries, and she capped those with her own from Greek classics. Heinrich, calmed by the mental exercise, soon fell asleep.

Another time, Sophia managed to get his mind off the persistent hooting by saying, "Tell me a story, Henry, and I'll tell you one. We must each imagine a story about the owl." He spun a fanciful tale about an Indian girl of low caste, who dreamed of being a princess. She worked hard on a garment made of metal threads, wasting not a minute of time by day and sleeping little at night. When she drowsed over her stitches in the evening, an owl's hoot wakened her. After a while the owl regularly flew to the girl's windowsill, and she, being lonely and friendless, talked to it. Finally she finished her handiwork, and in the light of the dazzling full moon, she held up a glittering cloak, silver and gold, for the bird to see. With a final ear-splitting screech the owl materialized as a handsome prince, who led the girl off to his kingdom and married her, turning to reality her dream of becoming a princess. When Heinrich came to the happy ending of his story, Sophia began: "Many centuries ago . . ."; but her husband, lulled by the sound of her voice, soon drifted into a deep sleep and wakened refreshed the next morning, ready for a day of vigorous activity at Hissarlik.

Sophia, beset by different kinds of pests, was constantly on guard against crawling bugs and flying insects. Centipedes had the nasty habit of dropping down from the ceiling in the house and from the roof of an excavated area. The most prevalent of the species had a name that meant "with forty feet." Those repulsive-looking centipedes, scavengers of smaller insects, were supposed to have a bite fatal to humans, but fortunately no one at the digs was ever bitten by one.

Workers often were bitten by snakes that, in great numbers, infested the whole region of the Troad. A common snake that Heinrich described as being "scarcely thicker than a rain worm" was the antelion, its name derived from the superstition that the person bitten by it would survive only until sunset. Schliemann said that if many antelions had not been destroyed in spring and summer by the thousands of storks over the Plain of Troy, it would have been uninhabitable "owing to the excess of these vermin."

Larger snakes that slithered among the stones of the excavation, even as far down as 36 feet, frequently were picked up by workmen, who enjoyed playing with them, a practice that repulsed Heinrich. One day, seeing a Greek workman beside him struck and bitten twice by the same viper, Heinrich grabbed at the man, indicating that he would split open the two fang-marked spots. The workman, laughing, pushed Schliemann away, explaining that, from early childhood, all people in the Troad were so repeatedly bitten by reptiles that they regularly drank a concoction made from a local snakeweed. Schliemann asked for some of the liquid so that he might also be safe from snake bite. Somehow he managed to get a dose of the bitter brew into Sophia, who was very finicky about drinking or eating anything unpleasant to her palate.

Schliemann thought a great deal about the antivenom liquid made from the weed of the Troad, and wondered "whether the decoction would be a safeguard against the fatal effects of the bite of the hooded cobra," which he had seen kill a man in India within half an hour. Ever the businessman, Schliemann considered that if the brew would work with the bite of a cobra, it "would be a good speculation to cultivate the snakeweed in India."

He really could not give serious consideration to growing snakeweed for profit, because too much was going on at Hissarlik. The excavation was being carried out with an efficiency previously lacking. His crews were working with pickaxes and spades from England, and had sixty sturdy wheelbarrows for carrying away the debris. Even that number of the barrows with iron wheels was not sufficient, so as work progressed, Schliemann sent for twenty more and wangled six horse-carts from a reluctant official in Constantinople. Through the kindness of Mr. Charles Cookson, the English consul at Constantinople, Schliemann procured ten man-carts, unique vehicles pushed by two men and drawn by a third.

Two foremen had been lent by Mr. John Latham, director of the railway from the Piraeus to Athens, "a road which I am glad to say brings the shareholders an annual dividend of 30 percent," wrote Schliemann, a stockholder of that line, as he was of several railroad companies in the United States. Latham's men, Theodorus Makrys and Spiridion Demetrios, who were overseers of large crews, received wages of 150 francs a month. The builder of the railroad from the Piraeus to Lanira offered Schliemann the services of a topflight construction engineer, Adolphe Laurent, whose fee was 500 francs a month. That spring, laborers were paid one franc, eighty centimes a day. Schliemann's account books were accurate to the centime, and he wrote in April, ". . . in addition there are other considerable expenses to be defrayed, so that the total cost of my excavations amounts to no less than 300 francs (12 pounds) daily."

He paid 7 francs a day to an invaluable man, Georgios P. Photidos, who for seven years had been a miner in Australia, working as pitman and tunnel-maker, an experience not matched by anyone else at the digs. Photidos, rugged and tough, wrote a surprisingly fine hand, and Schliemann used him as amanuensis for paper work on Sundays and Greek Orthodox festival days. Photidos made perfect copies in Greek of reports to newspapers and learned societies, relieving Schliemann of the tedium of copying long articles and freeing him for other work or for much-needed rest.

That Schliemann always called Photidos by his correct name was an indication of the man's importance. Schliemann either honestly forgot the names of the crew workers or chose not to remember them. He consistently addressed them by descriptive nicknames: Dervish, Short One, Tall One, Fat One, Gimpy, Peg-Leg. Most foremen were forced to answer to Homeric names: Telemon, Paris, Menelaus, Bellerophon, Ajax.

Schliemann never tampered with the name of Yannakis, the indispensable factotum, whose multiple duties were in no way defined. He handled so much money, all of which he signed for, that his signature appeared on the account books more often than Schliemann's. Yannakis wore a money belt filled with gold entrusted to him by Schliemann for payments as needed in "critical situation with some official or employee." The controller of bribes ran a private business, in partnership with his brother, selling wine, bread and brandy to the workmen. They bought on credit, but never owed large sums because Yannakis, as paymaster, collected what was due him when he gave them their wages.

Soon after the arrival of the Schliemanns at the digs in 1872, Heinrich told Yannakis that there should be at least one other woman on the Hill with Mrs. Schliemann, and asked if that could be arranged. Yannakis, to whom everything was possible, answered that if he might have a few days off, he would bring back a suitable female companion for Mrs. Schliemann. Four days later he returned with a young woman, very beautiful and sweet mannered. When Schliemann asked anxiously how long she would stay, Yannakis answered, "As long as I do. I married her." Because of the bride's handsome appearance, Heinrich nicknamed her Helen, the name by which she was known ever after.

Yannakis, who was the cook that spring, did as well as he could with limited food supplies; but there was an inevitable monotony to menus planned around fresh mutton, the only staple meat available. Practically no vegetables were grown on the Plain of Troy, where flowers flourished in wild profusion. There was a seasonal crop of spinach, and of hog and kidney beans that matured in June and July. The yield from potato patches was so small that potatoes had to be shipped in from the Dardanelles. Bread was the staple starch for the workmen. Heinrich, a connoisseur of wines, drank a local one, which, to his taste, compared favorably with the imported Bordeaux. A gourmet, when he could be, he tolerated the cuisine of Yannakis, writing, "We are not here to dine well. We are here to work, so we shall not worry about the food. We eat to live, and get on with the project at hand."

After an early breakfast, Schliemann was talking earnestly with Adolphe Laurent at six o'clock on a spring morning with the sun "glorious in the sky." The two men were standing on the rim of the great trench, and Heinrich noticed absent-mindedly that Sophia was below, directing a crew of ten. Suddenly she beckoned to him with her right hand and raised her left fist, tightly clenched, as if holding something. She spoke quickly to a workman, who nodded and started to clamber toward Schliemann. In midsentence he left Laurent and hurried to meet the approaching workman, who said that the lady had something to show. A find! Heinrich fairly tumbled into the trench. Breathless, he reached Sophia, who handed him a ring, saying, "The most precious possession I own."

Heinrich immediately recognized the diamond-studded piece of jewelry as the first ring he had given Sophia after their engagement in 1869. Naturally he had thought she wanted to show him an antiquity of great value, which was what she had wanted him to think. Disappointed and confused, he stared at her. Then he became angry and asked why she had tricked him "into coming when I was advising with M. Laurent on important matters." Before the incident got out of hand, Sophia smiled. "Henry, you have forgotten the date of this day?" He wrinkled his brow and then burst into loud laughter. To the amazement of the workmen, Heinrich kissed Sophia, hugged her, and swung her round and round so that her numerous voluminous skirts swirled out around her. "My beloved Sophaki! Yes, yes, it is the April first day of the fool!" Both of them enjoyed pranks and jokes at any time, and tried especially to trick each other on every April Fools' Day of their married life.

Two weeks later Heinrich outwitted laborers at the digs. Ever alert to wasted man-hours, he had begun to notice that these were mounting because workmen often stopped to smoke. Irritated by the costly delays, Schliemann issued an order that there would be no smoking during working hours. The day following that ultimatum, when he passed through the digs on inspection tours, entire crews seemed to be at work. Then he surprised idlers, smoking stealthily down in open trenches or behind walls. Infuriated, Schliemann threatened that any offender found smoking would be dismissed, never again to be taken on as employees. When that message was relayed by the foreman, seventy workers from Renkoï put down their tools, refusing to work unless Schliemann agreed that any man might smoke whenever he pleased. Schliemann was adamant.

The Renkoïts, in mutiny, threw down their tools and gathered in an angry group, muttering and shouting. Shortly they spread out around the excavation and stoned the thirty workmen who remained on the job. These, dodging pebbles and rocks, tried to continue with their digging, but it was impossible for them to carry on. With the permission of Schliemann, they left Hissarlik and started home.

The mutineers, instead of returning to Renkoï, lounged around the excavation, and at nightfall took up a vigil right outside Schliemann's house. Inside the flimsy frame building, Heinrich and Sophia made their meticulous notes of the day's activities, listing the objects unearthed from the excavation. Whenever a murmur from outdoors increased to a brief babble that then died away, they looked at each other across the worktable brightened by light from an oil lamp. A shrug, a lifted eyebrow, were the only signs that they were aware of the seventy men massed outside, only a few yards from the front door.

A cacophony of snores broke over a long line of sleeping forms. Small talk rumbled over a huddle of squatting men. In the dark a few solitary figures strolled up and down, their shuffling feet raising a spray of powdery earth. Probably no man doubted that, on his own terms, he would be back at work at dawn. There would have been no discussion of an alternative. The men knew that Schliemann drove forward with the digging in fine weather, such as they were then having. And to dig, he needed them. But they reckoned without Schliemann, a man equal to any emergency and determined to have things his way. The evening would not have been so relaxed for the Renkoïts, or their rest untroubled, had they known of a mission of Yannakis.

In the late afternoon he and Schliemann, after consultation, decided to try to recruit new crews from other villages on and near the Plain. Well instructed, Yannakis secretly rode away from the digs to spend a long night traveling from one small community to another in the hope of hiring workmen. His weary ride was a signal success. In predawn hours men on foot trudged across the rough terrain toward the excavation, or on burros jogged toward the site. At daybreak 120 workers were at Hissarlik.

The seventy strikers, dark faces sullen, grumbled to one another as they gathered for their return to Renkoï. The group moved slowly away from Hissarlik, a few stragglers looking back toward the Hill where crews were eagerly beginning to scrape, to shovel and to dig.

Schliemann wasted no time in gloating about his triumph over the Renkoïts. He was glad to be rid of them because they had been insolent and troublesome as a group from the time of their original employment in 1871. The smoking mutiny not only resulted in an increased number of workers, but proved to all that Effendi Schliemann meant what he said. Schliemann was then able to increase the workday by one hour. After the departure of the Renkoïts, the crews worked from 5 A.M. until 6 P.M., with a breakfast break at 9 o'clock and an hour and a half for eating and smoking in the afternoon.

Falling rocks were hazards at the digs where cave-ins were ever imminent. On a day in late April, Sophia was working at an isolated location with six men when three large boulders, dislodged from the earth, tumbled on four of the crew. Cursing and flailing their arms, they struggled in vain to get loose. Calm and controlled, Sophia pitched in to help the other two workmen move the rocks. Straining, pushing, pulling, the three inched the boulders off the trapped workers. Freed, one started to rise, but Sophia sternly ordered him to stay where he was. At her command all four remained on the ground while she expertly ran her hands along their limbs and rib cages, making sure that no bones were broken. Only when she was satisfied that the men had suffered just bruises were they permitted to get up.

Within minutes everyone at the digs knew that the young wife of Effendi Schliemann had with her own hands explored the bodies of four workmen. Astonishment gave way to respect for the compassionate lady, who, after risking personal injury in the successful attempt to rescue the men, had nonchalantly returned to work. When news of the mishap reached Heinrich, he hurried to Sophia, finding her with clothes ripped, fingernails broken, and hands nicked by stone. In a letter bubbling with pride, he described the accident to Madame Victoria, assuring her that her daughter was a heroine at the excavation.

The following month Schliemann was watching Photidos and a large crew excavating near a wall of huge stones, many of them hewn. Photidos thought that the stone wall was strong enough to hold up for centuries more, but Schliemann, to be on the safe side, ordered six men to shore it up with a stone buttress. Just after they started, the main wall collapsed with a thundering crash. "My fright was terrible and indescribable, for I quite believed that the six men must have been crushed by the mass of stones; to my extreme joy, however, they all escaped directly, as if by miracle."

Weeks later Schliemann was on the alert for three hours at a location where forty men were attempting to loosen a wall of earth that was 16 feet high, 16 feet long, and 10 feet thick. It seemed that the earth, hard as stone, would never yield to the pressure of huge levers operated by windlasses. Then, without warning, the earth wall fell, burying Photidos and another man who had been at work below a platform that was supported by wooden logs. The earth-mass crushed against the flooring, but did not cut off the men's air. Low moans from under the platform indicated that at least one of them was still alive. Rescuers had to work with extreme caution because of great gaps in the cracked wall. Schliemann with his own broad knife dug and scraped until he had cut a hole for the removal of Photidos who, like the second man, was only dazed by the experience.

In spite of precautions, earthslides and rockfalls were almost daily occurrences, and according to Schliemann, he thanked God every night for the blessing of another day without tragic accident.

The excitement of digging was so infectious that even the wife of Yannakis, who served Sophia as maid, scraped into the smooth earth close to the Schliemanns' house. Sophia, seeing the young woman, joined her, saying that together they would excavate. Using a garden hoe and a light rake, they scooped out a shallow trench, laughing and chattering as they worked. They looked like two young girls preparing a flower bed for planting; Sophia had on a bustled dress of exquisite cotton, and Yannakis' bride wore an underskirt of coarse cloth, her Sunday skirt rolled at her waist in the fashion of Greek women in the fields. After digging only a short time, Sophia and Helen were thrilled by the sight of first one terra-cotta whorl, then another. Within a few days they had excavated a sizable collection of whorls, some with decoration, some without.

Below the hilltop where they dug, daily finds were methodically excavated from the great trench, by then 233 feet wide and 46½ feet deep. Work crews removed from the earth evidences of the daily lives of ancient peoples: votive offerings, statues, military weapons, tools and household utensils, funerary jars, dung, and animal skeletons. Exposed remains of cities, buried one on another, disclosed the architectural constructions of dwellings, temples, and public buildings of specific early civilizations. Schliemann, tense with anticipation, expected soon to identify the real city of Troy—his Troy and Homer's Ilium.

THIRTEEN

Finds at Hissarlik accumulated so rapidly that Heinrich and Sophia were no longer able to examine every object excavated in any one day. A photographer, retained by Schliemann, took pictures of major objects, and a staff artist sketched smaller pieces. At night, in their house on the Hill, the Schliemanns discussed the day's discoveries in general, correlating facts and artifacts and comparing objects excavated with those they had seen *in situ* or in museums. The extensive studies made during their travels were proving to be invaluable as reference sources at Hissarlik.

Their method of research was typified by their study of large numbers of unearthed objects that were decorated with the head of an owl. Flat idols, carved from the finest marble, were enhanced by the head of an owl and a female girdle with dot decorations, and, in some instances, by two female breasts. "The striking resemblance of these owls' faces to those upon many vases and cups, with a kind of helmet on the owl's head, makes me firmly convinced that all of the idols, and all of the helmeted owls' heads represent a goddess, and indeed must represent one and the same goddess, all the more so as, in fact, all the owl-faced vases with female breasts and a navel have also generally two upraised arms; in one case, the navel is represented by a cross with four navels."

Who was the goddess? That was the important question. "*What* goddess is it who is here found so repeatedly, and is the only one to be found upon the idols, drinking cups and vases?" Together Heinrich and Sophia reasoned that "she must necessarily be the *tutelary goddess of Troy,* the *Ilian Athena,* and this indeed perfectly agrees with the statement of Homer, who continually calls her *'Thea glaukowpis Athene,'* the goddess Athena with owl's face. For the epithet *'glaukowpis'* has been wrongly translated by scholars of all ages, and, as I can show by immense numbers of proofs, the only possible literal translation is 'with an owl's face'; and the usual translation 'with blue, fiery or sparkling eyes' is utterly wrong. The natural conclusion is that, owing to progressive civilizations, Athena received a human face, and her former owl's head was transformed into her favorite bird, the owl . . . . The next conclusion is that the worship of Athena as the tutelary goddess of Troy was well known to Homer."

His major premise about Athena and the owl held true. Seeking facts to prove or disprove his theory, Schliemann wrote to dozens of European scholars, asking for information about discoveries of the owl symbol *in situ* or in museum collections. While awaiting replies, Schliemann studied books and journals in which he hoped to find clues to the logical development of the owl-headed design. Illustrations affirmed his theory; early owl-headed vases were eventually supplanted by the owl as a bird and by statuettes of Athena with human face. Scholarly answers to his letters of inquiry emphasized the evolution; excavated objects at archaeological sites and pieces displayed in museums demonstrated development consistent with Schliemann's literary research. All information gathered substantiated his theory that the owl-headed vases of Troy were symbolic of Athena, and that later the owl, as a bird not as a face, indicated Athena's dedication to knowledge. She herself was shown in sculpture in the form of a maiden with human face. Schliemann's owl-and-Athena concept was original and inevitably started a controversy. It was prolonged by chair-bound scholars, and, basically, Heinrich enjoyed their rebuffs because of the opportunities they gave him to expound on and clarify his correct theory.

Another symbol found on innumerable objects touched off further disputes. The symbol was a counterclockwise design, the *sauvastika*:

卍

Schliemann correctly judged the form to be a universal symbol "employed for unknown numbers of centuries." Reporting on the finds, he described an object decorated with little stars and three *sauvastikas*; another with rays of the sun across from two of the *sauvastikas* and eighteen little stars "of which twice three (like the constellation Orion) stand in a row." Schliemann repeatedly found the symbol posited with stars, and on occasion found the symbol on objects incised with three or four trees.

He began a study in depth that he was to continue for years, and he asked in print and letters for reports on the places where the symbol had been seen by archaeologists and other scholars and observant travelers. Émile Burnouf at once answered that three dots (stars) in a row denoted "royal majesty" in Persian cuneiform inscriptions, adding, "Indian scholars find these tree-crosses to represent the framework upon which our ancestors used to produce the holy fire. In other places, the tree is virtually the tree-of-life."

The mystery of the symbol was compounded when Schliemann found the *svastika,*

a clockwise design, the complete reverse of the *sauvastika.* The internationally known Orientalist Professor Max Müller of Oxford University wrote to Schliemann that the *svastika,* "derived from *su,* meaning well, and *as,* to be," was definitely from India. The other, counterclockwise symbol "is called *sauvastika* and is found outside of India."

An explanation of the dots on certain of the symbols, both

 and ,

was offered by Burnouf, who said the dots represented the wooden nails that held together crosses used in the worship of Maya, the reproductive force in nature. After Schliemann saw a cross symbol with dots in the vulva of a statue unearthed at Hissarlik, he frequently queried in print the relationship of that object to the deity.

Information about the distribution of the two cross symbols flowed in, proving that examples of *svastika* and *sauvastika* were evident in almost every civilization that flourished up to the 5th century. Schliemann unceasingly attempted to pinpoint the origin of each example and to correlate facts sent to him from many countries.

Sophia and Heinrich, drawing on his extensive knowledge of languages, searched for references to the symbols in world literature. They discovered the *sauvastika* in Ezekiel IX.4–6, where ". . . in the fork of the old Hebrew letter Tau . . . it is written as the sign of life on the forehead, like the corresponding Indian symbol." The Schliemanns, tramping through the Troad, wondered whether the two symbols, originating in one place, were carried to another by wanderers, or whether the symbols, by coincidence, were independently created in many countries. The amount of space given to the symbols in Schliemann's articles and books indicated how absorbed by the subject he and Sophia were. They mulled over advice, ideas, and theories without arriving at solutions satisfactory to them.

The key to their concentration on the problem of the symbols was contained in Heinrich's statement: "People say that my paramount purpose is to prove by any means possible that Troy existed. Since childhood my aim has been to uncover Troy, but my paramount purpose in this search is to uncover the development of mankind, and any clue to his [man's] interrelationship throughout the world is a prime contribution to my central purpose." The *sauvastika* and *svastika* symbols were definitely linked to the progress of mankind in many civilizations.

For most of his life, Heinrich lived without abiding faith in a specific religion. Sophia, although a member of the Greek Orthodox Church, was inherently attuned to the philosophy of the ancient Greeks and, through Heinrich's tutelage, was knowledgeable about the theories of life expressed in Greek classical literature. Her heritage and her learning enabled her to share in her husband's contemplation and discussion of a godhead. Heinrich wrote that they again and again returned to a common and positive belief: "My devoted and devout wife, my darling Sophithion, concurs with me that in this cosmos there is a *Supreme Being* because the cosmos is so orderly and simple. Because the cosmos is of such perfection, some *Being* must guide it, or all would be for nothing, and soon lost. My wife has shown me that, without doubt, there are four basic elements in mankind: curiosity, imagination, emotional feeling and faith. I find her declaration to be true. There can be no progress on this earth, or in the cosmos around it, without curiosity about everything, the imagination to interpret what one discovers, the inner emotion to feel, and the faith to carry the life we have been given by a *Supreme Being*. I would add to her summation a fifth (element) which is that quality of being without inhibition; that quality which made my wife's ancestors creatively without peer in the world."

Several years later, Sophia wrote, "How often my dear Henry and I spent hours, so important to our inner selves, in contemplating aloud on the verities of mankind. As we excavated and released the past for present-study, we found myriad objects; yet, fascinating as those objects were, they served only to illustrate the path followed by mankind from cave to temple. As a child, I learned the simple rules of my church; as a woman, I had the divine opportunity to delve deeply into the meaning of life. All this I owe to my dearest husband, Henry." The truths for which they searched, the conclusions they drew, the verities about which they philosophized, were guiding forces of their life together.

Heinrich and Sophia constantly were forced to make the transition from exalted cogitation to the grim reality of daily toil. On specifications drawn up by the engineers, Heinrich had a safety platform built the full length of the great trench. He consulted with his three foremen, and worked in spells with crews digging at various layers below the platform. Floors and walls of ancient buildings, pottery, small sculpture, molds for the making of metal instruments, and other artifacts were exposed on every workday.

But these were too few to suit Heinrich. Religious holidays so interfered with digging in May, that from the 11th to the 23rd the Greeks reported for work on only seven days. When Schliemann remonstrated with the crew members, they stubbornly insisted that the saint "will strike us if we do not observe his day." Heinrich told Sophia that he was going to offer wage increases for saints' days, but she knew that money would not influence the workers. And she was right. Their refrain again was "The saint will strike us."

In June, excavation was started on the portion of the Hill owned by Frank Calvert. Sophia and Heinrich were working together when he saw a thin edge of marble protruding from the earth. She, eager and curious to see more, scraped at the dirt around the stone with her bare hands while Heinrich sent for the staff engineers, Yannakis, and several trusted workmen. The group of experienced excavators made a horizontal cut into the trench and, with infinite care, slowly removed a block of marble. Under Heinrich's supervision, crusted earth was scraped and dusted from the marble, which was then washed.

Even the lowliest workman recognized the ancient object of Parian marble as a masterpiece. It was dominated by Phoebus Apollo reining four spirited horses. The bas-relief depicted the start of the sun god's globe-circling day, during which he took light to the world. The sculptured block conclusively indicated that a temple was buried at the digging location. Schliemann glowingly described the discovery in his diary entry of June 18, 1872: "Above the splendid flowing, unparted, but not long hair on the head of the god, there is seen about two-thirds of the sun's disc with ten rays 2⅓ inches long and ten others 3½ inches long. The face of the young god is very expressive, and the folds of his long robes are so exquisitely sculptured that they vividly remind one of the masterpieces of the Temple of Nike Apteros in the Acropolis of Athens. But my admiration is especially excited by the four horses which, snorting and looking wildly forward, careen through the atmosphere of the universe with infinite power. Their anatomy is so accurately rendered that I frankly confess I have never seen such a masterly work. . . . The grandeur and classical beauty of the style and happy character of the composition, the life and movement of the horses—all is admirable. This is a masterpiece of the first order, worthy of being compared with the best of Greek sculptures."

His judgment was confirmed by art historians and aestheticians excited by the published photograph of the Apollo metope, a work of fine quality and of inestimable artistic value. Experts, willing to undergo the rigors of travel in the Troad, made the pilgrimage to Hissarlik to see the sculpture. Schliemann, gratified by the reaction to his find, always gave credit to Sophia, the engineers, and the workmen for their skillful removal of the marble object that was without chip, nick or scratch on its surface.

The 1872 discovery of the first object of artistic merit spurred the Schliemanns to greater activity, and, with their crews, they returned to the drudgery of digging. Sophia, by intuition that Heinrich called "currents in the air," recognized as something special a broken urn with three legs extending from the bottom. Heinrich examined the contents of the urn and, with scientific directness, identified them. "In the vessel I found among the human ashes the bones of an embryo six months along, a fact which I can only explain by the mother's having died in pregnancy and having been burnt while the bones of the embryo, being surrounded by the membrane which enclosed it, were protected and remained uninjured. Yet, it seems wonderful that these small bones should have been preserved, for the bones of the mother are burnt to ashes and I found only a fragment of them. I have most carefully collected the bones of the Trojan embryo, and shall have the little skeleton restored by a skillful surgeon." His conclusion was later confirmed by two reputable medical authorities.

The identification of the embryonic skeleton was one more proof of Schliemann's extensive knowledge. His insatiable curiosity led him to inquiries and studies that he either failed to mention or referred to in passing. He never detailed how he was able to pinpoint the state of growth of the embryo in the urn, but he hinted at early discussions with an experienced midwife and with friends in the medical profession.

Announcement of the find of the embryo was received with mixed reactions by scholars. Those who accepted it as fact were in the minority. Some chose to ignore it, others made fun of it, and a few scoffed at it. Professor Hans Meister, a minor classicist, wrote, "Now the eminent Herr Doktor Schliemann has added the science of obstetrics to his limitless professions. Soon he shall become a specialist in metal and join the Gold Works Guild, then a chemist, then an astronomer, and for all this will be honored by learned societies around the world." Schliemann did not then deign to reply to the sarcastic remarks that Meister was in time to rue.

Occasionally a find turned over to the Schliemanns was faked by a workman hoping for the bonus of 10 paras (five centimes) sometimes paid for objects, particularly for those decorated with symbols. Uneducated but not unintelligent, the workmen quickly caught on to the kind of object for which a bonus was likely to be paid. A few dexterous men learned to incise pieces of undecorated terra cotta before taking them to Heinrich or Sophia. Suspiciously examining a large whorl with markings never before seen at Hissarlik, Sophia took off her glove and rubbed the clay surface with her hand while the workman who had handed it to her stood by, smiling. Looking him straight in the eye, she explained the meanings of the symbols on the whorl to the crew gathered round. She said that the carver's ancestry was unfortunate, his mother having been born out of wedlock, the daughter of a murderer. Since no one would perform a marriage ceremony for the carver's parents, he was born without blessing of church or sanction of government and, worse yet, was doomed, according to the final symbol, to be thief, liar and cheat. Concluding her remarks, Sophia made the workman-carver feel the rough edges of the incised symbols before breaking the object with his spade, as she ordered. Asking him for the pieces, Sophia flung them at his feet and turned her back on him. Other workers unmercifully taunted him, and he left the digs at the end of the day, never to return. But the faking continued, and the Schliemanns had to be on guard against the chicanery of workmen who mistakenly thought that they could outwit the experts.

Schliemann, who had been sure he would one day discover the two springs of Troy Homer had written about, did find two springs at Hissarlik. The water of one, situated directly below the ruins of an ancient town wall, was at a constant temperature of 60.8° F.; the water of the second tested at 62.6° F. Schliemann thought that it was "extremely possible" they were the springs that Homer described:

> They by the watch-tower, and beneath the wall
> Where stood the wind-beat fig-tree, raced amain
> Along the public road, until they reached
> The fair-flowing founts, whence issued forth
> From double source, Scamander's eddying streams.
> One with hot current flows, and from beneath,
> As from a furnace, clouds of steam arise;
> 'Mid Summer's heat the other rises cool
> As hail, or snow, or water crystallized;
> Beside the fountains stood washing-troughs
> Of well-wrought stone, where erst the wives of Troy
> And daughters fair their choicest garments washed,
> In peaceful time, ere came the sons of Greece.
>
> *Iliad* XXII, 145–156

Even the possibility that the springs were the Homeric ones was naturally challenged because the recorded temperatures were nearly the same. Schliemann pointed out that the geologic conditions had changed through the centuries, as evidenced by the shift of the river bed of the ancient Scamander. He contended that in Homer's day the springs might well have been *hot* and *cool.* Two springs, one really warm and the other cold, were located on Mt. Ida, but Schliemann refused to accept them as Homeric. No argument offered throughout years of controversy swayed him from his conviction that the two springs of Hissarlik were those of ancient Troy, the *Novum Ilium* of Homer.

Schliemann at first accepted as Trojan a tower uncovered in a trench at the south side of the Hill. After examining drawings made by the engineers, Schliemann decided there should be a channel for the runoff of winter rain water that, pounding at the tower, might destroy it. He personally examined every inch of the 40-foot-thick masonry tower and described it in a treatise, saying that experts asserted it had been designed by and built under the direction of a highly skilled engineer. Schliemann "presumed" that the structure was the Trojan Tower, the great tower of Ilium, which Andromache ascended because she heard that the Trojans were hard pressed and that the power of the Achaeans was great.

Schliemann's contemporary opponents declared that too often he was swayed by implicit faith in Homer and ruled by his own romantic nature. Both charges were to some extent true. His critics refused to recognize how often Schliemann employed the words *presume, suppose, my imagination* and *perhaps* in his personal diaries and published writings. Detractors ignored written passages and public addresses in which Schliemann expressed doubt concerning individual objects and theories. Many failed to credit his frequent requests to the scholarly world for aid and advice.

In his search for the remains of Troy at Hissarlik, Schliemann supervised digging that exposed more than three millennia of historic habitation. In all, nine cities with their subdivisions were later identified by 20th-century archaeologists, who, guided by facts unearthed by years of digging, had at their command more sophisticated methods and instruments than those available to Schliemann. The many cities of Troy extended from approximately 3000 B.C. to 850 B.C.

Schliemann thought that Troy II, the second city from the bottom, was the City of Priam, destroyed by Greeks in revenge for Helen's abduction by Paris, son of Priam. Schliemann used every available fact to substantiate that Troy II was *Novum Ilium*. But he was wrong.

Troy II actually existed from about 2600 B.C. to 2300 B.C., more than a thousand years before Priam's Troy. That fact was made public in 1937 by the American archaeologist Carl Blegen, after sifting the ruins of Hissarlik, and studying the objects excavated before his time. Most scholars today agree with Professor

Blegen that the city beseiged by the Greeks and made famous by Homer was Troy VII A. That city at Hissarlik was five and a half levels above the one that Schliemann declared to be the Troy of the *Iliad*.

Even before Blegen's announcement, archaeologists had good reason for doubting the Troy II theory. Sophia, who had provided large sums for the continuation of excavation at Troy after the death of her husband, was sure that he would have accepted later evidence. She wrote: "I am certain that Henry, faced with facts now available, would admit his error and freely agree that there is still doubt about the exact level of Priam's city."

Certainly Schliemann was well aware that there would always be doubt about many archaeological and historical beliefs. In 1875 he wrote: "For a fact we know that the Parthenon was the shrine of Athena, that Eleusis was the center of the rites of Demeter and Dionysus, that the ancient site of Delphi lies buried below the miserable modern city clinging to the heights of Parnassus, but there are many places about which man will never be absolutely certain." Those words of Schliemann displayed reason and prescience, but as with all mortals, Schliemann failed at times to be guided by objectivity.

When Heinrich and Sophia ceased the digs and left Hissarlik on August 14, 1872, Schliemann was certain that Troy II was the city of Priam, the city of the Trojan War.

Heinrich took Sophia home to Athens and left hurriedly for Paris, where he reported on his excavations of 1872 to four learned societies, checked on his real estate, conferred with his bankers, and shopped for Christmas. Laden with gifts, he rushed back to Athens to spend the holiday season with Sophia and their beautiful little daughter Andromache.

FOURTEEN

Sophia and Heinrich, in a state of excitement, reached Hissarlik in January 1873. They were prepared, as formerly, to give their minds and bodies to the work at the excavation, but both of them, sensitive and emotionally involved, had inexplicable foresight of successes in the months ahead. Sophia, in a letter of January 31, reported on their arrival: "We stood together, gazing at the Hill so bound within our lives. Encumbered with heavy clothing, we joined hands so firmly that I later noticed my ring pressed deep in my flesh. I had no doubt that this winter would be one long remembered for its events. Something within me told me."

Of the same moment, Heinrich wrote: "As my darling Sophithion placed her hand in mine, we looked toward the mound rising from the flat land, and allowed our eyes to sweep the Trojan plain we knew so intimately. Is this spot friend or foe, adversary or challenge? With our hands joined like two ends of electricity, we knew with certainty that our excavations would be memorable. My beautiful Sophithion would never have come here were it not for me; I would never have progressed so far were it not for her assistance—both physical and emotional. Together our love and faith has brought us to the brink. Never before has this love been so fully consummated as at the moment we paused, before attacking."

Both repeatedly wrote about their individual and mutual "feelings about the year ahead," even while enduring the tribulations of their early weeks at the digs. There were only eight good workdays in the first month; operations were delayed by the inevitable feast days and slowed by thunderstorms. The wind was bitter and "the cold is so intense that the workmen proceed at a fast rate in order to keep warm. In this way only does the cold work to our advantage." Later, after Heinrich reread that diary entry, he humorously questioned, "Why do I say 'the *workmen* proceed at a fast rate' when my most faithful Sophithion and I do the same?"

At night in the old wooden house, Heinrich and Sophia continued to suffer from the cold. Their new house, built of stone "from the old Trojan buildings," was temporarily occupied by three foremen who "were not sufficiently provided with clothes and wrappers, and would have perished through the great cold." The strong, icy wind blew with such violence through openings in the frame walls of the Schliemanns' house that they were not able to keep their lamps burning. They had a hearth fire, but the temperature of the room hovered around 23 degrees, and water, in containers placed close to the fireplace, froze solid. "During the day we could to some degree bear the cold by working in the excavations, but of an evening we had nothing to keep us warm except our intense enthusiasm for the great work of discovering Troy."

Sophia, writing to her family about the wind and cold, described how she and Heinrich huddled together at night, not only fully clothed but wrapped in every blanket and shawl in the house. Her fingers tingled with cold when she worked at the digs, although she wore four gloves on each hand. To protect her face, she wrapped her whole head in a woolen scarf in which she had cut eye slits for seeing. She wrote her mother: "My only anguish and concern is that my Henry shall not have suffered in vain." That winter Heinrich and she both suffered physical agony for an ideal.

After a routine for continuous digging was set up, 11,000 cubic yards of earth were removed in a month. Under the direction of Schliemann, Yannakis, and two of the foremen, Photidos and Georgios Barbar Tsirogiannis, five terraces were carved so that strata could be identified and first-datings preserved. The earth, separated and often sifted, yielded so many objects that it was no longer possible to record each and to give the depth at which it was found. The staff artist, Polychromos Lempessis, was able to draw in India ink only a small percentage of the objects excavated.

Walls of cities came into view. Small temples, paved streets and outlines of houses were laid bare. Workers collected numberless terra cottas, statuettes, vases and miscellaneous artifacts. Beautifully inscribed blocks of marble were released from centuries of entombment; some weighed two tons and their removal was slow and meticulous.

One of the objects that most intrigued Schliemann was a brilliant red hippopotamus of hollow terra cotta, with a ring on the left side. Schliemann concluded that the object must have been a vessel of some sort, and he took time to ruminate about the shape. The notes from his on-the-spot diary were almost literally transcribed as comments on the hippopotamus in his book *Troy and Its Remains*: "Extremely remarkable, nay, astonishing it is to find this animal; for this animal, as is well known, is not met with even in Upper Egypt, and occurs only in the rivers in the interior of Africa. It is, however, probable that hippopotami existed in Upper Egypt in ancient times; for, according to the historian Herodotus (II, 71), they were worshiped as sacred animals at the Egyptian town of Papremis. At all events, Troy must have been commercially connected with Egypt; but even so, it is still an enigma how the animal was so well known here as to have been made of clay in a form quite faithful to nature."

By March 1 there were 158 workers digging, shoveling, chopping, sifting, and cutting at Hissarlik. Working with a crew at a section where hundreds of objects were being excavated, Sophia reached out for one and thoroughly examined it. She took the object to Heinrich, who was excited by her interpretation of the unique find, a piece of stone, hard and black, two and a half inches in diameter. Some ancient sculptor had carved it into what Sophia identified as a primitive idol with head, two arms and two legs, all the same shape. The head was distinguished from the limbs only by horizontal lines that seemed to represent a necklace. Sophia thought the circular indentation in the middle of one side of the stone was intended as a navel, and Heinrich wondered whether the convex arch on the reverse side might not be a shield, symbolic of Ares, the god of war. Research later proved their combined interpretations to be correct.

As the digging continued copper was the only metal found. There were copper sickles, weapons and nails by the hundreds. During previous excavation only a few copper pieces had been unearthed. The Schliemanns, correlating copper objects from the same depth, decided that the metal had been vital to one early civilization.

On small and large objects, ancient Greek inscriptions were

carved or incised in capital letters, with no spaces between the words, in the custom of ancient times. Sophia and Heinrich, by lamplight, translated the inscriptions into modern Greek with capital and lower-case letters, proper word-spacing and punctuation, aspirate and pronunciation marks. They recognized famous names and events chronicled by inscription on the objects. Later they checked on names and facts unfamiliar to them.

By mid-March, days were pleasant, with the noon temperature about 72 degrees. Flowers bloomed on the Plain, and the storks returned to the Troad, the region governed by ancient Troy. On nights, still cold, the air was rent by the hideous croaking of thousands of frogs and the screeches of owls again nesting in the excavations.

The work pace slowed as sweating workmen stopped often to quench their thirst and to wipe perspiration from their brows. Heinrich and Sophia, working along with the crews, helped to uncover the ruins of Athena's Temple and a gate Schliemann called the Skaean, so important to the unfolding of the story of the *Iliad*. A temple of Apollo appeared. Remains of a theater were outlined in the ground. Schliemann had hundreds of stones removed, considering them to be impediments to the progress of his exploration of the past. He cared little for the importance of the stones, many of which were later recovered by other archaeologists, eager to study them in detail.

Without apology Schliemann wrote: "The many thousands of stones which I bring out of the depths of Ilium have induced the inhabitants of the surrounding villages to erect buildings which might be called grand for the inhabitants of this wilderness. Houses were built. Among others, they are at present building with my Ilian stones a mosque and a minaret in the wretched village of Chiplak, and a church-tower in the Christian village of Yeni Shehr. A number of two-wheeled carts, drawn by oxen, are always standing by the side of my excavations, ready to receive the stones which can be of any use as soon as they have been brought to the surface; but the religious zeal of these good people is not great enough for them to offer to help me in the terrible work of breaking the large, splendidly hewn blocks so as to make them more convenient to remove." Sophia's caustic comment about the stone collectors was: "Throughout the ages those who have little wish much free from those who have more, being unwilling to work for their own gain. This has been the way of man since the beginning, and probably will be until the end of time."

Workmen excavated two musical instruments that gave Heinrich pleasure; one was a flat bone with a single hole in one end and three holes in the other. He blew notes from the bone instrument and, as always, relating objects with people long dead, wondered if he was about to find "another civilization of higher culture to which fine music was added." The second instrument was a flute-shaped piece of ivory, magnificently ornamented. Heinrich blew a note on the flute and then another, fingering the holes cut into the ivory. Smiling workmen seemed about to break into song and dance as the *Effendi* tootled a series of notes "without doubt the first given forth by this flute for many centuries. Would that we could know by whom it was played, and the tune, and the circumstances, and the meaning!" was the wish of the romantic Heinrich, letting his imagination play with the idea. Sophia wrote of the flute incident: "How pleased I was to see my Henry so happy. Few are given the opportunity to share such moments with him."

They shortly shared an experience that might have ended in tragedy. A log fire had been burning for six days in the bedroom fireplace, primitively constructed with its stones, joined by cement, resting on floorboards. Flames from the fireplace escaped either through a crack in the boards or through a crevice in the cement. At 3 A.M. Sophia, half-awake, smelled smoke and roused Heinrich. Their bedroom was filled with dense smoke, and flames, which had burned 2 square yards of flooring, were licking up the north wall.

Although alarmed, Sophia and Heinrich both kept their presence of mind. He poured bath water from a storage jar onto the north wall, where small flames were being fanned by a strong north wind whistling through chinks in the frame siding. Sophia called out to Photidos, who was sleeping in the adjoining room, and he shouted to the foremen living in the stone house opposite. With iron levers and pickaxes, they pried up the burning floorboards. There being no more water at the house, scooped-up earth was thrown on the fire. Lower beams beneath the flooring were burning in several places, so it took a long time to extinguish the flames. Photidos carefully checked to be sure that there was no smoldering beam that might later burst into flame. Sophia and Heinrich, strong characters that they were, went back to bed and slept until dawn "roused us with its call to work in this magnificent spring."

With the coming of spring, Heinrich resumed his practice of swimming daily in the salt waters of the Hellespont, where he went for "exercise and the curative substances in the water." Before the sky was fully light, he would mount his horse and set out on the 3-mile ride, accompanied by bodyguards to protect him from the Troad brigands. One morning the guards were riding well ahead of Schliemann when his horse shied while crossing a wooden bridge. The rearing horse tumbled into a deep ditch, landing on Schliemann. The guards, concerned when the *Effendi* did not catch up with them, turned and galloped back along the road. Schliemann, having struggled free from the horse, tongue-lashed the guards; then dusting himself off, he remounted and, preceding them, rode on with dignity toward the shore for his swim.

A rise and fall of land between Hissarlik and the Hellespont corresponded with a conformation of ground described by Homer. He told of Trojan chieftains who saw their men move out from the city and disappear below a sloping summit, only to reappear at a distance along the road. Sophia and others on the Hill could see Schliemann, far off on his white horse, returning from the Hellespont. Always, at a certain place, he disappeared from sight for a few minutes; then, on the last stretch of road leading to Hissarlik, he could again be seen from the Hill. On his morning rides Schliemann often thought of the Trojan forces who had traveled the same road between the Hellespont and ancient Troy.

With rare caution, Heinrich slowed down the work of large crews excavating the Temple of Athena and the surrounding houses, walls, buttresses and paved streets. Realizing that a labyrinth of very ancient house walls was being uncovered, he asked for advice on procedure from archaeologists excavating elsewhere. Flexible when the successful outcome of his endeavor was at stake, he accepted the suggestions of experienced excavators.

Rooms on top of rooms, rooms beside rooms, were unearthed in the area of the Temple of Athena. Schliemann personally excavated one room with "tender care, meticulous work and absolute personal supervision. Aided by my wife, I found a room

10 feet high and 11¼ feet broad. One of the compartments of the uppermost houses, below the Temple of Athena, and belonging to the pre-Hellenistic period, appears to have been used as a wine merchant's cellar, or as magazine, for in it there were nine enormous earthen jars (pithoi) of various forms, about 5¾ feet high and 4¾ feet across, their mouths being from 29½ to 35¼ inches broad. Each of these earthen jars has four handles, 3¾ inches broad, and the clay of which they are made has the enormous thickness of 2¼ inches."

Sophia and Heinrich, digging 6 feet below the surface of the ground, came upon a red clay jar that was 7 feet high. Expecting to measure and study the jar at their leisure, they had it moved up to the Hill and placed in front of their new house. They were highly amused when the mammoth jar without handles became a night-shelter for one of the workmen, and served by day as a rain-shelter for two and sometimes three workmen. Lempessis made a scale drawing of the jar with a Turkish worker standing beside it.

Discovered 26 feet below the section Schliemann called the Palace of Priam was another container of much finer workmanship: a brilliant brown vase. Its mouth was molded with two eyes and a nose, the stem was encircled by a necklace, and two breasts stood out from the bulbous body. Heavy stones were layered in the hard earth above the smooth clay vase, and Heinrich carefully dug with his knife around the object, which he thought represented Athena. To his dismay, when he was gently removing the vase from the surrounding rubble, the weight of stone above broke the clay into several large pieces. An expert in Athens did a skillful restoration, and Lempessis then sketched the Athena vase, which was 24½ inches high with a handle on each side.

The excavation of the first complete skeletons gave conclusive proof of occupation of the Hill by ancient people. Helmets, lances, and other military gear were found beside some skeletons, and one skeletal head intact was adjacent to a collection of shattered head bones. An unearthed altar, shaped like a large throne, indicated the sacrificial worship of some deity. Sophia and Heinrich worked steadily toward the re-creation of life as it had been many centuries earlier.

When balmy weather settled over the Troad, the workmen

did not always return home at night but often slept at Hissarlik, in the open or down in the excavations. That arrangement Schliemann found convenient because he always had the workmen at hand. "Besides this, the long days are a great advantage, for I can continue to work from a quarter to five in the morning till a quarter past seven in the evening."

Work was speeding along when Sophia received word that her father was critically ill. Heinrich, leaving Yannakis in charge of the excavations, took Sophia to the Dardanelles and put her aboard a ship sailing for the Piraeus. She was too late: George Engastromenos died before she reached home. Sophia, saddened by the death of her ebullient father, was emotionally torn, and her letters to Heinrich were pitiful. She wanted to be with her mother and with Andromache, growing so fast, but Sophia also yearned to be with Heinrich at Hissarlik. With deep and loving understanding, he wrote to her from Troy:

Troy, May 14, 1873

MY DEARLY BELOVED WIFE:

Comfort yourself, my dear, with the thought that in a short while we too shall follow your splendid father. Comfort yourself for the sake of our dear little daughter who needs her mother, and whose whole happiness in life would be destroyed without her. Comfort yourself with the realization that your tears cannot bring your dear father back to life and that he, good and worthy person that he was, now—removed from the cares and sufferings of this world—enjoys the true blessed joy of the next and is certainly happier than we who mourn him. However, if you cannot overcome your grief for the dearly departed, then come back to me on the next steamship and I shall find a way to cheer you up. Our excavations have not progressed without you and all await [your] speedy return with tears of joy. . . .

Heinrich could be as tyrannical and egotistical, as selfish and thoughtless, as any genius driven toward the accomplishment of goals not set by lesser men. Yet he often displayed a rare quality of understanding denied to men without genius. His comforting words drew the pain of her father's death from Sophia's heart, gave her solace as mother, and demonstrated that without her Heinrich was lost and his work nothing. Convinced that she must be with Heinrich, Sophia prepared to leave for Asia Minor.

FIFTEEN

Heinrich, tense and impatient, waited at the Dardanelles for Sophia to land. Dressed for the occasion in the very best suit from his wardrobe at Hissarlik, he wore stark white linens and his travel hat. Face somber, he leaned lightly on a formal walking stick, restlessly tapping one toe. As Sophia, pale but with eyes glowing, stepped ashore Heinrich rushed forward and, uttering an emotional gasp, swept her into his arms. Clinging to her, he "whimpered like a small animal that needs and has found momentary refuge." Pressing against him, she sighed with the bliss of a woman loved and loving.

Joy attended Sophia's return, and as she and Heinrich started toward Troy he gave her highlights of activities during her absence. She, in turn, quietly told him of her father's fatal illness and funeral. Their conversation, as often, was like that of devoted friends, which, in fact, they were. Their letters to each other frequently contained expressions of friendship, interspersed with those of love. "My friend, Henry," she would write to him, or "Henry . . . my friend for life," or, in salutation, "Friend and dearest husband." He called her "My own Sophithion, adored wife and everlasting friend."

As proud father, Heinrich smiled and chuckled when Sophia told him about the new beauty and lively ways of Andromache, their cherished child. Suddenly interrupting Sophia, Heinrich, with the impetuosity of a young lover, ordered outriding guards to halt and, vaulting from his horse, bent down to uproot a poppy plant. No sound but that of the whining wind was heard as he presented to Sophia the bright wildflower, its red petals surrounding a velvety black center. A moment's silence, engendered by their unity, followed. "At such times, the heart is so full, one's gratitude for what the gods have given is so great, that words would only split the air like gunfire, and defile the sanctity of the moment."

At the digs foremen, guards and workmen greeted Sophia with cheers, and Yannakis stood mute, tears running down his cheeks, roughened by wind and sun. Helen, his wife, looking deep into Sophia's eyes, led her into the house, barring the door to Heinrich, who tried to follow. An hour passed before the two young women reappeared. What passed between them indoors was never known.

With his Sophithion again at his side, Heinrich was happy and his energy recharged. Work progressed rapidly through the long days. The Schliemanns were kept busy from the moment when Sophia gave Heinrich a kiss of welcome after his return from the predawn swim, until they settled for the night in the tiny bedroom of the house on the rim of the great trench.

Then in late spring 1873 came the day that justified their January predictions. "Something within me" told Sophia of a time to be "long remembered for its events," and Heinrich had known with certainty that "our excavations would be memorable."

Sophia and Heinrich, sweaty of body and dry of mouth, were digging together, but without a crew, on a level flagstone floor between two walls. One was the wall of the house that Heinrich thought was the Palace of Priam; the other, a high fortification wall. Heinrich, standing apart from Sophia, struck metal, a strike that triggered the most sensational archaeological news of the 19th century and sparked archaeological interest not matched until 1922, the year Lord Carnarvon and Howard Carter discovered the tomb of the Egyptian boy king Tutankhamen.

The word *Sophia* was spoken softly but with an urgency that she, sensitive to Heinrich's tones, immediately interpreted as "Come at once. It is vital. Be silent." In a flash she stood beside him, looking at a "big copper object of a most peculiar shape. . . ." Then she too saw the glint of brighter metal. Without speaking, she helped Heinrich dig into the wall, to scrape pebbles and dirt from around the copper object. On top of it there was a layer of red and calcined ruins, about five feet thick and hard as stone. The fortification wall rested on that layer.

The copper object was finally freed from the earth, and the Schliemanns stared at the hole. Gold gleamed from it. With his back to the opening, Heinrich turned to Sophia; soundlessly his lips formed the words: "None must see it. None can be trusted."

In a whisper he told Sophia to scramble up to the foremen and order *paidos.* She objected that calling for a rest period ahead of the breakfast hour would arouse the workmen's suspicion. Thinking fast, Heinrich said, "Tell them I forgot that this is my birthday. They must have extra time to rest today in my honor . . . a long extra time." Trusting that Sophia, with her charm and wiles, would carry off the deception, Heinrich shooed her away. She climbed the dirt incline, tearing stockings and undergarments in her haste. The crews were working quite far away that morning, and it took her a few minutes to reach them. Her announcement of the *Effendi*'s birthday *paidos* happily was accepted without question, even by Georgios Sarkis, the overseer representing the Turkish government.

Outwardly calm, Sophia climbed back down to where Heinrich was frantically digging and scraping. She placed a restraining hand on his arm and pointed up to the fortification wall. He nodded to show he understood her pantomime warning that careless digging might cause a cave-in or a perilous landslide. He "cut out the Treasure with a large knife, which it was impossible to do without the greatest exertion and the most fearful risk to my life, for the great fortification-wall, beneath which I had to dig, threatened every moment to fall down upon me. But the sight of so many objects, every one of which was of inestimable value to archaeology, made me foolhardy, and I never thought of any danger." Without the help of Sophia, as he wrote, it would have been impossible for him to remove the treasure.

Small stones and hard earth, loosened bit by bit, clattered to the flagstones, the sound echoing in the small enclosure. Shuddering at the noise that might attract the attention of the vigilant Sarkis, Sophia held out her voluminous skirt to catch debris, which she deposited on the floor, noiselessly. A jumble of gold, silver and copper objects began to pile up, and she gestured to Heinrich that she was going to their house. With many objects bagged in her skirt, she reached the Hill and nonchalantly strolled across it to the stone building, where she quickly placed the treasure in a pillowcase. She returned with a large square red shawl and laid it on the flagstone at the excavation. As more objects were removed from the earth they were placed on the shawl that was soon heaped with metal pieces of various shapes and weights. Gathering the four corners of the shawl, Sophia again went to the house. She gently spilled the contents of the shawl onto the great worktable, and left, turning the key in the front door, normally left unlocked.

Working against time, the Schliemanns dug into the wall from which treasure spilled with each cut. Even as Heinrich worked he imagined that the disorder of objects might be attributed to the speed with which they were stored. "Owing to the fact that I found all . . . objects packed together in the big wall of the gods, it seems certain that they lay in a wooden trunk like those mentioned in the *Iliad* (XXIV, 228) as having been in Priam's Palace. This seems to be still more certain as immediately next to these objects I have found a big copper key, which bears great similarity to the keys of today's banks. Apparently someone of Priam's family carried the treasure in great haste to the trunk, packed it there, but did not have time to take the key out . . . and had to forsake the trunk." The key fit an unearthed lock, but the trunk, if wood, had either been destroyed by fire or disintegrated with passing centuries. A helmet buried with the treasure made Heinrich wonder if "perhaps it belonged to the unfortunate man who was trying to save the treasure."

By the time the last visible object was removed from the opening in the wall and cuts into the earth released only dirt, Sophia's shawl was again filled, and she and Heinrich were encircled by mounds of treasure. Concealing objects in her skirt and blouse, in his pockets and under his hat, they started slowly for the Hill, she carrying her shawl weighted with treasure, and he lugging metal bundled in handkerchiefs.

With incredible luck, they reached the house without being seen. When Heinrich had deposited objects stripped from his person, he went outside in search of Yannakis, to whom he explained that Sophia had been taken ill with fever, "a thing to sadden me on my birthday, but I shall remain with her placing wet cloths on her forehead, after she has taken quinine. See that we are not disturbed so that Madame is allowed to rest."

Yannakis was properly sympathetic and acquiescent but, being observant and keen-witted, he must have noticed the disheveled condition of the usually neat Dr. Schliemann. His mussed hair glistened with drops of sweat and his dusty clothes were drenched from shoulder to ankle. Whatever Yannakis thought, he gave no sign that anything might be amiss as he turned from Heinrich and walked away.

Inside the house, Heinrich locked the door behind him; then he and Sophia covered the windows with makeshift curtains of shawls and blankets. Standing shoulder to shoulder, they gazed at the morning's extraordinary discovery, bright as twinkling candles in the gloom of the shaded room. Drained by their exertion, they were slow to react to the dazzling display.

What the real date of the day was may never be known. Guesses have ranged from late May, shortly after Sophia's return from Athens, to early June. Heinrich's diary entry about the treasure of Troy was dated June 17, 1873. The place name beside the date line was changed from Athens to Troy, in his own handwriting when he prepared to publish his findings. Since he gave exact weights of gold objects, the entry must have been written after the treasures were weighed by an Athenian goldsmith. Heinrich had the best of reasons for being devious about the date of discovery. But since there was no reason to falsify the order in which the treasures were examined by him and Sophia, his record of that was straightforward and exact.

Exhaustion nullified by elation, they began to examine the more than 10,000 precious objects they had dug from the earth that morning. Heinrich, with hands as steady as those of a surgeon, picked up the first piece of treasure. It was a copper shield, less than 20 inches in length. An inch-high rim surrounded the oval-shaped shield, which had a light furrow around a simple decoration at the center; the decoration, raised about 2 inches, was a little more than 4 inches in diameter. From years of study, Heinrich knew that the shield originally had been covered with oxhides; but before he could mention that fact, Sophia began to recite lines from Homer. Her face pink with a youthful flush and smudged by dirt, she stood dreamy-eyed, as if in a daze, and softly spoke:

> "Ajax approached, before him, as a tower
> His mighty shield he bore, seven-fold, brassbound.
> The work of Tychius, best artificer
> That wrought in leather, he in Hyla dwelt.

Of seven-fold hides the ponderous shield was wrought
Of lusty bulls; the eighth was glittering brass."

The shield of Ajax? No, but one of copper, perhaps like his of brass? Emotion and romance produced the momentary and quickly discarded questions.

Three other copper objects were examined next: a cauldron with two horizontal handles, a plate, and a vase. Then Sophia and Heinrich, with their four hands, lifted up a globular vase of pure gold (403 grams) that was 6 inches high and 5 inches in diameter at its roundest swelling. Heinrich, letting Sophia have the vase, reached for a superbly wrought cup of gold (226 grams); it was 3½ inches high, with a 3-inch opening and a rim-base aesthetically proportioned to the gently curving form.

Controlling hands trembling by then, they picked up a boat-shaped drinking cup, also gold (600 grams). The two-handled cup curved up to a drinking lip, 2¾ inches wide, at one end, and to a more steeply slanted lip, 1⅕ inches wide, at the other. The object reminded the Schliemanns of other words by Homer: "The guest is ever sacred and shall have the best of the household, without questions asked." They pictured a weary traveler welcomed to Troy by a host who first offered him a bath in a mammoth tub filled with water mixed with perfumed oils. Fair ladies of the household held towels for the guest, who emerged relaxed and rested from the soothing water. Standing in the full glory of his nakedness, he was gently rubbed dry, and then draped with fine raiment. Striding to the central court the proud guest joined his hospitable host, who picked up the golden boat-cup and himself took a few sips of the wine-and-water mixture from the smaller end of the vessel. The wayfarer then accepted the cup and drank deep from its wide mouth. The "best of the household" was for the guest, whether friend or stranger, and only after he had sipped wine were confidences exchanged or questions asked.

From fantasy the Schliemanns returned to reality and looked at a small cup of gold alloy, a natural mixture of silver and gold that the ancients called "electrum." Heinrich had seen modern electrum made in Germany.

Sophia, the back of her blouse damp with perspiration and

her skirt frayed by jagged rocks and sharp metal, slowly picked out from the heap on the worktable six silver knife-blades that she lined up in front of her. The blade of each knife was round at one end and V-notched at the other. Heinrich and Sophia puzzled over the probable use of the knives. They could not have been for fighting because the blade lengths were not uniform. Homer, the Schliemanns recalled, commented that women, cauldrons, tripods and knife blades were offered as prizes in sporting contests and as battle trophies. Perhaps the silver knife blades had been such prizes. They fit Homeric descriptions of trophies, but no one could be certain.

Quickening their pace, Heinrich and Sophia picked up three silver vases, delicately fashioned, a silver goblet, a flat silver dish, thirteen copper lances, fourteen copper weapons, seven large double-edged copper daggers and a bronze helmet.

They were so overcome by the beauty of a huge silver vase that they looked for a long time before touching it. "Not even our breathing could be discerned, if truly we breathed at all. Before us the silver shone. Why did we hesitate? Who knows? The extra sense with which the gods of Olympus have endowed us proved to us that here was an object of such magnificence that, at first, we dared not touch it for fear that it would crumble and disappear forever."

Sophia tentatively reached toward the vase, but Heinrich touched her hand and a wave of oneness surged through them. He firmly gripped the silver container and, lifting it to eye level, as if making a votive offering to the gods, shook the heavy object. Thuds, clinks and rattles reverberated in the room, startling Heinrich and Sophia. He, frowning, cautiously lowered the vase and placed it on its side.

Sophia, motionless, looked at him with shining eyes. "At the moment, it was my darling Henry who should touch for the first time in centuries that which was contained in the depth of this vase. His dream, his passion sustained him from childhood, and this should be his reward." His fingers explored the inside of the neck of the vase, and he gently pulled from it gold so glorious that Sophia involuntarily cried out, then swiftly covered her mouth with her hand to deaden the sound.

Heinrich held two diadems—two, not one—and both perfect in

design, workmanship and state of preservation. His descriptions of them were minute in detail. They were gold; thin gold plate and wire from pure ingots. The first "consists of a fillet, 22 in. long and nearly ½ in. broad, from which there hang on either side 7 little chains to cover the temples, each of which consists of 50 double rings, and between every 4 of these rings is suspended an hexagonal leaf having a groove lengthwise; these chains are joined to one another by four little cross chains. At the end of each of the side chains hangs a figure similar in shape to the Trojan idols. . . . Each idol is nearly an inch long; their breadth at the lower end is about ¾ths in. The entire length of each of these chains, with the idols, amounts to 10.4 in. Between these ornaments for the temples there are 50 little pendant chains, each of which consists of 21 double rings, and between every 4 of these rings there is an hexagonal leaf. At the end of each little chain hangs an idol of identical form, ⅗ths in. high; the length of these short chains with the idols is only 4 in. The number of double rings, of which the 64 chains of this diadem is composed, amounts to 1750, and the number of hexagonal leaves to 354; the number of suspended idols is 64." The grand total of pieces in the second diadem was 16,353.

As if the two elaborate diadems were not crowning treasure enough, Heinrich drew out a third fillet, 18 inches long and simple in design. Sophia slid her hand into the vase and pulled out four golden earrings. Each measured 3½ inches, including the swinging pendant of the Trojan goddess. The vase then gave up, in succession, six gold bracelets and fifty-nine more earrings of various sizes.

Heinrich, unable to restrain himself, impulsively tilted the silver vase, and thousands of tiny objects tumbled to the table. He and Sophia, sorting little pieces of gold, made separate piles of similar-looking objects. What seemed like sections of necklaces were collected in one group; single buttons, double buttons, miniature brooches, and pins, in others. When the tiny gold treasures eventually were counted, they numbered 8,700.

Not even a soaring imagination like Heinrich's could have envisioned such treasure as was spread out in the tiny room. The find was at once of inestimable worth, monetarily, and of incomparable value, archaeologically. When the day of triumph came to a close, the Schliemanns, physically exhausted and emotionally spent, forced themselves to the arduous task of storing the treasure out of sight. Before Heinrich wrapped the second of the two large diadems, he beckoned to Sophia, who, skirts swirling, glided to him. Raising the diadem, Heinrich placed it on her head and, voice unsteady, said, "Adornment worn by Helen of Troy now graces my own wife, Helen's descendant, before whose regal presence the world will kneel." Neither of the Schliemanns really thought that the jewels had belonged to the Trojan Helen. But later Heinrich, referring to the incident, stated, ". . . in my imagination I saw the Fair Helen and during this moment of overwhelming emotion I conjured up the picture of a Grecian queen on Trojan soil, bedecked with jewels."

After the treasure was well concealed, Sophia and Heinrich planned how to sneak it away from Hissarlik, outwitting the watchful Sarkis. They successfully smuggled out the treasure of Troy, but never said by what means. Heinrich far from suffering qualms about taking the treasure, justified his questionable action with several explanations. He declared that pilfering of small gold objects would have reduced the collection before it ever reached the new museum at Constantinople. There he thought that thievery by officials would have further prevented the whole collection from being maintained in trust for public viewing. Whatever his rationalization, his own experience with Turkish intrigue had made him wary. Schliemann publicly stated that the Turks had in various ways abrogated their agreements with him, and in consequence he was not bound to their terms. He felt that his boyhood dream, his own energy, his personal fortune, and his unshakable faith had directly led to the discovery of the treasure. Without him, so he held, the treasure would not have been released from its imprisoning walls. In short, Heinrich claimed the treasure as his rightful due.

Although normally, Schliemann was given to putting to paper every fact, trivial and important, he refrained ever from bragging about how the treasure of Troy was spirited from Asia Minor. And Sophia never mentioned the subject, not even when, in her old age, she reminisced about her life with Heinrich to her children and grandchildren.

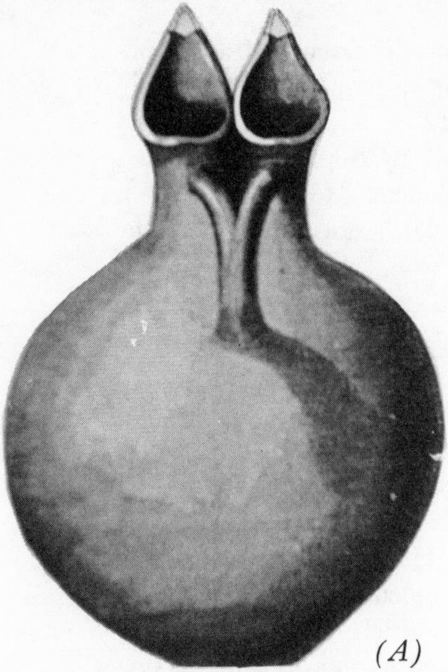

(A)

(GENNADIUS LIBRARY, ATHENS)

(B)

(GENNADIUS LIBRARY, ATHENS)

(C)

(GENNADIUS LIBRARY, ATHENS)

(D)

(FREE UNIVERSITY, WEST BERLIN)

Troy finds included (A) two-necked jar similar to modern French liqueur decanter; (B) owl-headed vase with eyes, nose, necklace, breasts, and belt running diagonally across body; (C) two-handled drinking cup; (D) lustrous black pitcher with breasts and incised design.

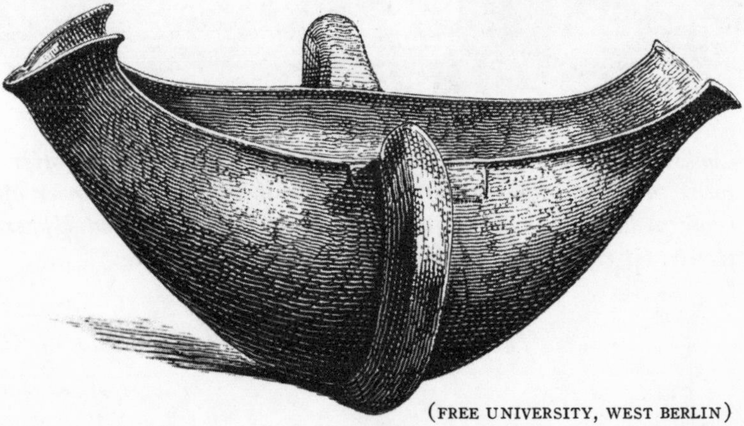

(FREE UNIVERSITY, WEST BERLIN)

Boat-shaped drinking cup found at Troy was shared by the host with his guest. Each drank from lips at opposite ends of the cup.

(GENNADIUS LIBRARY, ATHENS)

Looking north along the trench running through the Hill of Hissarlik, drawing shows what Schliemann thought to be Tower of Ilium at bottom, then Skaean Gate, Palace of Priam, and Upper House. At top of Hill are Schliemanns' living quarters.

(GERMAN ARCHAEOLOGICAL INSTITUTE, ATHENS)

Marble bas-relief found at Troy showing head of young man and horse.

(GENNADIUS LIBRARY, ATHENS)

For 14 months mammoth jar lay on its side outside Schliemann's hut. At night, one workman slept in it; during rain, two or three crawled inside it for shelter.

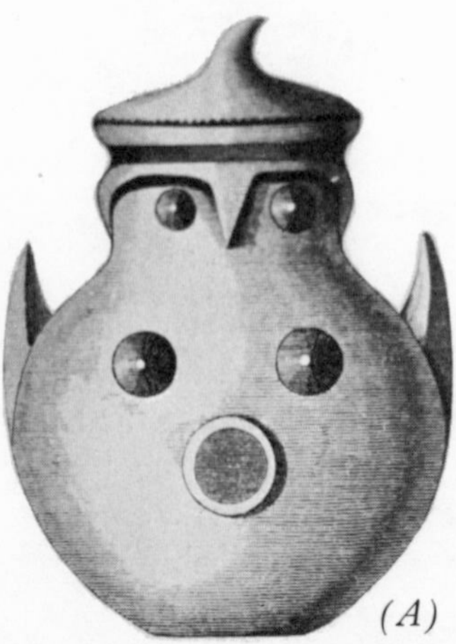

(A)

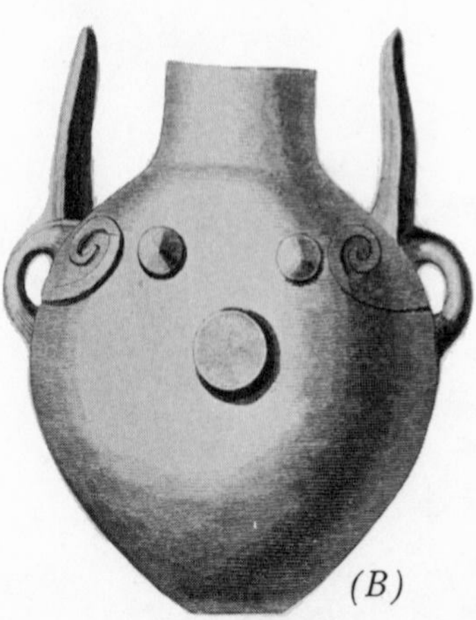

(B)

(ILLUSTRATED LONDON NEWS)

Beneath subsurface at Troy, workmen unearthed these giant jars whose size may be gauged by man at left. Wooden and stone huts above served as homes for Heinrich and Sophia and supervisory personnel.

(C)

Three of the hundreds of terra-cotta vases dug up at Hissarlik: (A) red clay vase with owl's head motif, two upraised arms, and two breasts; (B) black vase with appearance of owl's head, with arms, breasts, and a large navel; (C) red vase with human face, more realistic arms holding libation cup.

(GENNADIUS LIBRARY, ATHENS)

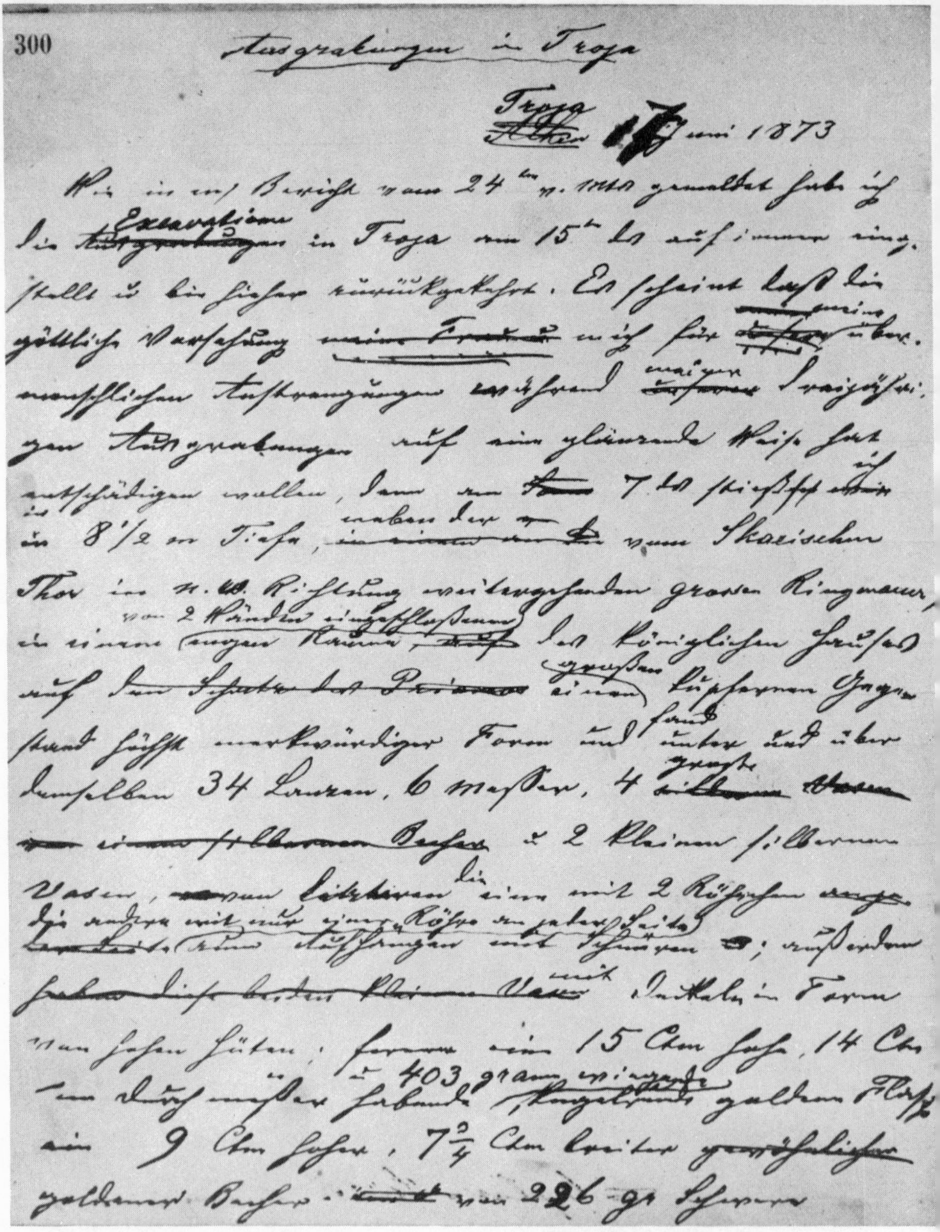

300

Ausgrabungen in Troja

Troja 17 Juni 1873

Wie in meinem Bericht vom 24ten v. Mts gemeldet habe ich die Excavationen in Troja am 15ten ds auf immer eingestellt und bin hieher zurückgekehrt. Es scheint daß die göttliche Vorsehung mich für meine übermenschlichen Anstrengungen während meiner dreijährigen Ausgrabungen auf eine glänzende Weise hat entschädigen wollen, denn am 7 ds stieß ich in 8½ m Tiefe, neben der vom Skaeischen Thor in N.W. Richtung weitergehenden grossen Ringmauer, in einem von 2 Wänden eingeschlossenen engen Raume des königlichen Hauses auf einen grossen kupfernen Gegenstand höchst merkwürdiger Form und fand unter und über demselben 34 Lanzen, 6 Messer, 4 grosse ... & 2 kleinen silbernen Vasen, die eine mit 2 Röhrchen ... die andere mit nur einer Röhre an jeder Seite ...; ausserdem mit Deckeln in Form von hohen Hüten; ferner ein 15 Ctm hohe, 14 Ctm im Durchmesser habende 403 gram wiegende goldene Flasche ein 9 Ctm hoher, 7¾ Ctm breiter goldener Becher von 226 gr Schwere

(GENNADIUS LIBRARY, ATHENS)

First description of the Schliemanns' discovery of priceless treasure of Troy is dated 17 June, 1873 on page 300 of Heinrich's diary. He wrote this in Athens, but crossed out Athens and wrote Troy in its stead when preparing to publish his findings.

(FREE UNIVERSITY, WEST BERLIN)

On flagstone floor next to workman, "a" marks the spot where the great treasure was found. Sophia and Heinrich, working alone, carried the objects to their hut without being seen, then spirited them out of Turkey to Greece.

(COURTESY: ALEX L. MÉLAS)

Sophia Schliemann wearing an elaborate headdress, a necklace, and two sets of earrings—one pair at her throat. This was only a small part of the treasure of Troy.

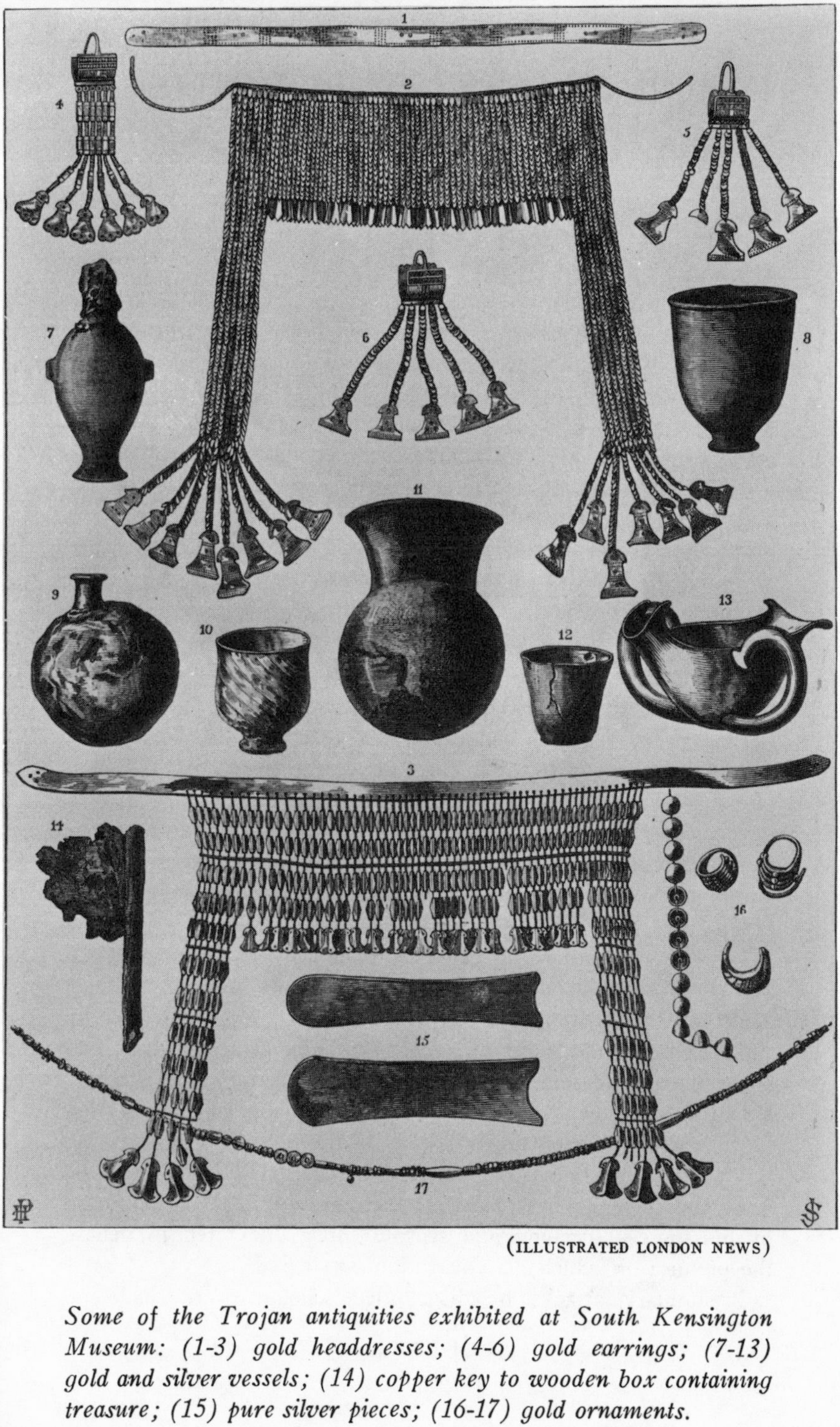

(ILLUSTRATED LONDON NEWS)

Some of the Trojan antiquities exhibited at South Kensington Museum: (1-3) gold headdresses; (4-6) gold earrings; (7-13) gold and silver vessels; (14) copper key to wooden box containing treasure; (15) pure silver pieces; (16-17) gold ornaments.

SIXTEEN

Secluded in his house at Athens, Schliemann studied the entire Trojan collection in the summer of 1873. Large objects were weighed, sketched, and described in detail. Only he and Sophia knew the extent of the collection, and outsiders, like the goldsmith who had to see individual pieces—but only one at a time—were sworn to secrecy. The cataloguing was rapidly completed, and before the announcement of the great find the collection was broken up. In securely wrapped packages, unlabeled, the treasure was sent to Sophia's numerous relatives throughout the Greek mainland and on Crete. They were instructed to hide the packages in houses, barns, and caves on their farms or estates. There was no written list of hiding places; Heinrich and Sophia memorized the locations and the package contents.

Reaction to the published announcement of the discovery of the treasure of Troy proved the wisdom of the temporary dispersal of the objects. The news unleashed the full fury of the Turkish government, which reviled the Schliemanns, and set into operation persecutions that were to plague them for more than a year. Turks shadowed Heinrich, and harassed Sophia and members of her family.

Laymen everywhere, in great cities and at remote outposts of the world, read about the rich discovery with intense interest; some were fascinated by the historical import, some intrigued by the adventure, and many envious of the two principals who had come into possession of so much gold. Open-minded scholars hailed the discovery as justification for Schliemann's assertion that Troy was buried under Hissarlik, the objects demonstrating the wealth of a flourishing ancient civilization. Negators of the Troy theory long championed by Schliemann were discomforted by his success; carping and scornful, they attempted to debase the premise on which his excavation was based.

Preliminary attacks by disgruntled scholars were made on

Heinrich alone, but in recognition of Sophia as partner, the trend of criticism shifted to include her too, the word *they* becoming more common than *he*. The change of emphasis resulted from Heinrich's praise of Sophia's contributions both at the excavation and to the study of the antiquities. He considered her to be an equal partner, sharing his passion for excavation of ancient sites and for interpretation of the civilizations that existed long before the classical age of Greece. She was aware of his acceptance of her as colleague but was self-effacing, answering with ire only those scholars who attacked "my husband who is both lover and friend, a leader others will be forced to follow if inquiry into the past is to go forward."

The triumphs of Troy behind them, the Schliemanns were eager to go forward with excavations at Mycenae, a famous site in the Peloponnesus. In February and March of 1874 they sank thirty-four exploratory shafts there, but exploration was halted by a lawsuit. With the Greek government's permission, Schliemann was being sued in Greece by the Turkish authorities, who charged him with illegal removal of the treasures he unearthed at Troy.

Returning to Athens, Heinrich retained outstanding attorneys to argue his case in the Greek court. It was soon patent that the Greek ministers, Eustratiades and Valassopoulos, were engaged in double-dealing, giving full cooperation to Turkish representatives while being obsequious to Schliemann at every encounter. The two Greek officials apparently thought that whatever the outcome of the suit, they were certain to be winners. A verdict in favor of the Turkish government would rid them of Schliemann for all time; a verdict for Schliemann might encourage him to turn the treasure of Troy over to Greece in gratitude. Like many other adversaries of Schliemann, they underrated him.

With his excavation at Mycenae interrupted and the civil suit dragging on in a court where the long-winded were never curtailed, Schliemann reacted as always when thwarted by circumstances beyond his control: He involved himself in feverish activity. Heinrich and Sophia began work on a book about their excavations at Troy. He constantly conferred with Dentopoulos, his Athenian banker, and studied daily reports from the New York Stock Exchange, cabling orders to buy and sell. He kept in touch by mail and cable with P. Beaurain, the agent in Paris, who managed Schliemann's real estate and kept the account books of his other investments on the continent.

The French and Russian governments, using the lawsuit as lever, tried to pry the treasure of Troy from Schliemann. He was so infuriated when the Greek government admitted the civil suit into its courts that he threatened to send the treasure of Troy to the Louvre. The French, certain that the treasure would be theirs, lost it by asking Schliemann to send samples to Paris for inspection. In refusal he answered, "My word and the word of other scholars must suffice to assure the French that the treasure is of more value than any tremendous sum they can raise to purchase the collection."

The Russians, coveting the treasure, offered honors to Schliemann, while condemning the Turkish government. In July a letter from Baron Nicolas Casimir Bogoushevsky invited Schliemann to accept honorary membership in the Russian Institute of Archaeology. By authority of Baron de Wrangell, Baron Bogoushevsky sent another letter imploring Schliemann to accept a place on the Institute's advisory commission, citing famous international figures who served on it. In the second communication the baron wrote: "The proceedings of the Turkish government have excited general indignation. Such proceedings are nothing new, the Turkish government being well known here."

The Turkish action caused universal indignation, and letters of protest by the hundreds were sent to Greek authorities and to Schliemann. Even some who had previously been his bitter critics closed ranks, praising Schliemann and his contributions to science.

Every delay in the courtroom gave Heinrich an excuse for trips to other European cities, from which he returned with each resumption of testimony. He wrote to Renan from Bologna that being forced to suspend excavation, he could not "waste time sitting in Athens. So, I am continuing my studies in the museums and archives of the Continent, the better to interpret my past and future finds."

Now and again, Sophia briefly joined Heinrich in Europe, conferring with him about the lawsuit. She returned to Athens with confidential messages to the lawyers and instructions for her personal dealings with officials.

Sophia and Heinrich were elected to honorary membership by the Greek Archaeological Society of which Eustratiades was a director. No sooner was Schliemann a member than someone in the Society suggested that he might enhance his public image by paying for the removal of an ugly Frankish Tower from the Acropolis. The Turks, who occupied Greece for four centuries of turmoil and bloodshed, constructed the Tower as a fortification that overshadowed the Propylea and the Parthenon. Under the supervision of members of the Archaeological Society, the Tower was razed at a cost of 9,000 drachmae, donated by Schliemann. The Society's vice-president, S. Fendikles, wrote on July 4, 1874, profusely thanking Schliemann for his contribution to the continuing restoration of the glories of ancient Greece.

It must have given Schliemann considerable satisfaction to finance the destruction of anything Turkish, because he was in a mood to do physical violence to Turks who persecuted him with words in the courtroom and with actions in Greece and Europe. Without warning Turks swarmed into the Schliemanns' house in Athens and into the homes of Sophia's relatives, vainly looking for Trojan treasures. It was embittering to the Schliemanns that the Turks made their raids by authority of the Greek government. In European hotels, Heinrich several times was awakened by Turks who forced their way into his room and left only after they were satisfied he had no treasure with him. On other occasions his hotel rooms were torn apart during his absence. He and Sophia were shadowed wherever they went, as were some members of her family.

Yannakis was a victim of Turkish cruelty. He had stayed on at Hissarlik to act as guide for ambassadors and scholars who came from all over the world to visit the excavations, some to observe and some to study the trenches and objects displayed at the site. The Schliemanns, pleased by reports from Yannakis, were heartsick to learn he had been placed under arrest by Turks who, raiding the Hill, had destroyed many objects in the storehouse and had set fire to the buildings. Schliemann's efforts to have Yannakis freed were thwarted by the wily Turks. They spirited their prisoner from the jail at Koum-Kale, incarcerated him at Erenkeny, and finally placed him in irons at the Dardanelles, from where he was released through Schliemann's intercession. But

Yannakis carried to his grave the scars of wounds inflicted by his Turkish gaolers.

To no avail, Heinrich and his friends made formal protest about the surveillance and indignities to which the Schliemanns and their family were subjected. Turkish and Greek officials completely distrusted the motives of Sophia, who regularly conferred with visiting dignitaries and entertained influential Greeks. Twice the Greek police physically forced her to remain at home when they knew she had planned to visit people suspected of conspiracy with her and Heinrich. A politician, seeking to call on Sophia, was recognized by police, who barred entry to him on one occasion, and on another, pushed him back into his carriage, whipping his horses into a gallop.

After months of lengthy deliberation, the Greek judges ruled that Dr. Schliemann could keep the treasure of Troy but must pay an indemnity to the Turkish government. Congratulations were sent immediately to the Schliemanns by their long-time adversaries Valassopoulos and Eustratiades. But when the latter presented his calling card at the Schliemanns' house, he was informed by a servant that Dr. and Mrs. Schliemann were not at home to Mr. Eustratiades.

Heinrich, jubilant in victory, invested in the future when complying with the court order to make payment to the Turkish government. Astutely capping his success, he sent to Turkey not only the 10,000 gold francs stipulated, but also an additional 40,000 as contribution to the Imperial Museum at Constantinople. Schliemann figured that his generosity would in time pay dividends. And it did.

SEVENTEEN

The Christmas holidays of 1874 were merry and lively. Heinrich was home with his family. Sophia, humming cheerfully, darted about the house putting up festive decorations and supervising the preparation of confections that gave off mouth-watering aromas. Friends and relatives called early and late, delivering brightly wrapped gifts that were added to a heaping pile.

Heinrich had been profligate when he shopped in seven countries, purchasing lavish gifts for Sophia and her many relatives, buying the greatest number for Andromache. She was permitted to open a few presents on Christmas, but the rest were saved for the New Year's first day, always celebrated by Greeks in honor of St. Basil, churchman and philanthropic founder of Basilias, a city for the needy.

Andromache, not yet three, was allowed to stay up on New Year's Eve. As the hours wore on, she tried to overcome drowsiness by toddling from doting uncles to her adoring grandmother to playful cousins. Heinrich was amused when Andromache, tugging at his trouser leg, asked him please to pinch her. Finally she sat on the floor, banging her head against a doorjamb to stave off sleep. Although she could not have understood the midnight ceremony, her piping voice joined with the others harmonizing through "Kalanda," a carol to St. Basil, that signaled the arrival of 1875.

Sophia was hostess at the family's traditional New Year's Day dinner, climaxed by the cutting of the *Vasilopeta.* Bishop Vimbos blessed the New Year's cake, and then Heinrich, as head of the household, cut the first slice. It was set aside for the Lord, the second slice was for St. Basil, and successive slices were for the family, by order of age. Heinrich dramatically prolonged the serving of the *Vasilopeta,* tantalizing grownups and children alike. When all were served, adults hastily separated their pieces with forks; youngsters crumbled theirs with fingers. Somewhere in the cake there was a coin, a lucky piece assuring a happy year to the finder.

Disappointed expressions already had crossed several faces when Sophia, coin in hand, let out a squeal. Licking the coin clean, she looked at it closely and her eyes filled with tears. She got up, walked to the far end of the table, and tenderly embraced her husband.

The coin, passed from hand to hand around the table, was recognized by the grownups as one always carried by Heinrich. Men and women alike began to shed tears and to exclaim with the animation and gesticulations so characteristic of the uninhibited and emotional Greeks. Seeing the coin, Bishop Vimbos also rose and went to embrace Heinrich. When they first were friends in St. Petersburg, Vimbos, the struggling theological student, had given the coin to Heinrich, the young businessman risking everything on ventures that became the foundations of his fortunes.

Heinrich had substituted his coin for the modern one given to the cook for the *Vasilopeta*. Sophia knew how much the coin meant to Heinrich and, on that New Year's Day she placed it in her jewel case where it remained until she died.

Celebration of the New Year continued after dinner with toasts by the adults, and games for the children. Heinrich played with the children, teased the menfolk, and even danced some sedate steps with Madame Victoria. Few ever saw Heinrich in holiday mood—jolly, witty, gay and gracious. He seemed another man entirely from Schliemann the dedicated archaeologist, the canny tycoon, the opinionated scholar. There was no resemblance to the man capable of smuggling treasure out of Turkey, of outwitting international financiers, and of establishing a reputation for recalcitrance. His obstinance was in evidence during the week following the New Year when he argued over details of the lawsuit with government officials of Greece and Turkey.

In the first weeks of 1875, Schliemann's study, normally well-ordered, looked like the command post of some major operation, which in fact it was. He analyzed international stock-market reports and gave orders for the management of his far-flung properties. He considered business propositions made to him, and initiated enterprises of his own. Messengers dashed to and from the study with mail and cables. There were daily requests to

Schliemann to write articles for scholarly journals, to speak at conferences, at universities, and before members of learned societies. Often the pace became too much even for him, and stretching out on the floor, he went through a routine of exercises.

Heinrich, in rare contentment, was happy at home, and his state of mind was reflected by Sophia's joy. Little Andromache enjoyed her father's undivided attention for part of every day. When the weather warmed enough for Heinrich to ride to Phaleron for his morning swim, he often took Andromache with him and showed her a trick that delighted them both. One morning an old servant went along and rowed them out from shore. Heinrich, expertly diving into the water, disappeared, and Andromache chuckled because she knew he was playing their game. The servant, nervous about anyone who swam in the sea, cried out in alarm, "The master has sunk! He is nowhere to be seen!" Andromache giggled.

Her father, suddenly surfacing, grabbed the side of the rowboat. His receding hair was plastered tight to his head; his mustache dripped with globules of salt water that glinted in the sun. Heinrich grasped the arm of the servant, who, dropping his oars, said, "Thanks god! You are not drowned!" Solemn-faced, he did not join in the loud laughter of Heinrich and Andromache that rang out over the Bay of Phaleron. Although he frequently drove Heinrich and his little daughter to Phaleron, the servant never failed to be distressed by Heinrich's dive and disappearance.

One morning at breakfast, after his swim, Heinrich, in a sepulchral tone, said, "Today I have decided, my darling Sophithion, to leave four days from now for the Continent." She smiled at him and, without comment, continued to eat. Did he think that she had forgotten, that she did not know the date? It was April 1, the day of the fools, the day when she and her beloved friend and husband always tried to best each other.

Heinrich was traveling in Europe during the summer, and on August 10 he wrote her a peevish letter from Copenhagen. He fussed about the climate of Denmark, decried the ruthlessness of the royal family, described the ugliness of Danish women, and complained about Sophia's management of their affairs in Athens. His captious words did not fool Sophia, who knew her Heinrich well. She answered him with a succinct letter in which she spelled out the truth for him. "Your state of mind and emotion, undoubtedly unfair to all mentioned in your letter, was obviously a result of not being feted as you feel is your due." Heinrich's answer to her was loving and cheerful.

From Copenhagen he went to Stockholm, and from there to Germany. At Dobberan he took the baths to freshen his body and mind. He refused a dinner invitation from the Grand Duke of Mecklenburg, but spent an hour with him, promising to send a gift of antiquities for his museum. Heinrich pressed on to Rostock, where he lectured at the university that gave him the doctoral degree. He visited his sister Doris at Röbel, en route to Berlin. In quick succession Schliemann visited museums at Danzig, Dillenberg, Pest, and Vienna; and doubled back from a brief stay in Paris to Leipzig, where he received a standing ovation from a lecture audience.

In late September, after a quick trip to Athens, he was in Naples and Rome, where he advised members of the government about Italian excavations. On October 10 he met with Minister Benghi in Albano, and three days later was in Palermo. While speeding from place to place in compulsive study of ancient objects and history, he answered voluminous correspondence forwarded from Athens. He complained that keeping up with his mail hampered his studies, but he refused Sophia's offer to write replies to routine communications. Many letters contained pleas for financial aid from the poor of the world who had read about his largess to the Turkish government. They could not have known that Heinrich's gift of 40,000 gold francs was a calculated investment.

Late in 1875 he went to Constantinople to call on Safvet Pasha, who had expressed in glowing terms his gratitude for the generous donation to the Imperial Museum. After exchanging amenities, Schliemann blandly broached the subject of a new *firman* for excavation at Hissarlik. Safvet Pasha, usually inscrutable, was visibly shaken by Schliemann's audacity.

The effrontery of Schliemann amazed even his friends in Turkey. However he had rationalized the smuggling of the treasure from Turkey, the fact remained that by his action he had broken his agreement with the government. Impressed by Schliemann's daring, his friends rallied to his cause, and the *firman* was about to be signed when the Council of State peremptorily rejected his request. As devious as the Turks, Schliemann called on His Excellency Rashid Pasha, Minister of Foreign Affairs, a cultivated and worldly gentleman, who was receptive to the idea of further excavation at the site of Troy. He went personally to His Highness the Grand Vizier, Mahmoud-Nedim Pasha, to say a good word for Schliemann. Negotiations were slow, but Schliemann had his *firman* by the end of April 1876.

Leaving Sophia at home, Heinrich went to the Dardanelles and encountered an old enemy with a long memory. The Governor of the Dardanelles and the Archipelago, Ibrahim Pasha, unforgiving about the stolen treasure, had ordered the raid and destruction at Hissarlik and the arrest of Yannakis. Ibrahim Pasha also had profited from the sale of rights for excavation at Hissarlik: with his official permission, wealthy tourists, provided with spades and shovels, took away such artifacts and objects as they were able to dig up.

By late spring of 1876 the Governor of the Dardanelles, although reluctant, was somehow forced to honor the new *firman*. But he sent as watchdog to Hissarlik a weasel-eyed overseer, Isset Effendi, whose instructions were to obstruct operations at every turn. He carried out his orders with such zeal that Schliemann, deeply angered, sent a scathing letter to the *Times* of London. He let it be known to all that the lengthy epistle about his treatment by the Turks had been written by him. The *Times* printed the letter on July 24.

I hear, with regret, that Dr. Schliemann, though powerfully supported by the foreign Ambassadors at Constantinople and by many of the more enlightened Turkish Ministers, has not been able as yet to carry on his excavations at Troy. The Porte granted him a Firman, and, after engaging a large number of workmen, Dr. Schliemann hoped that nothing would interfere with his further explorations of the ruins at Hissarlik. Unfortunately, the Governor of the Dardanelles and the Archipelago, Ibrahim Pasha, did not approve Dr. Schliemann's presence. During the last three years he had exercised a kind of protectorate over "the diggings" at Troy. All travellers had to apply to him for a permit to inspect the trenches opened by Dr. Schliemann, while, after the Doctor's return, the Governor's authority ceased. This seems to have offended his vanity. It is difficult, also, for any Oriental to imagine that people can spend large sums of money in digging for mere rubbish, and after the discovery of the gold and silver ornaments at Hissarlik three years ago, the people in the neighborhood and the Governor himself looked upon the place as a vast gold mine. Hence, Ibrahim Pasha, though obliged to obey the Sultan's Firman, threw every kind of obstacle in Dr. Schliemann's way. He appointed a delegate, a certain Isset Effendi, who was to receive a salary of 20 pounds a month, and whose chief object seems to have been to thwart Dr. Schliemann's labours. The Doctor had to dismiss his own servants and to engage Turkish navvies. He was not allowed to make drawings of the new objects which were discovered, and he was expected with regard to any new excavations to obey the orders of the Governor and his delegate. At last the Doctor's patience, which is great, seems to have given way. The Firman gave him 600 acres of land on which to build whatever houses and sheds he required for himself, his clerks, and servants. The Governor, putting his own interpretations on this clause, insisted on Dr. Schliemann covering the whole of these 600 acres with houses and magazines of stone and wood. After trying for two months to come to terms with the Governor of the Dardanelles, Dr. Schliemann, I am sorry to hear, has left the field of his labours, and I doubt whether, in the present state of public affairs in the Turkish Provinces, he is likely soon to return.

The Vilayet of the Dardanelles seems to have enjoyed the most perfect security under the governorship of Ibrahim Pasha's predecessor, Achmed Kaiserli Pasha, the present Minister of the Navy. At present it is infested by brigands and the whole country is in a state of utter misery. At Priapson (Caraboa) the Circassians quite recently wounded and killed a large number of Christians, and forced the remainder to fly naked to Peristasis, in European Turkey. At Bairamits, at the foot of Mount Ida, not more than 40 miles from the Dardanelles, the Redifs, on the 16th of June, ransacked the town and killed the Christian inhabitants. The Governor, Ibrahim Pasha, sent no troops to protect them, nor has any notice been taken to the murders lately committed at Chois. Whether Ibrahim Pasha will be supported by the authorities at Constantinople remains to be seen, but it is hardly likely that in present circumstances the Turkish Government will have time to pay much attention to Dr. Schliemann's just complaints. This is much to be regretted. As it is, the trenches opened at Hissarlik have been filled by rubbish washed down from the ruins, and are now 10 ft. less deep than they were three years ago. Dr. Schliemann intended more especially to explore the lowest stratum at Hissarlik, which ought to solve some of the most interesting problems connected with the early civilization of that neighborhood, but the difficulties are very great. If the stratum containing the gold ornaments is to be identified with Troy, then, as Dr. Schliemann has proved by measuring the accumulation of rubbish, its date could not be less than 3000 B.C. or about 2,000 years before the traditional date of Homer. The lower stratum, however, would go far beyond 3000 B.C. and yet, to judge from some specimens, the pottery found in it seems more perfect than that of the later cities. In examining again the layers of ruins of the first city in the great trench, Dr. Schliemann found that they slope towards the great tower, which belongs to the second city, and that, consequently, the first town must have been very small, consisting of a couple of large buildings only. There are powerful walls belonging to one of them, possibly the sanctuary of a Phrygian goddess erected on the rock of Hissarlik. Here are problems of the highest importance for students of historic and prehistoric antiquities, but unless Dr. Schliemann is powerfully supported at Constantinople, the evidence by which alone they can be solved may be lost for ever and Troy be destroyed once more.

Through the immediate reaction of influential diplomats representing powerful governments, repercussions to the letter were swift and far-reaching. Ibrahim Pasha was heavily fined and imprisoned. Safvet Pasha, a victim of high-echelon reorganization, was sent to a remote post, his career ruined. Schliemann wasted no time in celebration of victory over Turkish officialdom. His attention had already shifted to Mycenae, because the Greek government had granted him another permit for excavation.

EIGHTEEN

Schliemann had first visited Mycenae in 1868, rapidly exploring the citadel and the lower town of the place once ruled by Agamemnon, one of the aggressors of the Trojan War. Schliemann's research and his "extra sense," which he thought of as a gift from the gods of Olympus, led him to the conclusion that the thread of history binding Asia Minor, the Greek islands and the Hellenic mainland was much stronger than was commonly accepted.

The Mycenaean landscape was forbidding even in early summer when Schliemann made his initial investigations. The sky was often clouded above the horseshoe ridge of mountains dominated by two bare peaks to the east of the citadel. It crowned a hill more than 900 feet above sea level, with a sheer cliff to the south. Two gloomy ravines cut through the narrow flatland close to the fortification walls.

In prehistoric times that geological fastness was chosen as the seat of an empire that controlled the Argolid, a large area of the Peloponnesus. Nature's stark aspect symbolized tragedy, which climaxed every legend and all history of Mycenae. Blood flowed there in the days of Perseus, son of Zeus, and of Atreus, son of Pelops; and Agamemnon, on the day of his return from the Trojan War, died a gory death at the hands of his wife, Clytemnestra, and her lover, Aegisthus.

After studying the site in 1868, Schliemann propounded a controversial theory about Mycenae. It was one of the two prime theories about ancient civilizations published in his *Ithaca, the Peloponnesus and Troy,* a copy of which he had presented to Madame Victoria on the first evening he spent with Sophia's family. In that work, for which he was awarded his doctorate by the University of Rostock, he stated that royal tombs would be found within the extant cyclopean walls of the Mycenae citadel.

His theory was in direct contradiction to the one firmly held by most scholars who, like him, based their conclusions on a passage from *Descriptions of Greece* (II,16,6) written by the 2nd-century topographer and traveler Pausanias.

Amongst other remains of the wall is the gate, on which stand lions. They [the walls and the gate] are said to be the work of the Cyclopes, who built the wall for Proteus of Tiryns. In the ruins of Mycenae is the fountain called Perseia and the subterranean buildings of Atreus and his children, in which they stored their treasures. There is the sepulchre of Atreus, and the tombs of the companions of Agamemnon, who on their return from Ilium were killed at a banquet by Aegisthus. The identity of the tomb of Cassandra is called in question by the Lacedaemonians of Amyclae. There is the tomb of Agamemnon and that of his charioteer Eurymedon, and of Electra. Teledamus and Pelops were buried in the same sepulchre, for it is said that Cassandra bore these twins, and that, while as yet infants, they were slaughtered by Aegisthus together with their parents. . . . Clytemnestra and Aegisthus were buried at a little distance from the wall, because they were thought unworthy to have their tombs inside of it, where Agamemnon reposed and those who were killed together with him.

Pausanias' lines about Clytemnestra and Aegisthus were generally interpreted as meaning that the murderers were buried outside the walls that enclosed the lower town *and* the citadel. Schliemann claimed as erroneous the theory of scholars who ". . . thought that, in speaking of the wall, he [Pausanias] meant the wall of the city, and not the great wall of the Acropolis; and they therefore understood that he fixed the site of the five sepulchres in the *lower* city, and the site of the tombs of Clytemnestra and Aegisthus outside of it. But such was not his intention, and that he had solely in view the walls of the citadel he shows by saying that they were inside the walls of the Lion Gate."

Scholars who did not hold with Schliemann's theory about the location of the tombs were generally agreed that the fortress and lower town of Mycenae had existed for centuries. But few cared enough to search in the earth at the site. The Schliemanns, who did care, received a permit to dig from ministers of Greece, but only after lengthy negotiations.

Permission was given with the provisos that excavation was to be directed by the Greek Archaeological Society, and that all excavated objects were to be the property of the Greek government. To insure that not one artifact or fragment of treasure would be retained by the Schliemanns, a man named Stamatakis was assigned as inspector in constant attendance at Mycenae.

In early February 1874 he accompanied the Schliemanns to the Peloponnesus. That mulberry-shaped, southern part of the Hellenic mainland was tenuously connected to the north by an umbilical stretch of land little more than a mile wide. The cord, holding together the northern mainland and the Peloponnesus was not severed until the construction of the Corinth Canal was begun in 1881.

Schliemann's aim was to uncover remains that would distinguish myth from fact in the Mycenaean tales of incest, adultery, vengeance, and murder. His party on horseback rode toward the citadel through a landscape somberly colored from dark to ghostly grays. The citadel's great wall stood like a threatening sentinel, defying invaders, its cyclopean stones piled—by what superhuman strength—one on another.

On foot, the silent group made its way to the citadel's Lion Gate, the entrance blocked by the debris of ages. The lions, with timeless regality, stood above the lintel, their forefeet on a carved stone base separated by a Doric column. The kingly lions, symbols of power and feudal control, dominated the relief; it, carved from one slab of gray limestone, was thought to be the oldest architectural sculpture extant. Seeing the impressive lions for the first time, Sophia wrote: "For how many centuries have these animals stood their silent guard, daring a wanderer to pass through into the realm over which they alone are the custodians?" For decades scholars wrangled over that same question to which she and Heinrich provided the first clues to an answer.

Six years earlier, when Schliemann predicted that five graves would be found close to the Lion Gate but *within* the citadel walls, his interpretation of Pausanias had been mocked with scholarly invective. After it became known that the Schliemanns were to dig at Mycenae in 1874, an unsigned paragraph appeared in the *Times* of London:

> Schliemann continues to deny the world of intellectuals who have devoted their *entire* lives to the world of the past. But, let him proceed and prove himself to be but the butt of our amusement. Graves will never be found within the citadel walls unless the destroyer of Troy seeds graves during the night.

Unperturbed by the insulting item, Schliemann began the excavations, directing crews that sank the first exploratory shafts just inside the Lion Gate. Work was going forward rapidly when the Turkish lawsuit interrupted operations. Without opportunity to examine any of the thirty-four sunken shafts, the Schliemanns left Mycenae to which they would not return for two years.

Schliemann, requiring a renewal of his permit in 1876, anticipated opposition from Greek officials. He asked for support from no less a personage than the erudite Gladstone. The British Prime Minister wrote on a postal card to Schliemann: ". . . in much haste to say that out of respect for you I have taken the great liberty of writing direct through the F.O. [Foreign Office] to the person you name. I have made known to him all you say. But I must own to you that I have done this with great doubt and embarrassment for I can by no means say what he will think, or whether he may judge himself to have the slightest desire to interfere."

The person Gladstone meant was the British Ambassador in Athens. Schliemann correctly reasoned that if the British Ambassador were to intercede for him with Greek authorities, they would be receptive; the breach in their relationship with the British government caused by the Dilessi murders was one the Greeks could ill afford and wanted to close by every possible means.

After receiving Gladstone's note, Schliemann called on the British Ambassador and was told that, in spite of mutual recriminations in the correspondence between Schliemann and Greek ministers, they had granted the permit. It again designated the Greek Archaeological Society as the agency to direct the excavations, and Stamatakis as the *ephor* who would assure that directions were explicitly followed. Without delay the Schliemanns assembled their paraphernalia and staff, and reached Mycenae on August 7, 1876.

In ancient times the citadel on the Acropolis and the lower town, spread out in the valley, were encircled by a tremendous wall, measured in miles. Within the wall were houses, several treasuries, wells, and the citadel, itself walled. Some ancient remains were already exposed to view when the Schliemanns began their excavations.

The Treasuries were the most interesting remnants of the Mycenaean civilization, and were in fact *Tholoi,* underground tombs constructed in the shape of beehives. The most famous was the Treasury of Atreus, with an approach down a walkway, 20 feet 7 inches long, flanked by tremendous stones. The 18-foot-high entranceway was topped by two beautifully cut and polished slabs, weighing an estimated 300,000 pounds. The great domed chamber, 50 feet in diameter, resembled a vast beehive. It was constructed skillfully of hewn blocks, placed in regular layers and precisely fitted together without binding material. A doorway to the right of the main entranceway led into a second chamber, dark and square, cut from rough rock.

Immediately upon arrival at Mycenae, Schliemann ordered a crew to clear the approach to the Treasury of Atreus which has since awed millions of travelers. It took eight workmen two weeks to reach the upper part of open triangular space above the door; chopping through soil hard as stone, they often struck huge blocks of rock that impeded progress.

Several crews, comprising forty-three men, started a trench in front of the Lion Gate, an operation temporarily halted by Stamatakis, who reached Mycenae a few days later. He fired off a complaint to the Greek Archaeological Society, accusing the Schliemanns of proceeding without his approval. The suspicious *ephor* used violent epithets to discredit the Schliemanns, being particularly venomous about Sophia.

Stamatakis, who considered himself to be the assigned partner of Schliemann, resented Heinrich's consultations with Sophia. She gained the complete loyalty of the work crews, who obeyed all her orders and ignored countercommands by Stamatakis. He not only resented Sophia as colleague to her husband and favorite of the workmen, but could not be reconciled to a Greek woman of her social standing who would labor as she did at the digs.

In his letter of complaint to Athens, Stamatakis asserted that she was an evil influence on her husband and hinted that the aging dreamer could be managed if Madame Schliemann were barred from the excavations. The president of the Society received, along with the report from Stamatakis, a message from Schliemann containing a defense of his capable wife and countercharges against the inspector.

Schliemann and Stamatakis attacked each other in written notes sent to Athens, and in verbal confrontations at Mycenae. Face to face at the ancient site, the two men yelled at each other in fearful argument; Schliemann screamed, the high pitch of his voice raised in anger, and Stamatakis bellowed, the deep sound rumbling up from inside him. Schliemann, though slight, was tough, strong and wiry, conditioned by daily swimming, other exercise, and a rigid diet. Physically fearless, he faced up to the hulking Stamatakis, who towered over him. Peasants, attracted by the altercations, frequently gathered around in anticipation of a good fight; but Sophia remained calm, knowing that every argument would end without fisticuffs.

With the grudging consent of Stamatakis, the passageway to the Lion Gate and its aperture were opened. Just inside and to the left there was a chamber that Schliemann took to be an ancient gatehouse. Excavation inside the citadel wall was productive. Workmen turned up bronze objects, small gold pieces, combs and needles; terra-cotta goblets and figurines, many in animal shapes; keys, knives, and weapons of metal; and numerous other objects marked with both the *svastika* and the *sauvastika*.

Schliemann, following along an excavated water conduit, studied how it had been engineered for efficient use. Beyond reservoirs for water storage, two tombstones were positioned in a direct north-to-south line; both were ornamented with detailed bas-reliefs. One, carved from soft calcareous stone, was worn and ravaged by centuries of time. The other, in good condition, had beautiful rythmic designs of intertwined spirals across its upper section, and a chariot scene on the lower section. A seated warrior, head in profile and chest flat, without perspective, leaned toward a stallion with legs outstretched for running. The charioteer held in his left hand a knob-handled sword, still sheathed, and in his right, a long object more like a lance than reins, although it touched the stallion's mouth. A naked warrior, running ahead of the stallion, grasped its head with his right hand and clutched a double-edged sword in his left.

An average of 125 workmen dug at the site each day, and debris was carried away in four horse-carts that rattled over the rough terrain from dawn to dusk. Important examples of archaic pottery and innumerable idols were unearthed before workmen dug around other sculptured tombstones marking very simple graves. Schliemann described each find with such scientific precision and attention to detail that his diaries proved to be invaluable source material for later archaeologists at Mycenae.

Stamatakis and Schliemann continued their running battle, sending telegrams and letters to the Greek Archaelogoical Society and to Athenian officials. In a progress report, Schliemann addressed Valassopoulos: "Your Excellency, I and my wife are exposed here to all kinds of hardships, seeing that my life is always in danger, as I stand the whole day in the blazing sun; I pay out four hundred francs every day for the pure love of scholarship and pure love of Greece, in an endeavor to enrich her by the discovery of new worlds for archaeology, by which I shall attract thousands of foreigners to the country."

Stamatakis complained, not of the blazing sun but of the unreasonably long hours spent at the digs by the Schliemanns at whose side he was required to be. He stated falsely that he was forced to rise at 2 A.M. and remain on his feet throughout the day and into the dark of night.

In early September, Sophia assumed total responsibility for the excavation of a small Treasury near the Lion Gate where she worked with thirty laborers and two horse-carts. The workmen had difficulty in removing the hundreds of huge stones that had fallen from the vault's ceiling, but Sophia, refusing to call on Heinrich, figured out exactly how the work should be done and then directed the workmen in their labors. In spite of the difficulties encountered, Sophia persisted and finally cleared the debris. That Treasury was less sumptuous than the Treasury of Atreus; but inside, Sophia and her crew found archaic pottery, the *svastika* and *sauvastika* signs, vases decorated with geometrical patterns, and necklaces of large glass beads, white and colored.

Inside the citadel wall, Heinrich was busy directing the clearing of debris from the foundations of an ancient house with a number of parallel corridors and labyrinthian chambers. Sophia came often to watch the unearthing of the house and the progress being made on the graves near the area.

Once while digging, Heinrich found potsherds which, when put together, showed a procession of warriors in full fighting gear as though about to leave for battle. Much was learned about the prehistoric people from the manner, marching and armor of these men.

The relationship with the *ephor* deteriorated to such a point that Sophia made a September trip to Athens, where she demanded an interview with Valassopoulos. She advised him that Stamatakis from spite was deliberately delaying the excavation by ruses, diverse and malicious.

Stamatakis was thoroughly angered by instructions from Valassopoulos to do the assigned job and to cease the petty harassment of the Schliemanns. In answer to the minister, Stamatakis wrote that communication between him and Schliemann had to be through an overseer because the archaeologist would neither acknowledge the presence of Stamatakis nor speak to him. As always, Sophia was his main target. "Would that she had never come here. She is to blame for everything, and I fear all will go on as before." Although Heinrich was described as dogmatic and obstinate by the *ephor,* the refrain recurrent in his reports was that things are "even worse because of Madame Schliemann."

From his point of view, Stamatakis was correct. Sophia, determined that nothing should interfere with Heinrich's operations, protected him as a lioness does her cub. And he, well aware of her aid, wrote: ". . . the work here is condemned to come to a complete standstill, without you."

Sophia, a talented mimic, by acting out the exaggerated gestures, the rage, the violent words, and pompous poses of Stamatakis, often managed to relax Heinrich. In the seclusion of their room, she would turn herself into the image of the *ephor,* going through the irritating incidents of the day past. Her scenes always made Heinrich laugh, and usually ended with husband and wife joining their physical selves in sensual bliss.

At the close of each workday, the Schliemanns and Stamatakis supervised the loading of finds into a cart, which headed for the village of Charvati where the storehouse buildings were. The two Schliemanns and the glowering *ephor* rode behind, and stood during the unloading. Stamatakis, yawning, scratching, sighing with boredom, stayed with Heinrich and Sophia while they studied, discussed, numbered and catalogued the day's finds. Ignoring the *ephor,* who might have been a crude piece of furniture for all they cared, the Schliemanns animatedly talked with each other or, silent, were totally absorbed in the examination of objects.

On October 7 Schliemann received an official request from the Turkish government to hasten to the Troad to meet His Majesty Dom Pedro II of Brazil, a cultivated ruler intensely interested in Schliemann's discoveries. Over the babbling protest of Stamatakis, Heinrich left Sophia in charge at Mycenae and started for the Hellespont. His Majesty, with the Empress and a large entourage, arrived aboard the steamer *Aguila Imperiale* in the early morning hours of October 14. Schliemann, no stranger to the amenities of receiving royalty, impressed Dom Pedro by a courtliness that carried no hint of obsequiousness.

While guiding their horses toward Hissarlik, Dom Pedro and Schliemann gave scant attention to others in the party. The man born to a throne and the man born for greatness were deep in discussion of Troy. At Hissarlik, Dom Pedro and Schliemann, talking or in companionable silence, examined the major sections of the digs, then rode off to Bunarbashi. Dom Pedro, after exploring the terrain, said he was more than ever convinced that Schliemann was correct in declaring for Hissarlik as the site of Troy. The Emperor had come to that opinion previously from reading books and articles, not only by Schliemann but also by other authors with both similar and conflicting views.

On the return trip to the Hellespont, the two men talked animatedly about the realization of the dream of a parson's son from Germany. They spoke in Portuguese, Dom Pedro's native tongue, which Schliemann used fluently. In warm farewell, Dom Pedro sincerely thanked Schliemann for his hospitality, and accepted with alacrity an invitation to visit the digs at Mycenae.

On October 29 the Emperor and his party arrived at Mycenae. Dom Pedro greeted Heinrich with an affectionate *abrazo,* and bent low to kiss Sophia's hand before presenting her to the Empress, who, exhausted from the long and tiring trek, asked if she might rest. Sophia was pleased to accede to her wish, and Heinrich later wrote in his diary: "My joy knew no bounds because my devoted and wonderful Sophithion could accompany us through the citadel and His Majesty could see for himself the divine creature who is my wife."

No greetings were wasted on Stamatakis, although he was the official representative of the Greek Archaeological Society. His presence, disregarded by the Schliemanns, was barely acknowledged by Dom Pedro, after which the *ephor,* shifting from one foot to another, remained on the party's periphery.

Climbing to the Lion Gate, Dom Pedro was moved by the power of the sculpture, and said to Heinrich, "Dr. Schliemann, these timeless animals with all they convey should hereafter form your Coat-of-Arms." Tears welled in Heinrich's eyes, and Sophia moved to his side, grasping his hand in her own that shook with pride. "The Emperor attentively examined our excavations, the large circle of two parallel rows of tombstones and three straight lines of tombs. He paid particular attention to the pieces of sculpture, and one attracted his attention so much that he lost himself in it for more than half an hour. He conjectured and discussed with me why the parallel tombs should have been made as they were, and on what purpose the area in between might have been used for."

Schliemann's innate and keen sense of the dramatic was seldom more clearly emphasized than by the midday meal he gave his distinguished guests. With flair, Schliemann chose to have it served in the depth of the Treasury of Atreus. The Emperor, much fêted on his foreign tour, had not previously been entertained in a subterranean building forty centuries old. The mysterious setting seemed to heighten the animation with which he discussed archaeology with his hosts. The handsome Latin face of Dom Pedro was mobile as he talked, and Schliemann responded with discussion of work accomplished and the expectations of things yet to be unearthed. The flicker of candles, too weak to reflect against the smooth surface of the stones of the dome, 50 feet above the table, played over the faces of those around it. Heinrich's eyes, deep-set, dominated his face in spite of his prominent nose. His expression was intense and intelligent; his statement lucid and lively.

The lackluster Empress seemed to be spellbound by the young Madame Schliemann, who spoke with charming directness. Sophia, becomingly dressed in a full-skirted frock of exquisite material, did not look like the day-laborer she was at Mycenae. Her shining black hair was piled high in a becoming coiffure, and her olive skin glowed with health. She could not have been more gracious or attentive a hostess had she been in her elegant Paris home.

At the conclusion of the successful party in the Treasury, the Emperor insisted on visiting the storehouses at Charvati. The large collection of prehistoric Mycenaean antiquities the Schliemanns had excavated fascinated Dom Pedro, who particularly admired the archaic sculptures and the Mycenaean pottery. After a tour of the quarry at Charvati, the Emperor left for Argos and Nauplia.

On the following day Heinrich and Sophia, standing on the citadel, looked down and saw a company of riders approaching slowly along the rugged trail below. Within minutes a horseman, led up the steep incline to the Acropolis of Mycenae by a running peasant, dismounted and called out to the Schliemanns. It was Dom Pedro, eager for further inspection before he left Greece.

With Dom Pedro's entourage scattered below, trying to find shaded protection from the hot autumn sun, the Emperor and Schliemann made their way around the excavations. The tall Brazilian wore a dashing hat at a rakish angle; the wiry Schliemann, a sun helmet pulled down on his forehead. With the Emperor taking long strides and the archaeologist moving with his characteristic floating gait, an effortless walk, the two followed narrow paths and disappeared into tunneled areas. Exacting a promise from Schliemann to forward photographs of certain objects to Cairo, Dom Pedro reluctantly left for Athens.

Two years later, when Schliemann's *Mycenae* was published, it contained a preface by William E. Gladstone, British Prime Minister, and was dedicated to Dom Pedro II with the profound respect of the author.

But the October day when Schliemann bade goodbye to his royal guest was not to be the end of their immediate contact. As the Emperor passed through Nauplia on his way to Athens, he gave a tip to the Chief of Police for his courtesy to the Emperor and his entourage during their stay. Stamatakis, seething with fury at having been pushed into the background, seized on the incident to make trouble for Schliemann. The *ephor* immediately reported to Athens that bribes of large amounts had been given to the Chief of Police, one being passed to him from Schliemann through Dom Pedro. The fantastic accusation sent Heinrich into one of his Olympian rages.

No less eager to clear the Chief of Police at Nauplia than to expose the prevaricating Stamatakis, Schliemann sent a cable to Dom Pedro, then in Constantinople, giving him brief details of the bribery charge and asking for a statement of the purpose of the money given to the Chief of Police, and the amount offered. Dom Pedro settled the matter, and the Chief of Police was exonerated.

Stamatakis was bested, but Schliemann wished that he "could place the devil Stamatakis in a grave shaft and cover him for eternity." Unfortunately for Sophia and Heinrich, Stamatakis lived on and remained at Mycenae.

NINETEEN

At Mycenae, in November 1876, Sophia and Heinrich dug alone, without either crews or Stamatakis. The *ephor,* slow thinking, had at last worked out a system that relieved him of constant supervisory duties and freed him from standing around in the cold throughout the day. He had placed a cordon of guards around the citadel to make certain that neither Sophia nor Heinrich slipped away from the digs carrying excavated objects.

The arrangement pleased the Schliemanns, who could work rapidly when uninterrupted by the dour-faced *ephor*. Digging to the right of the Lion Gate, they found two tombstones, undecorated, and a tomb filled with natural earth brought from another place. That distinction was made without the aid of scientific instruments by Heinrich, who, keenly observant, noted the difference between the earth in the tomb and the soil of the citadel.

Beyond the earth-filled grave, the Schliemanns excavated a tombstone and tombstone fragments in an area since called the great grave circle. Working with intensity, but much more slowly than at Troy, Sophia and Heinrich unearthed, from five tombs, skeletons and fabulous gold objects that were only a small part of the Mycenaean collection.

The fourth tomb yielded twenty bronze swords, numerous lances, a copper vessel filled with gold buttons, and a silver cow's head with two long gold horns and a sun, more than 2 inches in diameter, centered in the forehead. The skulls of five bodies in the fourth tomb were in such a state of decomposition that nothing could be done to preserve the crumbling bone remnants. Two of the skeletons, with heads toward the north, had large face masks of gold plate, and all five skeletons were blanketed in jewelry. Two gold signet rings fascinated the Schliemanns who ". . . together spent many, many hours looking at these two delicate rings, studying them for the pure joy of their beauty." The workmanship of the intaglio design of one ring was typical of both.

The scene on the one represented a hunter in a chariot with two spirited and straining stallions in front; no visible straps attached them to the chariot. The bushy tails and bodies of the animals were delineated as equine, but the heads bore a stronger resemblance to camels than to horses. In a number of written statements, Schliemann referred to the intaglio designs of the rings as "non objective." "The scenes on the intaglio signet rings have tremendous force and power. They evoke from the viewer a complete sense of reality; nevertheless, the carving is non objective in detail."

The design of another ring, a gold seal, was representational, showing a palm tree, four women, a child, a double axe and, along the right border, a design of six objects, strange in form, like helmeted heads and eyes. The ring was important as a comparative object: A tall seated woman had noble Grecian features like those carved on figures of the Parthenon; the double axes were identical with those found on metals in other parts of Greece and in Asia Minor; the figure holding a long staff or lance probably was Pallas Athena, whose image was for ages unchanged. After studying that figure, Schliemann wrote: "This rudely represented woman in the presence of the splendidly dressed women can in my opinion be nothing else than a *Palladium* . . . of a very ancient and primitive type. . . ." The border forms strongly resembled Trojan idols found at Hissarlik, which, when discovered, were also thought to be *Palladia,* statuettes of Pallas Athena. There was also close similarity between the six forms and the helmeted Pallas Athena, as she appeared on Corinthian coins of the 4th century B.C.

From the opening of the first treasure tomb, in December 1876, Heinrich and Sophia dug for forty-five days in the grave circle, using only small shovels, penknives and fingers. Delicate handling was essential to the preservation of skeletal remains and of many of the objects, which were incredibly fragile. Sophia, working almost exclusively with a penknife, sat on the cold ground shivering as she patiently cut around objects with fingers trembling inside thin gloves, the only kind she could wear for the tedious task.

The finds compensated for every back-breaking, miserable minute spent in the great grave circle. There were gold diadems and masks of incredible beauty and immeasurable archaeological importance. And terra-cotta, stone and gold vases; large goblets, silver and gold; gold drinking cups and silver flagons; a stag of silver and lead alloy; gold shoulder belts; pins, clasps and brooches of silver and gold; amber bead necklaces; a three-handled alabaster vase; bone lids for jars; copper spears; wooden buttons covered with highly ornamented gold veneer; 118 gold buttons with intaglio work of 15 separate designs; models of temples and statuettes of gods in gold, silver and ivory; a gold cuttlefish; gold knobs for sword handles; gold, silver and copper pots; copper, bronze and terra-cotta tripods; metal lances; and two-edged bronze swords with alabaster handles. The *sauvastika* symbol ornamented many objects. The treasure of Troy, magnificent as it was, paled in comparison with the treasure of Mycenae, excavated, not in a few hours but over a period of nearly seven weeks.

Fifteen gold diadems were taken from the second tomb, which contained only three graves. Each of the three skeletons had five diadems of thin gold plate. All showed the same *repoussé* ornamentation of thin lines separated by a row of triple concentric circles that increased or decreased according to the breadth of the diadem, the largest circles being in the center. Many other pieces of jewelry and small gold objects were taken from the three graves, and the glitter of the collection was almost blinding.

Ashes on the tombs indicated that funeral pyres had topped the graves after the burial of the dead. In the second, third and fourth tombs, the bodies with their gold ornamentation had been covered with a three-inch layer of white clay and a thinner protective layer of pebbles.

The first tomb uncovered was the last to be fully excavated; in it there were three male skeletons, all with their heads to the west, lying about three feet from each other. The most important tomb of the five, it alone showed unmistakable signs of grave robbery. Ashes covering the center skeleton had been disturbed, and no ornaments were found on the body or around it. Schliemann, commenting on the condition of that one grave, stated, "Most likely someone sank a shaft to examine the tomb, struck the central body, plundered it recklessly, and for fear of being detected carried off the booty in such a hurry that he thought of saving only the large massive gold ornaments, such as the mask, the large breast cover, the diadems and bronze sword, and remounting to the surface." Silver and gold buttons and other little objects scattered on the earth covering the other bodies indicated that the grave robber might have dropped small treasures during his escape.

Since the three skeletons were large-boned and long, it seemed that the bodies must have been forcibly squeezed into the small space of only 5 feet 6 inches left for them between the inner walls of the tomb. The head of the first man was covered with a massive gold mask, and its removal caused the skull to crumble when exposed to the air; the skull of the body in the plundered grave also disintegrated on contact with air.

The third body, at the north end of the tomb, had a round face with flesh well preserved under a gold mask. There was no vestige of hair and the nose was gone, but both eyes were intact as was the wide-open mouth with thirty-two perfect teeth. Schliemann hoped that the body could be kept in its condition long enough for medical examination; but, failing that, he was determined to have the figure in the tomb reproduced in an oil painting, and sent for an artist to come at once. The news that the skeleton of some hero of an ancient age was on view at Mycenae spread throughout the countryside, and peasants from miles around came to see it. On the second day after its discovery, Spiridon Nicolau, a pharmacist from Argos, arrived at the citadel and, with permission, hardened the body with a mixture of gum sandarac dissolved in alcohol. Schliemann had a small trench cut into the rock and, by horizontal incision, removed the skeleton from its tomb in a 2-inch-thick slab. The skeleton was shipped from Charvati to the Greek Archaeological Society in Athens. Physicians who later studied the skeleton confirmed it as masculine, and estimated that the man was thirty-five years old at the time of death.

No find at Mycenae created more interest than the glorious gold object that Schliemann called the Mask of Agamemnon. The bearded noble face of the mask had an intelligent expression, and the hooded eyes seemed real. The romantic Schliemann wanted to believe that the three graves in the first tomb were those of King Agamemnon and his two companions, murdered by the treacherous Clytemnestra and her lascivious lover Aegisthus.

Schliemann relinquished that theory when later evidence proved that the gold mask had not been made during the time when Agamemnon lived.

Schliemann, in a telegram to King George I of Greece, stated that according to the tradition following Pausanias, the tombs were those of Agamemnon, Cassandra, Eurymedon and their comrades, as well as the tombs of Clytemnestra and Aegisthus. His Majesty was assured by Schliemann that the treasures, belonging to the Greek government, would attract strangers from many countries. He stated, too, that his work had been for the pure love of science and not for the purpose of finding gold, as so many of his detractors claimed. That accusation, which persisted long past Schliemann's lifetime, is not supported by ranking archaeologists today.

Contemporary archaeologists, reassessing Schliemann's accomplishments, are certain that he was motivated by a passionate desire to uncover past history and to realize his dream of discovering Troy. His success there led him to Mycenae and to other locations for excavation. Nowhere in diaries, letters or published works did Schliemann state or imply that he sought gold. He did reiterate that he had to make a large fortune with which to support his work. He found gold, but the gold finds at Troy and Mycenae were fractional to the total number of objects on which Schliemann based his deductions about those two sites.

Scholars of his own time resented the fact that most journalists in 1876 reported principally on the gold finds when printing stories about Schliemann's telegram to King George. Archaeologists of subsequent decades stressed the historical value, not the monetary worth, of Schliemann's contributions as the father of modern archaeology. The late Professor D. Papadimitriou, chief of archaeology for the Greek government, stated: "When Schliemann made his discoveries, newspapers headlined the discovery of gold. This was natural, because more laymen are interested in gold than in bits of broken pots and inscriptions. This is true of contemporary popular writers who fasten on to the glamor of gold, and, without conscience, ascribe to Schliemann a total motivation as a gold seeker."

King George, through his secretary, A. Calinkis, answered Schliemann's telegram: "I have the honor to inform you that His

Majesty the King has received your dispatch, and has quickly charged me to thank you for your zeal and your love of science and to felicitate you on your important discoveries, and His Majesty hopes that your efforts will be always followed by more happy successes."

Disgruntled scholars in cloistered studies muttered about Schliemann's luck but Schliemann's great finds simply proved the old saying that "luck comes only to those well prepared." At Mycenae, as at Troy, Schliemann searched for evidence of early civilizations; and treasure, an inevitable adjunct to a flourishing culture, was but one proof of its existence and high rank.

A success that was bitter for Schliemann to accept was achieved at Mycenae in January 1877. Lieutenant Vasilios Drosinos, the engineer who had worked with Schliemann at Mycenae, went there from Nauplia on January 20 to do some work for Schliemann. Close to the house where Heinrich himself had excavated, Drosinos noticed masonry similar to that of the large tombs. Returning to Nauplia, he ran into the *ephor,* Stamatakis, who was en route to Mycenae to arrange for the construction of a wooden hut for watchmen. Stamatakis, learning of the precise location of the unexcavated tomb, went to it and instructed a workman, who struck gold with the first or second blow of the pickaxe, according to Schliemann. In a short time, Stamatakis had assembled a considerable treasure from a section of the digs not more than a few feet from where Schliemann previously had excavated. He stated in writing that Drosinos had been quite correct in his identification of the masonry, and in passing on the information to Stamatakis. But both Sophia and Heinrich must have had many anguished thoughts about the *ephor's* success. They had been within a few feet of an important archaeological find made by the man with whom they had so long been in conflict.

(GERMAN ARCHAEOLOGICAL INSTITUTE, ATHENS)

In 1876, the Schliemanns began excavations in the Peloponnesus at Mycenae, home of Agamemnon. Tragedy climaxed the legends and history of this site, which was "rich in gold, bathed in blood."

(GERMAN ARCHAEOLOGICAL INSTITUTE, ATHENS)

Great grave circle inside the Lion Gate at Mycenae, as it looked from the fortress walls. Here the Schliemanns were visited by Dom Pedro II, the Emperor of Brazil, and his Empress.

Standing atop the Lion Gate and leaning on lion's back is Schliemann. His associate and friend Wilhelm Dörpfeld is framed in opening at upper left. Sophia, wearing elegant white hat, sits with visitors below.

(GERMAN ARCHAEOLOGICAL INSTITUTE, ATHENS)

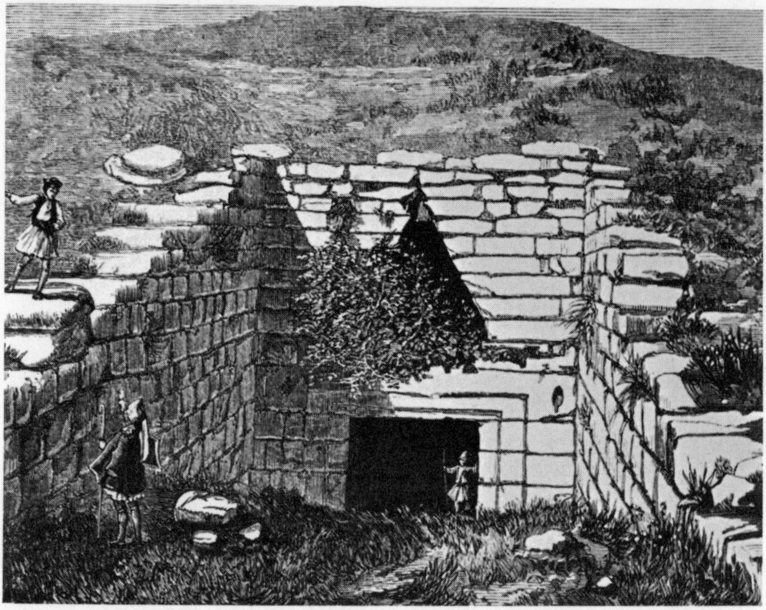

Most interesting discoveries at Mycenae were the Treasuries, which were Tholoi, *beehive-shaped tombs. Top left is the entrance to the famous Treasury of Atreus; bottom left is the Second Treasury,*

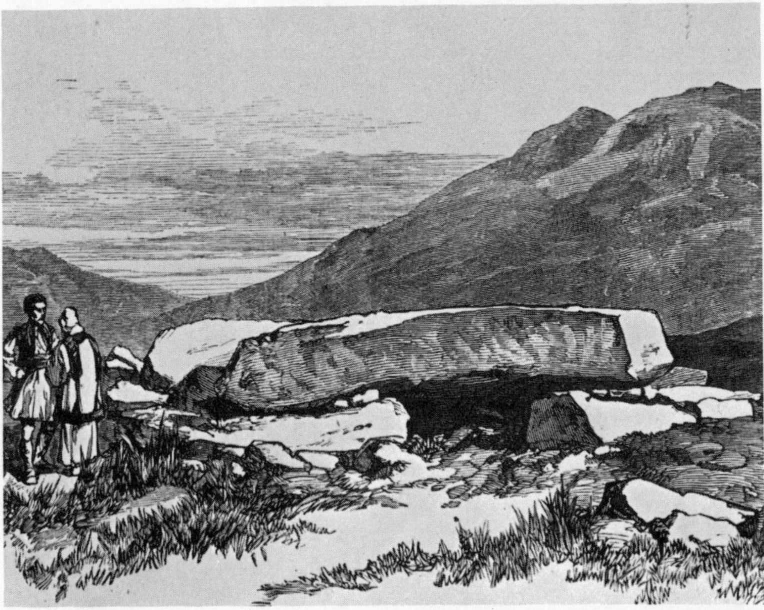

(ILLUSTRATED LONDON NEWS)

excavated by Sophia (shown in drawing) and her crew. At right are the Third (top) and Fourth Treasuries.

(GERMAN ARCHAEOLOGICAL INSTITUTE, ATHENS)

(ILLUSTRATED LONDON NEWS)

Eighteen-foot-high entrance to the Treasury of Atreus is approached by a walkway 20½ feet long. Interior is constructed of hewn blocks skillfully fitted together without any binding material. Drawing shows Heinrich, at left, explaining details to two Athenian visitors.

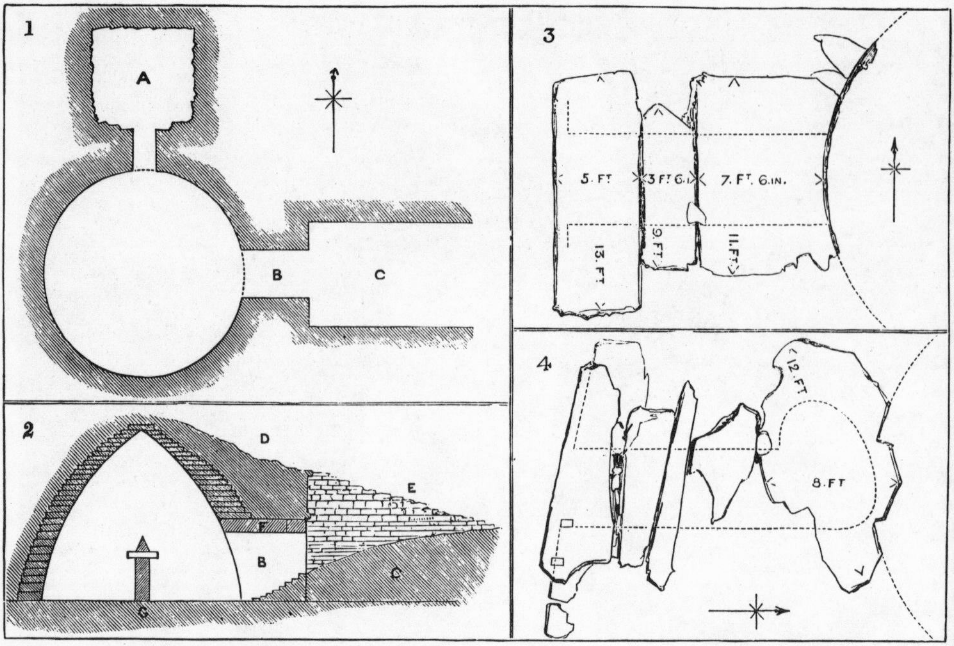

(ILLUSTRATED LONDON NEWS)

1. Plan of Treasury of Atreus: (A) rock-cut chamber; (B) doorway; (C) approach. 2. Section of above: (C) earth-filled approach; (D) slope of ground; (E) wall on north side of approach; (F) lintel stone; (G) door to chamber A. Numbers 3 and 4 are sketch plans of Third and Fourth Treasuries respectively.

Mycenaean tombstone has bas-relief of intertwined spirals on upper portion, chariot scene below.

(GENNADIUS LIBRARY, ATHENS)

(FREE UNIVERSITY, WEST BERLIN)

(FREE UNIVERSITY, WEST BERLIN

(FREE UNIVERSITY, WEST BERLIN)

Five skeletons in fourth tomb were blanketed in jewelry. Two gold intaglio signet rings fascinated the Schliemanns: one shows hunters in chariot; the other, warriors fighting. Large ring has four women, child, palm tree, double axe. Six heads on right side resemble Trojan idols found at Hissarlik.

(FREE UNIVERSITY, WEST BERLIN)

Clay potsherds, assembled by Heinrich, show procession of armed warriors in battle gear.

(V. & N. TOMBAZI, ATHENS; COURTESY: GREEK NATIONAL TOURIST OFFICE)

Gold mask which Schliemann supposed to be that of Agamemnon (above) was uncovered in first of five graves of Great Grave Circle. At right is one of the cows' heads from Mycenae. Both are now in National Archaeological Museum in Athens.

(PAVLOS MYLOFF, ATHENS; COURTESY: GREEK NATIONAL TOURIST OFFICE)

(COURTESY: ALEX L. MÉLAS)

(COURTESY: ALEX L. MÉLAS)

Two drawings made at Great Grave Circle in citadel of Mycenae show Sophia (above) and Heinrich (below) with members of local work crew.

(ILLUSTRATED LONDON NEWS)

In frock coat and white tie, Schliemann delivered a speech before the Royal Society of Antiquaries at Burlington House in England. Heinrich's low collar was specially designed by London shirtmaker to minimize his short neck.

TWENTY

Schliemann's field notes were so detailed that he was able to assemble a definitive book on Mycenae in an amazingly short time. He was impelled to answer criticisms of his brief reports on Mycenae, already published, chiefly in the London *Times,* which he considered to be the world's most prestigious newspaper. His scholarly critics ranged from insignificant, like the contentious Ernst Boetticher, to illustrious, like the German archaeologist Ernst Curtius and the Oxford University philologist Hans Müller. They eventually were to contribute immeasurably to general understanding of Schliemann's discoveries by placing them in proper perspective and interpreting them factually. But neither Curtius nor Müller could accept as valid every conclusion of Schliemann, who coveted the approval of both men.

When the manuscript was completed in the early spring of 1877, Schliemann went off to lecture in Russia, Italy, France and Germany. When in Germany he arranged for publication of the Mycenae book, collaborating with translators. He also talked with a prospective publisher in England, the country where Schliemann's archaeological accomplishments were first hailed and he was highly esteemed.

Perusal of the columns of the *Times* and the *Illustrated London News* discloses that much linage was given to Schliemann in the first six months of 1877 and that many correspondents were sent to Greece. Accelerated interest in that country was in large measure due to the Schliemanns' excavations that incited travelers and journalists to learn more about Greece, ancient and modern. A reporter from the *Illustrated London News* wrote a story about the comparatively new Royal Palace in Athens, indicating that many readers would be familiar with the landmarks mentioned:

The view given in our illustration represents the southern side of the palace, which has most architectural pretensions, and here are the rooms occupied by the Royal family. This side looks to the south over the gardens, and commands a fine view of the Acropolis. From the windows some very interesting points connected with old Athens can be seen. The fine Corinthian columns of the Temple of Zeus Olympus appear not far beyond the garden enclosure; the Arch of Hadrian is also seen; and over the Ilissus is the hollow of the old stadium. Away to the left is Hymettus, and in the distant south is the open Mediterranean, with some of the Isles of Greece visible in the blue haze of the horizon.

In the same weekly, an article about the impressive celebration of the Greek Orthodox Easter contained the brief paragraph:

We regret to say, however, that one person at least among the Carnival Sunday masqueraders was seen next day in no befitting condition of mind and body. This was a rollicking, popular humorist of the town, who had put on the classic helmet of the Princely Agamemnon, King of Mycenae, making a little fun of Dr. Schliemann's recent discoveries there.

When that inconsequential squib was called to Schliemann's attention, he huffily observed that it was beneath any British journalist to include such a minor incident in his dispatch. Appeasing Heinrich, Sophia said, "Let the swine mock. Instead of being angry, my love, accept it as praise that you are so famous that one of the lowly herd must seek fame through making fun of you."

That Easter, the Prince of Wales, later to be Edward VII of England, was the guest of the King and Queen of Greece, who shortly after were visited by the King's sister Her Royal Highness the Princess of Wales. It may have been coincidence that the Princess of Wales chose to make the first visit to her brother King George I in the same spring that the Schliemann name was prominent in England. It was reported to Heinrich and Sophia that Her Royal Highness, well informed about their excavations, had read articles by and about both of them in widely circulated periodicals and in specialized journals.

Sophia, as a native-born Greek, was upset by the Hellenic royal family's failure to invite her and Heinrich to court functions honoring visiting royalty, dignitaries and heads of state, who evinced an interest in the Schliemanns. It hurt both of them to be slighted in Greece, especially after the success at Mycenae for which they were being widely acclaimed, particularly in England.

The first of several letters offering honorary membership to learned societies of England was sent to Schliemann from London in February 1877. Heinrich's first invitation came from the British Archaeological Association, requesting that he speak about his excavations and accept a diploma as well as honorary membership of the society.

After Schliemann's acknowledgment of the honor, he was invited to address the association on April 11. He received and accepted similar invitations from the Royal Institution, the Royal Geographical Society, the Royal Institute of British Architects, the Royal Society of Antiquaries, the Royal Archaeological Association, and the Royal Archaeological Institute of Great Britain and Ireland.

With a tentative schedule for an extended stay in London, he put up at the Atheneum Club in early April, subsequently moving to the Charing Cross Hotel. The tone of letters of arrangement from Loftus Brock, a noted architect and a secretary of the British Archaeological Association, showed with what respect Schliemann was regarded.

Courted by intellectuals and lauded by scholars, he often addressed meetings at which he was also extolled by others. At the spring meeting of the Royal Geographical Society, Schliemann spoke, and a Mr. Hutchison read a paper for Bishop Crowther, who could not be present; the Bishop's paper, entitled *Journeys Up the Niger and Notes of the Neighboring Countries,* contained innumerable references to Schliemann's excavations. By such indirection, various speakers sought to show how much they knew about Schliemann's accomplishments.

Even the London Grocer's Association, without even a tenuous connection to archaeology, invited Schliemann to lecture at a meeting and elected him to membership. That fact was reported by the press, which assiduously made news of Schliemann's every appearance before an audience. A line portrait of Heinrich made by an artist of the *Illustrated London News* was reproduced throughout the world in newspapers, periodicals and professional journals.

Another drawing in the *Illustrated London News* showed Schliemann delivering a speech before the Royal Society of Antiquaries at Burlington House. In frock coat and white tie, he wore a collar much lower than those of members crowded around him.

The standard height of his collar had been set years earlier after consultation with the London shirtmaker who designed a style that would de-emphasize Schliemann's short neck, and give the illusion of greater height to his stature.

Clothes-conscious, Schliemann was accompanied to London in 1877 by his valet who kept Schliemann's apparel in perfect condition—brushing, pressing and shining as required. But Schliemann inspected everything as he dressed, often rebrushing garments that were lint- and dust-free. For years his suits, as well as his shirts, were tailored in London, where he also purchased boots and shoes, and headgear from a hatter who made bowlers and beavers to Schliemann's specifications. Although he itemized in diaries the high sums paid to his tailor, hatter, shirtmaker and shoe designer, Schliemann never identified any of them by name. He once mentioned in passing that his current wardrobe contained fifty suits, twenty hats, forty-two pairs of shoes, thirty walking sticks and fifteen riding crops.

A gentleman of fashion, Schliemann did not look the part as he stood before the members of trade associations and learned societies. The invitations of many of the latter had included Sophia, who did not accompany him to London. He gave the excuse that his wife was not well, which was not the whole truth. Sophia, again pregnant, was suffering only from morning sickness.

The Royal Archaeological Institute of Great Britain and Ireland planned to present diplomas of honorary membership to both Sophia and Heinrich, and he urged her by letter to join him in London. Until the last possible day before the Institute meeting, Heinrich delayed in expressing his regrets that Mrs. Schliemann could not be present on Friday, May 4. Unfortunately, the Institute could not postpone its meeting, so Heinrich attended alone.

A large and distinguished company assembled in Schliemann's honor. The program was opened by the Institute's president, The Lord Talbot de Malahide, who highly praised the archaeological activities of Schliemann. The president asked the honored guest "to remember how entirely those labours are appreciated by your friends in England, and how sincerely they will welcome their completion and your presence again amongst them." The Lord de Malahide then addressed himself to the absent Sophia: "As the first lady who has ever been identified in a work so arduous and stupendous, you have achieved a reputation which many will envy—some may emulate—but none can ever surpass."

Heinrich, briefly responding, signed the membership book, and received elegantly embossed diplomas for himself and Sophia. Her absence was so sincerely regretted by the Institute's members that they planned a special session for paying homage to her. Heinrich received a formal invitation from the Institute's secretary asking Sophia to be the honored guest of the Royal Archaeological Institute of Great Britain and Ireland. She was requested to "read a paper upon such a subject as may be agreeable to her."

Proud of the invitation to his Sophithion, Heinrich wrote imploring her to journey to London. She, sufficiently advanced in her pregnancy to have recovered from queasiness, was eager to join him. In a letter saying that she would accept the invitation of the Society, Sophia tenderly phrased for Heinrich her feeling about the baby she was carrying, which was theirs together. As devoted wife, she looked forward to being publicly honored as partner to her husband. In Athens, she wrote the paper she would give at the special meeting planned in her honor for Friday, June 8, 1877, at five in the afternoon.

Waiting for Sophia's arrival, Heinrich worked with the secretary on the list of invitations to be sent to those who were not members of the Institute. His list included the names of friends, colleagues, and even some critics in other countries. Certain of the scholar detractors Heinrich had forgiven—but not Hans Meister, who had issued the petty and sarcastic statement when Schliemann had made his identification of the skeletal embryo found at Troy. The name Hans Meister, which might have been expected to be on Schliemann's invitation list, was noticeably missing.

Sophia duly arrived in London with the paper she was to read. There were conflicting views on the paper's authorship. Some maintained that Heinrich wrote the paper in London; others thought Sophia had composed it in Greek, which Heinrich then translated into English, rewriting as he chose. Neither opinion was correct. His diary and their correspondence about the paper confirmed that she had written it in English, and Heinrich, reading the paper in their London hotel room, had corrected certain phrases so, as she said, her words would be immediately understood by her British listeners.

On June 6 Schliemann received from Hartshorne twenty additional tickets for the meeting and the request that "Mrs. S. and you arrive here about *five minutes* after five o'clock on Friday next. Please to send up your name to me and then I will arrange that Mrs. S. is properly met in the staircase and conducted to her seat by the president."

Dressed well in advance of the appointed hour, Sophia read her speech aloud while Heinrich paced up and down their room. A servant at the door announced the waiting carriage. Heinrich lightly kissed Sophia on the left cheek and offered her his arm. The famous couple, heads high, sallied forth to share together yet another memorable experience.

At the precise minute set by Albert Hartshorne, Sophia and Heinrich reached the top of the sweeping staircase leading to the meeting room of the Royal Archaeological Institute of Great Britain and Ireland. The Lord Talbot de Malahide, President of the Institute, greeted them cordially. At his side was the Honorable William Ewart Gladstone, leader of the British Liberal party and four times Prime Minister during the reign of Her Majesty Queen Victoria. Gladstone had asked if he might share the privilege of escorting Mrs. Schliemann to her place in the hall.

With one hand resting lightly on the arm of The Lord de Malahide and the other on the arm of Gladstone, Sophia descended the stairs. Her elegant costume that she wore with grace was accented by a hat elaborately decorated with flowers, in the fashion of the day. She accepted with a radiant smile the welcome of the assembly that rose at her entrance, applauding and cheering.

Heinrich, overcome by emotion, followed behind The Lord de Malahide, Gladstone and Sophia. "As I heard and saw the ovation given to my Sophithion by such a notable assemblage, and as I gazed upon this divine creature, I could only wonder why the great gods of Olympus had given me this woman as wife, friend, colleague and lover. My eyes ran with tears so I could barely see; my shoulders, arms and hands trembled; my legs shook so I could hardly walk. Unashamedly I wept copiously and my skin was aflame with bit-bumps as I saw my own Sophithion face the cheering group of distinguished people and merely incline her flushed, smiling face in recognition of this reception."

When the members and their guests were at last quiet, the chairman presented Sophia with a bouquet of blue and white flowers, the colors of the flag of her native Greece, and graciously introduced her as speaker. It was less than eight years since she had stood up at the Arsakeion School to quote a lengthy passage from Homer for the foreigner and stranger visiting her classroom. That schoolgirl had had the simplicity and composure that marked the appearance of the matron, who only twenty-five was yet worthy to be honored at a special meeting of the august Institute. Her intelligent mind, in less than a decade, had absorbed facts and philosophies that she had put to her own use, translating them into ideas productive of scholarly conclusions and interpretations. Sophia's experience in excavation was much more extensive than that of most of the Institute's members, whose dedication to the science of archaeology was primarily based on concepts and the written word. Her speech reflected strong attachment to her Greek heritage, stressed the labors and wonder of excavation, and contained a plea to British mothers for the instruction of their children in Greek so that the classics of her country might be fully appreciated. The sincerity and dignity of young Mrs. Schliemann was admired by the large audience, which gave her a tumultuous standing ovation at the end of the speech. (Sophia's complete address appears in Appendix A.)

It was followed by remarks from Heinrich, Gladstone, and Lord Houghton, in that order, at the request of The Lord de Malahide, again presiding. The three men each talked briefly about various pronunciations of ancient Greek words, but their mild controversy did not dim Sophia's triumph. Heinrich, beaming, remembered his 1869 promise to his bride: "You, my Sophithion, shall be honored as few women have been privileged. Learned men will one day bow to your greatness."

The Schliemanns lingered on in London for a few days and were honored at a dinner reception given by the Lord Mayor. Again Gladstone was escort to Sophia, who sat at his right. A sumptuous banquet was served, and guests vied with one another in proposing toasts to the Schliemanns. Letters, cables and telegrams of congratulations were read by the chairman. One of the telegrams, signed Ernst Boetticher, read: "Our differences may remain forever. But, no one dares dispute the fact that Dr. and Mrs. Heinrich Schliemann have persevered in the face of every possible disputation and danger in following a path of personal conviction that cannot help but add greatly to the scholarship of mankind and an understanding of the past."

Sophia and Heinrich regretted many more invitations than they could possibly have accepted before their departure on June 17. Their last public appearance was at a meeting of the Royal Historical Society held June 12, at 11 Chandos Street, Cavendish Square. Greeted with loud cheers by the members, the Schliemanns were both made Honorary Fellows of the Society, and were presented with beautifully bound diplomas signifying their unanimous election. After they signed the album of membership, Heinrich gave a speech about the excavations made by him and Sophia.

The day the Schliemanns left England, they were accompanied to the boat train by a group of well-wishers that included Gladstone, The Lord de Malahide, and M. Gennadius, Greek chargé d'affaires.

TWENTY-ONE

Most Europeans went to watering places on the Continent because it was the fashionable thing to do; but in 1877 the Schliemanns went from spa to spa consulting doctors and taking cures for specific ailments. Sophia was suffering from a recurrence of her abdominal pains; Heinrich, from persistent earache. Doctors examined his ears and superficially treated them, without conclusive diagnosis.

The Schliemanns did not stay long in one place, nor did they really rest. Both were reading final proofs of the Mycenae book, and Heinrich was, as always, busy with voluminous correspondence and with rebuttals of attacks on his work published in periodicals, both popular and scholarly. After they had spent some time at Boulogne-sur-Mer, Sophia decided she was tired of watering places and went to Paris. The house at 6, Place St. Michel was rented, so Sophia took a large flat on the Rue de Tilsitt.

Heinrich, restless and far from well, began a city-hopping jaunt. He was concentrating on plans for an exhibition of the Trojan treasure in London, a project that distressed Sophia. She was afraid he would decide to leave the collection in England permanently, depriving Greece of antiquities that, she thought, rightfully belonged in a museum at Athens. Heinrich had long vacillated about the disposal of the treasure of Troy, which was sought by the Russian and French governments while the Turks were suing Schliemann. When he had won the case, he tentatively suggested that the one or the other might buy the Trojan collection, but neither government would set terms of purchase. Schliemann, half-hearted about selling, repeatedly stated later that he had never seriously thought of profiting from the sale of the treasure of Troy.

He did offer it as an outright gift to the British Museum in October 1876, and a four-page letter of refusal to Schliemann was signed by J. Winter Jones of the museum's staff. While acknowledging the "world famous value of the treasure," Jones explained that the British Museum was already too full to accommodate another exhibition. Confirmation of the museum's decision is documented in many of Schliemann's diaries and letters. The rebuff cost the museum the ownership of the treasure of Troy, a tragedy in light of the ultimate disposition and eventual fate of the collection.

The London exhibition, which distressed Sophia, resulted from negotiations that Schliemann had initiated while in the north of France. The London *Times* of August 16, 1877, printed the following notice:

> Dr. Heinrich Schliemann wrote to us from Boulogne-sur-Mer where he is now staying:
> "I have much pleasure in informing you that, in order to show my gratitude to the English people for the warm receptions I have found with them during my three months' stay in London, I have resolved to bring my Trojan collection, including the treasure in gold and silver, to England and to exhibit it provisionally at the South Kensington Museum. Of course, it is not for sale. I have taken great care to note on every one of the thousands of objects of which the collection is composed, the exact depth at which it was found, and it may, therefore, at a glance be seen to which of the four historic cities, built one atop the other on Mount Hissarlik, each belongs."

Schliemann's public offer was accepted at once by the South Kensington Museum, and he centered his complete attention on the arrangements. Sophia, in Paris and without a bank account of her own, was dependent on Heinrich for funds, which he, preoccupied and thoughtless, forgot to send. The 400 francs that he had given her when they parted at Boulogne-sur-Mer were soon gone, and at the end of August Sophia wrote him a pitiful letter, saying she was ashamed not to have money for necessities. One of her brothers had travelled from Greece with little Andromache who was then in Paris with her mother.

Berating Heinrich for running from place to place, Sophia reminded him that he had promised to join his family in Paris and to send money. He was informed that she, worried about finances and distracted by loneliness, often spent her nights agitatedly pacing the floor. Sophia received no tender messages of love and solicitude like those Heinrich had sent when she had been pregnant with Andromache. Their letters of the next few months showed that their personal relationship was at a low ebb, as it was whenever they were separated.

Heinrich, again studying the collections in museums throughout Europe, was increasingly troubled by earache, and sought medical advice, which he then ignored. Sophia wrote to him in November: "I am desperate that the ear so dear to me continues to ache. I hope it will end very soon. It is strange that last night I felt an acute pain in my right ear which lasted five minutes only, and I thought of what you are suffering, my little Henry . . ." Dream conscious, he fixed the time of Sophia's pain as coinciding with an almost unbearable earache he had suffered in Würzburg. She asked her beloved whether that coincidence did not prove they were bound together to share joy and pain. "The gods have decreed it, Henry, my dearest friend. Please, please return to me so I can hold your head to my bosom." He did not join her, but continually hinted at dreams that he was afraid to commit to paper; he customarily indicated any important dream by signing H., not Heinrich or Henry, to a letter written the following day.

Sophia, alone with Andromache, felt herself to be abandoned. She moved to 53, Boulevard Haussmann, and often summoned a doctor for Andromache, then six, who was frequently ill with colds, earaches and stomach upsets. Sophia pleaded with Heinrich to consult with doctors in England and Germany so their daughter might be restored to health. When he failed to do his duty as father and husband, Sophia wrote bitterly, "My heart, do not you consider me one of your occupations? I know I am worth nothing, but do not show it to me."

In vain, helpful Parisian friends tried to comfort and cheer Sophia. With good reason, she resented a letter in which Heinrich criticized her for not properly managing her affairs, and in answer wrote:

Blvd. Haussmann

Dear Henry:

Is it not enough that I remain here in poverty by your request? Do not complain that I cannot manage what I do not have. Were it not for friends like the Rallis, I could not make all things come together. They know you do not provide. So, it is your responsibility that all know.

Your wife?

That letter elicited from Heinrich the assurance, "All I do is for you alone. Do you think I consider myself? Not for a moment." Unconvinced, Sophia pointed out how selfish he was, and wondered to him, "How the human mind and soul can delude itself and find in every action a justification." He answered with one line: "Believe what you will, but my adoration is for you alone."

The Schliemanns seemed hardly to be the same devoted couple who had shared the labor at Troy and the honors in London. Sophia reminded Heinrich that she was not the Sophia of "eight years ago" when they were married. She was indeed a woman of maturity.

Knowing her to be both worldly and wise, Heinrich did not hesitate to enlist her as ally in a difficult family situation that involved Serge, Schliemann's son by his first wife. Serge, enjoying a liaison with a Parisian actress, threatened to marry her after his father called her a "painted, wanton woman." No record exists of how the affair between Serge and the actress was broken up by Sophia, but soon after Heinrich asked for her help, she wrote assuring him that the actress would never again see Serge, and that the illicit romance was definitely over.

Heinrich could depend on Sophia to solve his problems, but she could not count on him. He frequently went through Paris without stopping off to see Sophia and Andromache, and sent money grudgingly and sporadically. When it did reach Sophia, she often had to use the cash not for immediate necessities, but on bills long overdue.

Her husband thought only of the London exhibition. In Greece, Sophia's brother Alexandros and other agents of Schliemann collected the treasure from its various repositories; some objects had remained hidden even after the legal ruling that Schliemann owned and could keep the collection. By consent of the Greek government, a few Mycenaean artifacts were added to the exhibit material. Schliemann himself made three quick trips to Athens in late autumn, supervising plans for the shipment of the objects to London. There he rolled up his elegant shirtsleeves and personally worked on the installation with two staff members of the South Kensington Museum as aides.

When Heinrich was in England, working on the project that absorbed his total attention, Sophia wrote: "Dearest husband and friend, my hand meets yours across the land and channel.

Our love for each other is enough for me. May we expect you for Christmas? Your own and only yours, Sophia." Heinrich promised not only to be with her and their child in the apartment on Boulevard Haussmann, but that the Christmas would be one "none will ever forget."

Schliemann was delighted with the attention his exhibition attracted even before its opening, scheduled for December 20, 1877. Three days earlier the *Times* ran a full column story, giving a detailed description of the exhibit. The report began with the paragraph:

> The sightseers of London have a new and original treat in store for them in the remains from Hissarlik, on the plains of Troy, now being arranged by Dr. Schliemann, in some twenty cases, in one of the Courts of the South Kensington Museum. On the much-vexed question of the antiquity and historical value of these remains we do not intend now to enter; we wish simply to give an idea of the number and variety of the objects to be seen, which form but a part of the whole disinterred by Dr. Schliemann.

Sophia, close to the time of her delivery, was disconsolate in Paris. In a letter phrased with an anguish comparable to a lament from some ancient Greek tragedy, she wrote to Heinrich: "Are the praises of the English, the obeisance of the world, the sight of more and more objects, the selfish travels from place to place by yourself of greater importance than your family? Answer me, my friend. Tell me what is in your mind and heart. Why? Why do you demand, yet ignore? I thanks god for you, yet wonder what manner of man you are. No, my friend, I do not wonder because I know. I understand you and know the fate of every woman who is joined to a genius. How do I know? Because I have lived with you, been your partner, friend, lover and slave since our marriage. Also, I know because I have asked for books about men whose fame has lasted through the centuries, as will yours, my Henry. These books tell me that their wives have suffered as do I, but were privileged to share moments of glory as I have. A woman's place is but nothing in the shadow of her husband, and I thanks god that my fortune has been to be your wife, your shadow, rather than the wife of a man who works, spends time with his friends in the coffee house and comes home to his meal and his bed."

Although ill, Heinrich was sustained by elation. The *Times* of December 20 mentioned a forthcoming handbook of the Trojan collection, and thoroughly reviewed the exhibition. Heinrich, pleased with the long article, wrote about it to Sophia: "Be proud with me, my own darling wife, that the Times today saw fit to say that '. . . Dr. Schliemann may fairly be called the creator of Homeric archaeology. This title is his after finds at Mycenae, a scantling of which, it may be remarked in passing, enriches the collection opened to-day, have helped make good.' How I would you were here to share this with me, especially since you, my love, are a full partner in whatever I have been able to do."

She must have been ambivalent about that letter. By the time she received it, the Christmas that Heinrich had promised would be unforgettable was past, and his one passion had taken precedence over his love of family. He remained in London for the holiday season, and Sophia had a dreary Christmas in Paris, cloudy and cold, with only her brother Spiros and Andromache for company.

In London, Heinrich, partially deaf and tortured with earache, strolled through the exhibition hall with friends, and confronted those detractors who had come from many countries to see for themselves the discoveries of Schliemann. On his last day in England, as Schliemann was leaving the South Kensington Museum he ran into Hans Meister, the man who had sarcastically attacked Schliemann's embryo discovery at Troy. Reporting on that incident to Sophia, Heinrich wrote: "As our eyes met, we looked deep into each other. At that moment, a young scholar said to a friend, 'That is Meister who was never invited to any of Schliemann's public triumphs in London. Something must have passed darkly between them in the past.' My darling, I heard and Meister heard; we looked and I was the first to pass on."

Irritable from illness and driven by his uncontrolled energy, Heinrich again passed on, but not to Paris. With nothing else to complain about, he wrote a letter chiding Sophia for her inability to write and speak as many languages as he. She answered with a short note written in four languages, the last English, in which she wrote: "You must come here because I did not have any joy at Christmas time. Love, Sophia."

She wrote again to say their child Andromache was well and

the "one to come tries to make his presence evident with all his force." From the time of the child's conception in less stormy times for the Schliemanns, Heinrich had referred to the coming as the birth of "*my* child" or "when *he* will be born." He discussed the future of the anticipated boy child in glowing terms.

But Sophia was alone in Paris for the birth of their son. Informed of the infant's arrival, Schliemann announced the birth to the world, and rushed to Paris. Sophia immediately was comforted by Heinrich's love and strength, and without hesitation forgave him for his heedless behavior of the months past. In reunion, the Schliemanns rejoiced together over the new heir, who was called not Odysseus, as they had so long planned, but Agamemnon, in honor of the great king of Mycenae, scene of their latest triumph.

At Agamemnon's christening in a Greek Orthodox church, Heinrich was difficult, stopping the bearded priest just as he was about to lower the infant into the baptismal font. The finicky and hypochondriacal Heinrich took a thermometer from his pocket and placed it in the water, forcibly holding back the sputtering priest. He threatened to leave and not to continue with the ceremony, but Sophia, as so often in times of crisis with Heinrich, was able to charm the priest, persuading him to stay. He was intoning the baptismal rites when Heinrich, again interrupting, placed a copy of Homer's *Odyssey* on the baby's forehead and recited one hundred lines from the classic before the priest could resume the religious ceremony.

Schliemann had his way at the baptism, but the ritual with the Homeric volume did not influence Agamemnon to follow in the footsteps of his father as scholar and archaeologist. The son, who inherited Heinrich's business sense, became a successful financier.

TWENTY-TWO

Heinrich, publicly triumphant in London and elsewhere, was, as usual, egotistical and outwardly self-satisfied. But a new thoughtful point of view reflected a mellowing and a willingness to cooperate with others in the world of archaeology. He noted that established scholars were being forced into a re-examination of their discipline, which was attracting new men from whom Schliemann thought he could learn. Stimulated to more profound study, not of antiquities but of theories, he traveled widely, seeking out men who questioned archaeological interpretations made both by himself and by others with field experience.

Schliemann's transition from impetuous excavator and starry-eyed romantic to realistic scholar was due in part to the considerable influence of Rudolph Virchow, an internationally known German medical scientist, whose broad interests encompassed anthropology, archaeology and politics. Virchow, three months Schliemann's senior, had been a brilliant student with sufficient money to explore several professions before deciding on medicine. He became a professor of pathological anatomy and leader of the German school that dominated world medicine in the mid-19th century. In 1862 Virchow was elected to the Prussian Diet, and thereafter was an active liberal in his country.

Intrigued by Schliemann's reports on his excavations, Virchow initiated a correspondence that led to friendship, to joint investigation in the Troad, and to travel for archaeological study. Virchow's association with Schliemann had far-reaching effects of historic significance.

Both men were imaginative and dynamic, but Virchow, also cool, contained, intrepid and imperturbable, had a knack for calming Schliemann. He advised Schliemann to disregard the libelous attacks of certain classicists, and to take into account only those scholars well disposed toward him and the universal support of the mass public.

Encouraged to be his own man, Schliemann returned to the

island of Ithaca in the summer of 1878 to carry out an exploration he had started years earlier. Ithaca was the Homeric kingdom of Odysseus, who, after the Trojan War, spent ten drama-packed years trying to regain his home. Schliemann thought that his added experience in excavating would now help him find ruins of importance. At the site of Ithaca's capital on Mount Aëtos, he uncovered ruins of 190 houses, built of cyclopean masonry; and crews, under his direction, excavated the home of Ithaca's kings, situated at the very summit. Guided once again by the writings of Homer and Pausanias, Schliemann compared the excavated areas with their descriptions. He found, to his own satisfaction, the spring of water that fit the identical description of the Homeric place where the swine of Eumaeus were watered, and identified stables mentioned by Homer. Two coins unearthed at the foot of Aëtos delighted Schliemann: One side of each coin showed a cock and was marked with the word *Ithakon;* the other side was decorated with the head of Odysseus, wearing a conical cap.

When Schliemann had to leave Ithaca, he said a reluctant farewell to the wealthiest man on the island, Aristides Dendrinos, and his wife Praxidea, who had been most hospitable, as, according to Heinrich's published works, he asserted they would be to any traveler to Ithaca. He noted that their two children were named Telemachus and Penelope, after the son and wife of Odysseus, classical names that Schliemann considered to be only proper for children of Ithaca.

"Rare is this island with its beauty, its history and its people. In such a short time I have been rewarded with finding the ancient capital and made welcome by the people who now dwell here. When I left today, a large number of the populace swarmed around me, urging upon me presents for my wife and children. Their tears, matched with my own, were evidence of their love of Homer and affection for me. Thanks god for my life! To have experienced such honor as the diverse London and Ithaca is a thing few men warranted. I shall return, as I promised, in the company of my darling Sophithion and my two children."

At Athens, Heinrich packed for a return to Hissarlik and begged Sophia to accompany him, but she refused. She would neither leave her children nor spend another miserable winter at Troy, for which she had already sacrificed too much. Accepting the inevitable, Schliemann proceeded alone to the Dardanelles in late September 1878. Months earlier he had applied for another *firman,* the one of 1876 having expired. There were the usual difficulties over the new application, which, through the intercession of Sir Austen Henry Layard, British Ambassador at Constantinople, had been pushed through with the *firman* predated to September. Layard had been first to excavate Nimrud.

It could only have been cupidity that led the Turks to grant *firman* after *firman* to Schliemann, known to them as a troublemaker, not to be trusted. The Turks tolerated him as the only man with funds and the ability to excavate antiquities for their Imperial Museum. Surprisingly, in the *firman* of 1878 they did not insist on keeping all objects from Troy, but gave Schliemann the right to a third of the finds. He was required to pay the wages of eleven guards—one overseer, who would carry the key to the storehouse, and ten gendarmes. Schliemann wrote: "The ten gendarmes, to whom I paid 20 pounds and 10 shillings monthly, were all of great use to me, for they not only served as guards against the brigands by whom the Troad was infested, but they also carefully watched my laborers whilst they were excavating, and thus forced them to be honest."

Five days after the excavations were reopened in 1878, a workman, stuffing a small stone idol into his pocket, was caught in the act by a Turkish guard. The guard twisted the workman's arm behind his back and, with the butt of a gun, beat him until he dropped unconscious. Schliemann was revolted by the display of cruelty, which increased his loathing for the Turks; but he knew better than to interfere and, sickened, turned away.

Schliemann accepted the guards as necessary evils. In October an armed band swept down on Kalifatli, a small community about twenty minutes by foot from Hissarlik. It had been rumored that one of the villagers had a hoard of 10,000 francs, and his house was the target of the brigands. The intended victim ran to the roof to sound an alarm that brought out his neighbors, armed with rifles. Two villagers and two brigands were killed before the arrival of the ten Turkish gendarmes, whose torture of captured brigands was soon common knowledge in the Troad. The presence of the guards at Hissarlik was a deterrent to other lawless bands of the region.

Schliemann, in his fourth season at Troy, concentrated on an extensive section near the Skaean Gate and confirmed his opinion that a building there had been the home of the last chief of Troy. He uncovered hundreds of objects of historical value, and fumed when the Turks locked up two-thirds of each day's find in their section of the warehouse. He had to abide by the rules or leave the digs, but his letters and diaries indicate that he took advantage of the ignorance of the Turks. When sorting the objects with the overseer, Schliemann sometimes gave up gold ones that were much less important than those of terracotta and stone which he kept for himself.

Troy was so well known by 1878 that it attracted many visitors who tramped around the digs, delaying work to a certain extent. When the importance of the visitors required Schliemann to be cordial, he stopped whatever he was doing to guide them through the excavations. On October 21 officers of the British ship H.M.S. *Monarch* paid an official call on Schliemann at the very moment when he discovered several magnificent vases in the ruins of the house where he was digging. News of that latest find reached the outside world long before Schliemann was ready to announce it, because the *Monarch*'s officers wrote about the vases in letters to relatives and friends.

Although Schliemann had improved his techniques for digging, he still was attacked by scholars who read of new discoveries. In January 1879 a squib in the *Times* stated that "it is rumored that Dr. Schliemann will never again excavate at Troy. His anger at libels and a dire trouble in his ear which causes deafness are combined to force him to retire." The rumor of retirement had no basis in fact. In February Schliemann was granted another *firman* and soon was at Troy with 10 armed guards and 150 workmen. The weather conditions would have forced a lesser man to close down the excavations, but Schliemann, though plagued by severe pain in his right ear, stayed on. "Up to the middle of March, I suffered cruelly from the north wind, which was so icy cold that it was impossible to read or write in my wooden barracks, and it was only possible to keep warm by active exercise of work in the trench. To avoid taking cold, I went, as I have always done, very early in the morning on horseback to the Hellespont to take my sea-bath, but I always returned to Hissarlik before sunrise and before the work commenced."

Schliemann was Spartan but foolhardy, as he was told by Virchow, who arrived at Hissarlik late in March. He advised against the daily sea baths as being detrimental to the ear condition, but Heinrich would not heed the warning. He insisted that the morning swim in salt water kept him tough and healthy.

Schliemann and Virchow were joined in April by Émile Burnouf, the French scholar who had so often been consulted by Schliemann during earlier excavations at Troy. Sharing his work and accepting in-the-field advice for the first time, Schliemann was unable to resist a slight condescension, saying that Burnouf and Virchow "both assisted me in my researches, to the utmost of their ability." Their respective abilities made the team of three remarkable. Burnouf, an engineer, artist, and authority on ancient architecture, had worked with an archaeological group at Olympia and was experienced in making maps of excavations. His mission to Troy was underwritten by the French government. The erudite Virchow, a keen observer, studied the flora and fauna and geology of the Troad, and not only practiced medicine but did important research in that field. His stay at Hissarlik was subsidized by Schliemann, who sharply reminded Virchow of his generosity at a later date.

The three men uncovered town walls at the digs, Virchow and Burnouf interpreting many things that had escaped Schliemann when he had worked alone. They examined various layers of specific cities, carefully removing debris at a pace slower than that to which Schliemann was accustomed. His snap judgments were tempered by the more deliberate ones of Virchow and Burnouf. Fourteen *tumuli* were excavated on the plain beside the Scamander River, the tombs yielding little immediate return for the large amount of money Schliemann spent on the project. But Virchow and Burnouf both thought that the *tumuli* would be of considerable value when, after closer investigation, the data amassed was correlated with facts learned at other sites.

Climbing to the peak of Mount Chigri, the three men studied the vast Hellenic ruins first explored by Frank Calvert. Their examination added to the accumulating knowledge about the Mycenaean civilization, by comparative and confirmative links with excavations at Troy, Mycenae, and other sites subsequently explored. Schliemann was the first to admit that he alone unveiled the Mycenaean age, a picture at first dim and shadowy that became clearer through restoration by archaeologists who followed him.

Burnouf made maps of the Plain of Troy, and at Hissarlik, sketched scale drawings of Trojan walls, of building- and floor-plans of exposed sections.

Alone, Virchow rambled across the plain, studying the wildlife and cataloguing botanical specimens. As doctor, he attracted patients to an informal clinic, similar to the one that had previously taken up so much of Schliemann's time. Virchow treated the workmen and prescribed for peasant patients who reached Hissarlik on foot and on horseback, in carts and on litters; he even made house calls in distant villages. He soon discovered that there was not one qualified physician or apothecary in the entire Troad; quacks treated patients with mumbo jumbo, and village priests sought to effect cures of all diseases by bloodletting. He decried the narrow-mindedness of priests who insisted that the hard-working people fast during Lent. Virchow found that by Easter, at the conclusion of the holy season, the entire population was debilitated and many people were dangerously ill, the lack of food having made their bodies breeding places for disease.

Schliemann willingly paid for medical supplies sent from the Dardanelles to Virchow. Gathering peasants in small groups, Virchow identified for them the camomile and juniper that grew wild, showing how those plants could be prepared for use as palliatives and cures for certain ailments. Virchow had with him a large supply of vaseline, efficacious in the treatment of sunburn and of the chafing from riding; for the latter, vaseline "proved to be highly beneficial."

Through an interpreter Virchow questioned his patients about their daily habits, and observed their living conditions when he visited their homes, many as far as 50 miles from Hissarlik. As a result of his medical practice he became, by chance, an expert on residential architecture of the Troad. Virchow's study of malaria, a disease rampant in the region, was immeasurably important to doctors elsewhere. Although the peasants suffered from fever and other diseases, Virchow was tremendously impressed by their general good health. He compared the tall, well-built men, virile and rosy-cheeked, with males in "what we call civilized cities," and the Troad's women, pure of complexion and healthy, with the pale, bloated, anemic women in Constantinople and the "barely better women on the continent."

Schliemann was preparing material for his book *Ilios, City and*

Country of the Trojans, which was to be a monumental work when published in 1880. The dedication was to William Ewart Gladstone, M.P., D.C.L.; the scholarly Preface was by Virchow, who also contributed a treatise on Troy and Hissarlik, a treatise on medicine of the Troad, and the catalogue of its flora. The book contained an article by Professor J. P. Mahaffy on the relationship of *Novum Ilium* to the *Ilios* of Homer, an appendix by Professor A. H. Sayce on inscriptions found at Hissarlik, an article on Thymbria and Hanaï Tepeh by Frank Calvert; and maps and drawings by Burnouf.

While working on the final preparation of the book, Schliemann heard that Virchow intended to publish an article about his own work at the excavations. Unreasonably angry, Schliemann fired off an arrogant and demanding telegram, reminding Virchow that he had been a guest at Hissarlik, with all expenses paid. Schliemann stated that publication rights were his alone because he had put up his hard-earned cash to carry on the work no one else dared attempt, all others lacking the vision to invest. He demanded that Virchow cancel whatever plans for publication he had. Fortunately, Virchow ultimately wrote and published various treatises on the causes and cures of pathological problems of inhabitants of the Troad.

But on receipt of Schliemann's rude telegram, Virchow graciously withdrew the archaeological article intended for publication. He had a major design that required the total cooperation of Schliemann, and did not want to jeopardize that project by alienating him. Virchow had laid the groundwork for it in January 1879, two months before he joined Schliemann at Troy. A master at diplomacy, he had written to Schliemann: "It is tragic that you, although understandably, feel yourself estranged from the country of your birth, and that because of this we [in Germany] must be content if only a few little crumbs of your collection fall on us." He ended the letter with the information that Schliemann had been elected to membership in the Frankfurt Academy of Arts and Sciences, but did not add that the election was the result of Virchow's machinations.

Virchow coveted the Trojan collection for Germany. While in the Troad, he frequently mentioned to Schliemann his birthplace, his fatherland, always choosing moments when Schliemann was content and in good humor. Virchow made it his business to know the status of governments in regard to the collection. He knew that Greek ministers had rebuffed Schliemann, refusing to accept his offer to give them not only the Trojan collection but funds for the construction of a museum to house it. Virchow was aware of eager attempts by some countries to obtain the collection, and of Heinrich's tentative offers, with stipulations he had every right to make. There was no denying that Schliemann had spent a small fortune in the excavation of Troy; that because of it, his family had suffered physical and emotional strain; and that he personally had faced danger, from man and nature, in acquiring the collection, only a small percentage of which was gold treasure. Virchow completely understood Schliemann and knew to what psychological pressures he would respond.

The Trojan collection was still in England on the spring day in 1879 when Virchow and Schliemann started to climb Mount Ida, tramping through beautiful forests of oak and pine interspersed with chestnut, plane and lime trees, and firs. A sudden thunderstorm drove the two men into a sheltering cave, where they talked of many things. After the storm, they began a leisurely descent to the Plain. Along the way, Virchow, bending down, picked a flowering twig from a blackthorn bush and handed it to Schliemann, saying, "A nosegay from Ankershagen." Virchow's subtlety and his deep understanding of his friend were implicit in those four words. They touched the sentimental Schliemann. Ankershagen was the village where, at age seven, he had first vowed to excavate Troy and prove to the world that Homer's writings were not fiction but fact. At Ankershagen, with emotion far from juvenile, he had explored secret caves, searched for ghosts and buried treasure, and believed in local legends and myths.

By the end of the day's outing on Mount Ida, Schliemann was casually discussing the possibility of having his Trojan collection shipped from London to Berlin for temporary exhibition. Virchow had planted a seed that, for months after, he assiduously tended.

Sophia, who also knew Heinrich the sentimentalist and romantic, was frantic when she heard that the Trojan exhibit might be sent to Germany for a showing. Had she worked and suffered only to have the greatest single archaeological collection in the world go to a country other than her beloved Greece?

TWENTY-THREE

Heinrich and Sophia moved into their palatial home in Athens exactly one decade after the day of their honeymoon when Heinrich had promised to build such a house for his wife. Late in 1878, while Heinrich was digging to find ancient houses, excavators were scooping out a massive hole for the foundation of his modern home on University Street.

Plans for the huge three-story building were drawn up by the German architect Tsiller after many conferences with Heinrich, who knew precisely what he wanted down to the smallest detail. As his own contractor, he made arrangements for the quarrying of marble and other stone, selected what little lumber was needed, consulted with foundries about metalwork, engaged artists and artisans, and while traveling in Europe chose bathroom fixtures and kitchen equipment.

Heinrich in the roles of master builder, interior decorator, and landscape architect advised the experts and consulted Sophia only about minor details. She wrote to him in 1879, "Please do buy the necessary you describe. Its price is good, too." But the tenor of their correspondence about the house and its furnishings was better typified by his "Today I purchased a chair for your boudoir. It is functional and will serve many purposes." Sophia's palace, built to Heinrich's specifications, was furnished with what he thought was suitable, not with what she might have liked. Except in the matter of furniture, Heinrich's judgment was sound and his taste impeccable.

He placed no budgetary limits on the construction and decoration of the residence, a square building with well-proportioned rooms. The ground floor contained two exhibition halls for the display of ancient objects, the kitchen, the servant's quarters, and areas essential to the upkeep of a large household. From the street, marble stairways curved up to an exterior landing, with French doors that opened into a vestibule; here, inside steps led up and down. There was an inner vestibule, the Great Hall, the dining room, salons for entertaining, and three bathrooms. The family sleeping quarters, dressing rooms, the library and Heinrich's study were on the second floor.

Curious Athenians gathered daily to watch the construction of the largest private residence in their city and to stare at the procession of workmen, many of them foreigners, going to and from work at the building. Shouts in German, Italian and Greek could be heard above the sound of hammers.

All three stories had mosaic floors in colorful patterns and interesting designs; even the servants' quarters and kitchen had floors in mosaic. A corps of Italian artisans, experienced at tessellation, stayed for more than a year completing the intricate flooring of the palace.

When the basic structure was finished, Bavarian artists began the murals on walls and ceilings, painting in detail the designs roughly sketched by Schliemann. There was one ceiling mural showing the marble metope of the sun god found at Troy; other objects unearthed at Troy and scenes of Schliemann's excavations at Troy and Mycenae were depicted in stylized forms. Additional murals were added after Schliemann dug at Orchomenus and Tiryns. The exquisite ceiling murals, flowing and rhythmic, were in pastel tones; inscriptions and murals over doorways and above staircases were vibrant in color. There were even murals in soft shades on the exterior arcades off the first and second floors on the street side of the house.

Elaborate metalwork, bronze, in classical designs, formed the railings of the two arcades and of balconies and fences closing in the grounds. The *sauvastika* and *svastika,*

卍 and 卐 ,

were prominent in the design of the fences and the two double gates, one opening into the formal garden, the other into the entranceway to the house. On the two pairs of gates the *sauvastika* was on the right wing, the *svastika* on the left.

The spacious gardens were landscaped by Italian gardeners with whom Schliemann worked untiringly. Some shade trees already on the property were left standing; more leafy trees, citrus and other fruit trees, and flowering shrubs were planted. Sod and seed provided the sweeping green lawn where the children played.

Schliemann called his palace ΙΛΙΟΥ ΜΕΛΑΘΡΟΝ, the House of Ilium, and had the words cut into marble at the center of the front of the building between the first and second floors.

A great ball given on February 14, 1880, was the Schliemanns' first formal entertainment in their new home. A steady procession of carriages rolled up to Iliou Mélathron, and fashionables of Athens and the Continent passed through the entrance gates, attended by the gateman Belepheron, who was proud of the ancient name given him by Heinrich. Telamon, another faithful servant, stood at the French doors at the top of the sweeping outer staircases. In the entrance vestibule maids took wraps of the guests, who stepped into the large vestibule, where they were welcomed by Heinrich and Sophia. Eagerly the guests entered the Great Hall and wandered through the house, admiring its splendors. Men who normally walked erect and proud ambled with heads down, marveling at the mosaics underfoot. Elegantly gowned ladies, who usually coquetted with eyes cast down in mock demurity, gaped at the murals overhead. Even the most sophisticated, in wonderment, inspected the house that was indeed a palace.

Nothing marred the grand opening of Iliou Mélathron. Contented hosts, the Schliemanns bade goodbye to their last guest and retired. But before Heinrich dropped off to sleep, he puzzled briefly about one little incident. Late in the evening, he had surprised four ministers of the government in deep discussion. At his approach, three of them, obviously embarrassed, moved away; the remaining minister, in confusion, stuttered inanities to Heinrich.

Before noon the next day Schliemann completely understood the discomfit of the ministers whose impromptu conference he had interrupted. A government messenger delivered to Heinrich a document closed by the official seal of the Council of Ministers. Inside was a demand for Schliemann to either remove or cover the naked statues on the rooftop balustrade of Iliou Mélathron, lest the sensibilities of Athenian citizens be offended by the repugnant display of nudity. Heinrich was absolutely furious and at once took the letter to Sophia, who burst into almost hysterical laughter. At first puzzled by her reaction, he then recovered his sense of humor and laughed along with her.

They held their own brief conference and dispatched every available household servant to fetch as many seamstresses as possible. Throughout the evening and late into the night five rooms of Iliou Mélathron were bright with light needed by dressmakers, working steadily. There was a hum of animated talk in the rooms, and giggles, chuckles, and laughter rose from the busy women. Like all Greeks the seamstresses enjoyed a good joke, and all the more if on the government.

The next morning Athenians en route to work along University Street looked up at the statues atop Iliou Mélathron with an amazement that turned to delight and laughter. Heinrich mingled with the throng, and in strictest confidence, told here one man and there another that the Council of Ministers had ordered him to clothe the nude figures. The secret spread rapidly through the city as Heinrich hoped, and soon the sidewalks were jammed with hundreds of people mocking the ministers. Shopkeepers, bankers, clerks, errand boys, domestics, waiters, fishmongers, fruit vendors, and sponge sellers rubbed elbows in front of Iliou Mélathron. On its roof the marble statues, standing two to a plinth, were dressed in flowing garments of gaudy cloth, the most unattractive and garish Heinrich and Sophia could find.

The Greek ministers, after meeting in Cabinet session, dispatched a messenger to Schliemann shortly before noon. Their official communication literally begged Schliemann to remove the mirth-provoking garments from the statues in order that business in Athens might return to normal. With great glee, Heinrich mounted to the roof, and in full sight of the crowd below, ostentatiously and dramatically removed each garment, waving it triumphantly before going on to the next statue.

Not long after, Heinrich himself attracted a crowd on University Street. Sophia, noticing that the servants were laughing to themselves and pointing toward the garden, looked out and saw Heinrich walking up and down, shading his head with a large Japanese paper parasol of brightly colored design, and carrying a red handkerchief with which he continually mopped his brow. She went right out to him and said that he was making himself a laughingstock and should not be seen in public with that red handkerchief and gay umbrella. She should have known better than to chide Heinrich about even so trivial a matter. He turned on his heel and walked through the bronze gates into University Street, where he paraded for some minutes, accumulating in his wake and at curbside a sizable group of gawkers. If Sophia sighed with relief when he returned to Iliou Mélathron, her feeling was premature. Heinrich mounted to the roof and paced up and down along the front balustrade, clearly visible to all who passed below.

Sophia and Heinrich engaged in a real battle of wits when he decided that her stomach upsets would be improved by a daily glass of wine, a beverage she did not enjoy. He promised that he would place a gold coin under her wineglass every day at lunch, and she might have the coin whenever the glass was drained. At table she would lift her wineglass and say, "Henry, look at that tree outside; I think it needs some attention." When he looked where she pointed, she would pour the wine into a pottery bowl she always had close beside her. As soon as he turned back, she put the empty glass on the table and continued to talk about the tree or whatever she used as ruse to distract him. After about four months of her feinting, he said to her, "Sophithion, do you not know that I am on to your little trick? I am certain that in your room you have a storehouse of gold coins and that some servant in the kitchen has a treasurehouse of a healthy stomach. Perhaps it is better that I just place the wine there without the gold coin."

Looking him straight in the eye, she answered, "My darling Henry, I think you should do whatever you wish to do." The next day the wineglass had no gold coin under it. Sophia did not drink the wine, and Heinrich made no comment. The second day and the third, the glass of wine was placed beside her without the coin. Heinrich observed, "You seem not to be as interested in the garden or fixing household matters, Sophithion." Unruffled, she answered, "Your attention to these things is so much greater during your stay at home that I have no comment to make." On the fourth day, no wine was served to Sophia.

Four months was about the longest continuous time that Heinrich was at home in any one year, and during such stays he devoted a great deal of time to the children. Like many another self-made man, he wanted the best for his children, and was a taskmaster about their education. He had a fetish about the waste of spoken words, which was peculiar for a man whose writing was so verbose. If the children called, "Please come upstairs," he would correct them, saying that "please come" would suffice.

He held that when one person was below or upstairs, the other would know which way to go without the extra word *down* or *up*.

At the completion of Heinrich's digs at Hissarlik in 1882 he had found a tiny kitten, straggly and wobbly, that was too small to feed from any utensil at the house on the Hill. Heinrich made containers for food and water from an orange that he cut in half, nailing each scooped-out half to a board; one half he filled with water, the other with gruel. Stroking the matted, filthy fur of the kitten, Schliemann held it down to the gruel, and dipping his finger into the liquid, put the finger into the kitten's mouth. A little tongue flicked around the finger and very soon was lapping up gruel and water from the orange halves. Growing stronger by the day, Djindjinata followed Schliemann everywhere; and when he sat at his desk, she settled on one corner of it, preening her fur until it shone pure white.

When Schliemann left for home he took Djindjinata along, and aboard ship decided it was time for his "little white cotton ball" to change her eating habits. The first night out, Schliemann put her food in a metal saucer instead of in the orange halves to which she was accustomed. She refused to eat, and plaintively mewing, rubbed against Schliemann's shoes. He walked to his cabin, shutting her out; but she cried so pitifully that he opened the door, and picking her up, took her back to the saucer. Talking to her gently, he pushed her face into the food, repeating the motion three times; ". . . my cotton ball looked at me first with an expression of disbelief, the second time glared balefully and the third, resignedly." Smug with his small success, Schliemann returned to his cabin, leaving the door open for Djindjinata; but she showed how irritated she was by sleeping just outside the open door, not inside the room with him as she had done at Hissarlik.

Heinrich was usually the center of attention at his homecomings, but on that one Djindjinata stole the show. Sophia, the servants and Andro, his adored little daughter Andromache, made a great fuss about the beautiful white kitten, the family's only pet for the next three years.

One morning Agamemnon—called Memeko by the family—who had repeatedly asked if he might have a dog, saw a small black one on the road from Phaleron. Heinrich, on horseback, was returning from his morning swim, and Memeko, seated behind, had his arms curved around his father's waist. Seeing the dog, Memeko asked Heinrich to stop and pick it up; but he refused, explaining that the dog probably belonged to some family living near by. The horse trotted on and the dog followed. Finally Heinrich agreed that he would take the dog if it trailed them for five more minutes. At the end of that time, which must have seemed like hours to the little boy, Heinrich swung Memeko to the ground. He touched the dog; it whimpered, wagged its tail, and licked Memeko's hand.

At home, everyone was excited about the coal-black puppy. But the pure-white Djindjinata recognized him as an enemy on several counts and sprang at him with claws out. Memeko, grabbing up his new pet, just did manage to keep him from being scratched. At breakfast Andro held the cat; Memeko, the dog. Schliemann had once told the children the story of Nero, called the black Emperor because he fiddled while Rome was burned to charred black ash; and remembering that thrilling tale, Memeko pleased his father by asking if the dog might be called Nero.

Not long after, Nero, struck by a carriage, suffered a broken left front leg, which Heinrich expertly set, using two pieces of wood for splints. Nero, hobbling while the bone knit, was much pampered and spoiled by the family. When Heinrich removed the splints from the leg that he knew was quite healed, Nero limped about, whimpering. Some hours later, Schliemann went out to the garden where Memeko was laughing at the antics of Nero, racing back and forth to retrieve a thrown stick. The dog slowed down and limped as soon as Schliemann appeared. Suspicious, he went back into the house, and peeking out, saw Nero playing again. Concealed from view, Schliemann called to Memeko; and Nero, hearing the voice, went into his lame act.

At lunch, Heinrich explained to the children that "animals, like people, must learn not to take advantage of those who protect and care for them. Together we shall teach him [Nero] a lesson in gratitude."

After their naps, Andro and Memeko went into the garden with their parents. Nero started to run to Memeko and then, seeing Schliemann, limped toward the group. Heinrich put new splints on Nero, but instead of placing them correctly, extended them a couple of inches below Nero's paw, making the left front leg longer than the other three. After tottering uncertainly for a few minutes, Nero slunk under some bushes, refusing to leave even when Memeko called. The little boy wanted his father to remove the splints after supper, but Heinrich said that they should wait for 24 hours. He deliberately spent most of the next day in the garden, reading, and in midafternoon Nero staggered up to him and raised the left paw. When Heinrich removed the splints, Nero bounded across the lawn, raced back, and looked up at Schliemann, who stared down at the dog.

One day when strolling with Andromache in the garden, he saw her break a full-blown flower from a plant. He sat down with her on a marble bench and said gently, "Andro, my little love, would you like to have someone cut off the fingers from your dear brother Memeko? Don't you know that when you cut a flower, it and the plant have the same kind of pain your brother would have if someone cut off his fingers?" This was the same Heinrich who once, in the Troad, had uprooted a poppy plant that he presented—root, stem and bloom—to Sophia. But unaware of his inconsistency, he continued to discuss what he termed the "biology of botany" with Andro, reiterating that flora have a sense of feel and, therefore, must experience pain. He never allowed Sophia to take cut flowers into the house, and barely tolerated any sent to her as a gift. Iliou Mélathron was beautified by flowers that were in profusion for every party, but the blooms burst from the stems of plants or the branches of flower bushes set in pots.

The Schliemanns' palace was an architectural and decorative showplace, but it was sparsely furnished with utilitarian tables and chairs. Heinrich had no use for curtains or draperies, for upholstered or overstuffed pieces that might be comfortable to relax in. The house was so bare that, in Heinrich's absence, Sophia and the children picnicked on the floors of various rooms. They dressed for a jaunt, and picnic hampers packed in the kitchen were delivered to them at the front door. From there, the three set out for whatever destination in the house they decided on as the place where they would "be seated low where we and the food can be spread out." The Acropolis was the second-floor gallery; the Queen's Garden was a back bedroom with windows overlooking the real garden.

One day Memeko, then seven, suggested that they picnic at the top of Mount Lycabettus. Sophia and Andro were puzzled. Which room could that be? With solemn face, Memeko led his mother and sister by a circuitous route to the stairway that led to the roof. Stopping at the top of the steps, Memeko, mimicking the voice of a boring friend of the family's, read a passage from Hesiod, the Homeric poet, painted on the wall to the right. Completing his recitation, the little boy beckoned to Sophia and Andro to follow him out onto the roof. There, he turned to the right, walked a few paces, and unrolled the picnic cloth. With a sweep of his chubby arm, he said, "To you, my ladies, I give Mount Lycabettus." The famous mountain towered beyond the roof.

Schliemann honestly thought that his family should live like ancient Greeks with the minimum of furnishings; his refusal to have luxurious furniture in his palace was a matter of principle. Had his point of view been different, he would have spent as he wished to obtain the luxuries he wanted.

He was at some times pinchpenny and at others spendthrift. A letter to Sophia from the Netherlands epitomized his niggardliness. On a visit there in 1875 he dined with Queen Sophia of Holland, who was so fascinated with his tales of adventure and excavation that she invited him to breakfast the following day, and that night gave a banquet to which dignitaries from her tiny kingdom were invited. In gratitude to Her Majesty, Schliemann offered to obtain a governess for her children, and to send her Greek statuettes. Writing to Sophia about how graciously he had been entertained, he asked that she select the statuettes, but cautioned her to "find very nice ones at a very low price. I can't pay much because I have to give them away."

This was the same Heinrich who sent his shirts and underthings from Athens to a laundry in London, by fast ship. At Troy he daily changed shirts and underwear, which, being second best, he entrusted to a Turkish washerwoman. But he could find in Athens no laundress who could properly wash and iron his best linens, so he shipped them to England. In his diary for March 1877, he wrote: "If I live in this country much longer, I shall have to stop my excavations because it is costing me so much to have my laundry done. Yet, I am happy to say that because of my constant shipment to England, the laundry person is making me a better offer because I threatened to stop sending my laundry. I'm hoping that my 218 shirts will be enough to last me throughout the year."

In his introduction to *Ilios, City and Country of the Trojans,* he gave an explicit financial statement in answer to critics who asserted he was squandering his entire fortune on excavations. "As on my last journey to England and Germany I have heard it repeatedly stated that, carried away by ambition, I am ruining myself in my archaeological explorations, to the prejudice of my children, who will be penniless after my death, I find it necessary to assure the reader that, although on account of my present scientific pursuits I am bound to keep aloof from all sorts of speculation and am compelled to content myself with a small interest on my capital, I still have a yearly income of 4,000 pounds as the net proceeds of the rents of my four houses in Paris, and 6,000 pounds interest on my funded property, making in all 10,000 pounds; whilst, inclusive of the large cost of my excavations, I do not spend more than 5,000 pounds a year, and am thus able to add 5,000 pounds annually to my capital. I trust, therefore, that on my death I shall leave each of my children a fortune large enough to enable them to continue their father's scientific exploration without ever touching their capital."

After Heinrich and Sophia had lived at Iliou Mélathron for seven years, he told her one day that he was pleased to have just purchased the most beautiful piece of land with a splendid view of Athens, Phaleron, and the Ilisis River. He explained that the land was so situated that the magnificent view could never be obstructed. When Sophia, probably shaken, asked when he was going to start to build their next new home, he answered that Tsiller would at once begin to work on the plans, adding, "I do not intend to build a house there, but to build our grave on this spot where always we shall lie together and know that the beautiful view of Athens is all around us."

TWENTY-FOUR

Archaeologists who studied the results of Schliemann's excavations at Troy and Mycenae arbitrarily gave the name Mycenaean to the ancient civilization that linked the great cities of Asia Minor, the Greek islands, and the Greek mainland. Schliemann, after searching the literature and history of ancient eras, thought that the Mycenaean civilization was widespread in Greece. To find confirming evidence in northern Greece, he went to Livadia, 28 miles west of the ancient city of Thebes on the Boeotian Plain, north of Athens.

He began his investigation of the historic terrain at the deep gorge of Hercyna, a steep V-shaped formation of impregnable rocks with a small river flowing under them. Niches for votive offerings were hewn from the stone, and high on one side of the gorge was the ancient Oracle of Trophonius, a legendary divinity. Pausanias wrote of two springs that flowed from the rocks into the river of the gorge: one spring was called Lethe (forgetfulness) and the other, Mnemosyne (remembrance). Both springs were symbolic of the Trophonian rites, the bad of the past forgotten and only happiness remembered. The cool gorge was used, during the four-hundred-year occupation of Greece by the Turks, as a retreat from the heat by governors of Livadia, who went into the small niches to smoke their *narghiles,* water pipes, in comfort.

Sophia, worried that Heinrich would not be well fed in that remote area, offered to send fruits from their garden and food from their kitchen. Assuring her that the fare was excellent, Heinrich asked if Sophia would join him there. She and the children, with their nursemaid, met him at Skripa, near Orchomenus, which in prehistoric times was the capital of the Minyas, powerful leaders of the Boeotian Plain. From that rich farmland the sons of Ares, Ascalaphos, and Ialmenos departed to join the Greek forces sailing to do battle at Troy. The Minyas were rich, fabled, and famous; and Heinrich, certain that their capital was another link in the great chain of Mycenaean cities, hoped to find evidence to support his theory.

He and Sophia, in the fall of 1880, tramped the countryside looking for suitable sites for digging. No major excavations had been made there, but extensive sections of the citadel's fortress walls were still standing. Nearby there was a ruined beehive tomb.

Schliemann had a number of shafts sunk around the tomb, and Sophia supervised a crew at one location. Heinrich excavated without success. Sophia, depending on techniques learned from him, reaped the reward of long experience. News of her discovery, printed first in the Athenian paper *Ephemeris* and then in the *London Builder,* appeared on January 16, 1881, in the *New York Times*:

> Dr. Schliemann and his wife have been staying in Skripa energetically searching for prehistoric sites at Orchomenus. Several shafts Dr. Schliemann sunk afforded little result. His wife, who has been conducting researches in another portion of the ground, has been fortunate enough to find what is believed to be the remains of the Treasury of the Minyas. On November 23, according to the newspaper *Ephemeris,* Frau Schliemann came upon a door and passage lying to the right of the Treasury, leading apparently to a tomb or chamber and barred with a stone tablet covered with beautiful reliefs. The Government Commissioner who is attached to the excavating party, writing of Frau Schliemann's discovery, stated, "The door opens into a fine passageway running in a northerly direction from the Treasury. At a distance of three meters, however, lies a large stone, which had fallen down from the roof and completely blocked the passageway. This stone is adorned with sculptured flowers, which may be taken as indicating that the decorated portion of the interior commenced here." The remains of the Treasury of the Minyas lie at the foot of Mount Acontion . . . .

The articles in all three newspapers stated that it was Sophia who made the major discovery of the inner tomb. But Heinrich, in his subsequent articles and books, was not as generous to his wife as he had previously been. Instead of crediting her with the discovery of the buried chambers of the Treasury of the Minyas, he gave the impression that it was he who had made the find at Orchomenus.

Portions of the beehive tomb had been destroyed in 1867 on instructions from the local governor, who wanted the stones for the construction of a chapel. There was enough of the original structure left to prove it had been a *dromos,* and Sophia's crew unearthed the entrance to the previously unknown second room that created great interest in archaeological circles. The unique chamber, cut from native rock, had been sunk from above like a shaft, its walls rising vertically, not curved. The ceiling had fallen in, probably shaken loose by a severe earthquake that had rocked the region in 1870. The Schliemanns had the ceiling slabs pieced together, restoring exquisite sculptured patterns of rosettes and spirals. The patterns were typically Mycenaean. The rosettes were like those on alabaster friezes at Troy and Mycenae; the interlacing spirals were almost identical with those on wall-paintings at Tiryns, which was subsequently excavated. Like the Treasury of Atreus, that of the Minyas consisted of a *dromos,* or vaulted chamber, with a square tomb adjacent to it.

While Sophia and Heinrich were occupied at the digs, the children were cared for by the nursemaid. Nine-year-old Andromache, accustomed to city life, was amazed by the simple play of the local children and upset by the primitive conditions in which they lived. She gathered a group of new friends, and taught them games and recited stories about Trojan heroes whose names were household words to her. Children from nearby villages first gawked at Andromache and Agamemnon, then became friends with the two youngsters from Athens whose parents were famous the world over. Sophia was amused when she overheard one child say to another, "The father of Andro knows people on the other side of Athens."

Sophia did not think it was funny, however, when Andromache told her little friends that the tomb her father was excavating was that of an ancient ancestor of her two-year-old brother, Agamemnon. According to the nursemaid, Andro embellished her story by recounting the history of Mycenae where her father had uncovered the grave of another of her brother's ancient ancestors, that one having fought in the Trojan War.

Andro, sternly reprimanded by her parents, was ordered to set the record straight. At the end of the next day she said, "I have done as you demanded." Apparently she managed to save face and to remain the leader of the playmates who joined her and Memeko at their games.

Throughout 1880, Schliemann and Virchow were in constant touch by letters containing expressions of their friendship; it was *Embistos philos,* which expresses the love, faith, and mutual trust of two superior people. There is no doubt that their friendship was of that caliber, but there is no question, either, that Virchow was concentrating on the acquisition of the Trojan collection for Germany.

Sophia talked often with Heinrich about the collection, and when he was away, wrote letters that indicated her agitation about the matter. She reminded him of the goodwill of the citizens of Greece, so unlike the attitude of the Greek officials. "You may think me selfish if you wish, my friend and husband. But is my love, my labor and devotion for nothing?" she asked. "Do foreigners who praise you, give you honors and fawn on you count for more than do I and the land of Homer and Greece, the country you freely chose to adopt as your own?"

Heinrich's vacillation caused her feelings to fluctuate. She wrote in one note: "Please assure me again, my beloved Henry, that the treasure will come to Athens"; and in another: "I received your cable from Brindisi which gave me great joy. I am wondering why you did not cable Virchow's answer. I think that the museum did not accept your offer [of the collection] and I am very happy about it . . . ." Sophia steadfastly tried to persuade Heinrich to give the collection to Greece, but when doubts about his decision nagged, she said, "I write no more on this matter, I fear I am talking in vain." As indeed she was.

She was no match for Virchow, who had on his side shrewdly planned emotional arguments, political power in Germany, and access to Prussians of high rank. Influence was essential because Schliemann was asking for many concessions in return for the gift of the Trojan collection to the German people. He wanted, in addition to personal honors such as membership in the Berlin Academy, the assurance that the Trojan collection would be cared for in perpetuity in a building constructed for the Schliemann Collection.

While Virchow schemed to obtain what Schliemann wanted, others accused him of making excessive demands. Ernst Boetticher, for one, stated publicly that the demands should not be met, dismissing as trivial the great collection by saying, "Why should these items be given space in our state museum?" Virchow immediately suggested to Schliemann that by giving the Trojan collection to Germany, he could forever silence his malicious adversary Boetticher.

Although a political opponent of Prince von Bismarck, Virchow willingly waited outside the Chancellor's office for an interview about the collection. In time, Virchow won Bismarck's approval of acceptance of the collection, as well as the Kaiser's. Other backers were Puttmacher, Minister of Public Education, and the director of the Staatliche Museum, a complex of exhibition buildings, a new one of which was to be named for Schliemann.

When the Kaiser issued a public letter accepting the Trojan collection, Sophia wept in her boudoir, but bravely smiled as she helped Heinrich pack the Trojan objects that were still in Athens. Large cases filled with finds from the last expedition to Troy were sent from a warehouse at the Dardanelles to Berlin. Going to London where the major part of the Trojan collection was on exhibit at the South Kensington Museum, Schliemann supervised the crating of the objects for shipment to Berlin.

TWENTY-FIVE

Heralded by royalty and hailed by the populace, the triumphant Schliemann arrived in Berlin to receive the greatest honor he was ever to know. It was headlined in the July 2, 1881, issue of the *Leipziger Illustrierte Zeitung,* which reported on a meeting of the Berlin Town Council: "The town-councillors of Berlin have approved with enthusiastic applause the motion of the municipal council to name Dr. Heinrich Schliemann honorary citizen of the capital city of the German Empire." That distinction had previously been accorded to only two men, both former opponents of Schliemann. One was Bismarck, who had refused Schliemann safe-conduct during the Franco–Prussian War; the other was the amateur archaeologist and German military hero, Field Marshal Helmuth Karl Bernhard von Moltke, who had championed Bunarbashi over Hissarlik as the probable site of Troy. The achievement of equal rank with Bismarck and von Moltke was a victory sweet to Schliemann who made no secret of his feelings.

Virchow obtained for Schliemann all but one of the honors he demanded in return for the gift of the Trojan collection to the German people. Only membership in the Berlin Academy was denied him, because the Academy's roster was limited to scholars of professorial rank in Berlin universities. Even Virchow, as he reminded Schliemann, was not a member of the Berlin Academy.

Schliemann's disappointment about the Academy was minimized on July 7, 1881, when he and Sophia stood in distinguished company in the mammoth drawing room of their suite in Berlin's Thiergarten Hotel. There, at 1 P.M., the Lord Mayor of Berlin, Forckenbeck, read the proclamation making Heinrich Schliemann an honorary citizen of Berlin. Royalty, prominent citizens, diplomats, and scholars were present, and Dr. Strabmann, president of the City Council, thanked Dr. Schliemann for giving the treasures from Troy to Berlin. Heinrich held the certificate of honorary citizenship in his hand while he briefly spoke to the assembly, which broke into wild cheers when he finished. Heinrich and Sophia, tightly holding hands in support of each other, smiled through happy tears and acknowledged the plaudit.

Forty-three years had elapsed since the fourteen-year-old Heinrich, leaving school, had apprenticed himself to a village grocer; thirty-six years, since he had become the corresponding clerk and bookkeeper for Messrs. B. H. Schröder and Company in Amsterdam, before serving as their Russian representative; and thirty-five years since he had set himself up in business in St. Petersburg, where his first great fortune was made. Eleven years before that momentous occasion in Berlin, he had sunk the first spade into the Hill of Hissarlik, beginning then his second career, that of archaeologist devoted to the resurrection of ancient civilizations.

With a sense of destiny, Schliemann always recorded his feelings; and he wrote, after that day, that during the ovation the years swept over him.

"Today the road I trod seems short. Yet, in another manner it appears long. My emotions are mixed. I am at this moment uncertain of fact, time and sequence, because my very soul is elevated. Yet, of one thing I am sure—today is not the end, it is a beginning because the years of productive scholarship ahead of me are many and varied. Perhaps today is but a semi-colon of a paragraph in my life. Yes, I know this is true and it sustains me through the turmoil of today's events."

The reception for the distinguished honorary citizen and Frau Schliemann was lavish. Wine flowed freely, and toasts rang through the great hall. Bouquets by the dozens were presented to Sophia, and, in the continental custom, sheafs of flowers were given to Heinrich, too. Bewhiskered gentlemen with medals lined across their chests bowed low over Sophia's hand and congratulated Schliemann. Full-blown matrons, bedecked with diamonds, were presented by their husbands to Heinrich, and made small talk with Sophia. In that brilliant company two elderly ladies were conspicuous by their frumpishness; they were Heinrich's sisters. Dressed in the dowdy clothes of provincials, they watched every move made by their Greek sister-in-law and their brother, whose guests they were for the day never to be forgotten.

After the reception Heinrich and Sophia, laden with flowers, retired to their suite. There for more than an hour of silence, they held hands or embraced, alternately calm and tearful. Sophia was torn by conflicting emotions, being proud for Heinrich but still sad that her country was not to have the glorious Trojan collection. At last she spoke, and her words reflected her inner sorrow. "My devoted Henry, you did what was best in your own mind and what is best in your mind is right, for it was you who labored to make your boyhood dream come true."

Heinrich put his fingers to her lips. "My little darling, without you this day would not be. Rejoice not for me, but for yourself because together we shall be remembered in history for centuries after our bodies lie together in death and our souls joined in what hereafter has been planned by God for mortals."

They parted finally to get ready for the evening's banquet, Sophia to be dressed by her little maid, and Heinrich attended by his valet. When Sophia stood before Heinrich, he admired her as he had on the night, so long before, when they had given their great ball at 6, Place St. Michel. As always, Sophia's intelligence and beauty shone inseparably. Placing a flowing evening wrap around her shoulders, Heinrich kissed her, and they went down to the carriage waiting to take them to Berlin's Rathaus.

The mall before the city hall was thronged with curious Berliners gathered to watch the arrival of the famous couple whose every movement was publicized in the daily papers. Loud cheers from the crowd gave Heinrich his customary bit-bumps and again made tears well in Sophia's eyes. Rudolph Virchow and other dignitaries were the official welcomers. When he handed Sophia down from the carriage, Virchow kissed her and looked deep into her eyes, as if seeing her soul. Softly he said, "My friend and great lady, I understand. But always remember, Heinrich has done what is right." Tears flowing, Sophia squeezed Virchow's hand. He did understand the torment and happiness within her.

The party moved up the steps of the Rathaus, through the entrance, down a corridor to the door of the banquet hall. At nine o'clock exactly, Sophia stood at the entrance with Heinrich a few paces behind. Guests rose from their chairs and made the room vibrate with their cheers. Heinrich moved to Sophia's side, putting his left arm around her shoulder and, with his right hand, grasping her left one extended across her bosom. They stood regally, surveying the hall transformed into a flower bower by myriads of blossoms that perfumed the air; the kaleidoscope of flower petals was accented by the green oak wreaths that spiraled each column of the tremendous hall.

When the cheering died away, musicians from the Royal Berlin Orchestra played the triumphal march from *Tannhauser*. Sophia, on the arm of Forckenbeck, the Lord Mayor of Berlin, moved into the room; Heinrich followed at the side of Dr. Strabmann, President of the City Council. As the honored guests and dignitaries moved toward the head table, cheers could be heard above the music. Present as guests were the Minister of State; Hanseatic Resident-Minister Krüger; Chief Administrative Privy Councillor Rösing; Privy Councillor of the German Archives, Dr. Gollmert; the President of the German Geographic Society, Dr. Nachtigal; the General Manager of the Royal Museum, Dr. Schöne; as well as the President of the University of Berlin and prestigious professors.

After the long and elaborate banquet, congratulatory messages were read. Gracious greetings were sent by the Kaiser; his son the Crown Prince, later to be Kaiser Wilhelm II; and the Count von Bismarck. Schliemann must have been disappointed that those three were not present, but according to the official German archives and newspapers of the day, there were good reasons for their respective absences. The Kaiser was ill in Coblenz; Crown Prince Wilhelm was on a mission in southern Germany; and Bismarck was taking the cure in Bad Kissingen, where he had frequently encountered Heinrich and Sophia.

The major address of the evening was delivered by Virchow, and the newspaper account stated:

> With spirited words of welcome to the newest honorary citizen of Berlin and his wife, Virchow praised Heinrich's great academic accomplishments and described how Schliemann, who had been out of his native Germany for 40 years, was reawakened by a love of fatherland, and how out of this reawakened love came Schliemann's decision to give the overly-rich results of his discoveries to the fatherland and to make Berlin the guardian of his treasures. These treasures shall reside for all time in our city as a monument to Dr. Schliemann's devotion to fatherland and science.

Schliemann made a gracious acceptance of the honor and

praise bestowed on him. Very briefly he described the poor conditions under which he had worked while gathering the collection, and the privations he and Frau Schliemann had suffered. He said frankly that he had been convinced by Professor Virchow to give the finds to Germany "where they shall remain forever." He spoke eloquently of the joy of discovery and satisfaction of contributions.

Replying to Schliemann, Dr. Schöne proposed a toast to the new honorary citizen and his wife, addressing her also as honorary citizen. At that, the guests rose and let out a deafening roar that reverberated through the corridors of the Rathaus. Virchow proposed toasts and cheers to His Majesty the Emperor and King, and when the three cheers echoed into silence, the orchestra played the national anthem.

As Heinrich was leaving the Rathaus, he paused to speak to an alert and handsome young man he had only recently met, Wilhelm Dörpfeld. They shook hands and Heinrich went down to the carriage where Sophia, waiting, was animatedly chatting with admirers crowding around her. The carriage rolled toward the hotel, and Heinrich told Sophia that he expected to return soon to Troy with Dörpfeld. She was stunned. It had not occurred to her that Heinrich would do more excavating so soon at Troy. Heinrich explained that much could be done with the aid of the competent and experienced Dörpfeld, who "I know will carry our work to unprecedented heights. He impressed me and I have faith in him."

TWENTY-SIX

A divergent cast of characters was assembled to play out the drama at the digs of Troy in the spring of 1882. There were scholars and muscle-men; house servants and workmen; a traitor and a faithful; a corps of newspaper reporters; and, offstage, two nonsensical Turkish officials.

Schliemann had obtained a *firman* through the intercession of Bismarck, and the services of Dr. Wilhelm Dörpfeld through personal persuasion. Continuing with a policy of teamwork, Schliemann depended on the assistance of men with background in architecture such as Joseph Höfler of Vienna, and Dörpfeld. Dörpfeld's academic record was brilliant, and his experience included four years with the architectural division of a group excavating at Olympia, site of the ancient Olympic games.

Yannakis, the oldtimer of Troy, secure in his indispensability, chose that spring to demand a substantial pay increase. And as always, he had his keep and the informal franchise to sell tobacco, bread and brandy to the day laborers. Below him in the echelon were three overseers. One was an ineffectual nepotic appointee, Gustav Battus, the son of a former French consul at the Dardanelles. The other two were Gregorios Basilopoulos and Gregorios Paraskevopoulos, whose names Schliemann could not be bothered to remember. As usual, he gave them Homeric names, respectively Ilio and Laomedon. The latter had herculean strength and a gigantic frame with muscles that bulged beneath his tight shirt.

Brigandage, under control in Greece, was on the upswing in Asia Minor where incidents of mayhem and bloodshed were common. At Schliemann's request, Hamid Pasha, civil governor of the Dardanelles, sent to Hissarlik eleven trustworthy gendarmes armed with rifles, pistols and daggers; the *shaush,* or sergeant, of the detachment was assigned to twenty-four-hour duty by Schliemann. Three of the other ten always accompanied him on his predawn ride to the Hellespont for a swim.

The house on the Hill of Hissarlik was staffed by Heinrich's valet, Oedipus Pyromalles, and a cook, Jocasta. Food was in good supply that year, and in addition to edibles available from the Troad and the Dardanelles, Schliemann imported, from England, corned beef packed in Chicago; peaches, fine cheese, ox-tongues, and 240 bottles of pale ale. "I was the sole consumer of these 240 bottles of pale ale, which lasted me for five months. I used it as medicine to cure constipation from which I had suffered for at least 30 years, and which has been aggravated by all other medicines, and particularly by the mineral waters of Carlsbad. The ale cured my ailment."

Sophia, never one to be fooled by Heinrich, commented: "My father, too, a true Athenian *gagaris,* had his own special kind of drink which he assured my mother was purely medicinal. I seem to recall that on our last trip to take the cure at Carlsbad, my friend Henry extolled most highly the virtues of the mineral water. Perhaps Henry has some special reason for needing this ale at Troja. Who knows?"

He indeed had a reason, by name Beder Eddin Effendi, one of two men delegated by the Turkish government to watch over Schliemann "for what reason, I cannot imagine." Beder Eddin was in constant conflict with Dörpfeld, Höfler and Schliemann, who wrote: "I have done archaeological work in Turkey for many years, but I have never had the bad fortune to have such a monster as Beder Eddin whose arrogance and conceit were equalled only by his total ignorance. He considered that his only job was to place every obstacle in my way."

Early on, in spite of Beder Eddin, operations progressed well with 150 workmen supplied with adequate equipment: 40 iron crowbars, 2 jacks, 100 large shovels, 120 pickaxes, a windlass, 104 wheelbarrows with iron wheels, and 20 man-carts.

Full-scale work began on March 1, and crews uncovered several large complexes of buildings in Troy II, the second city above the native rock. Dörpfeld and Schliemann eventually proved, by comparison of those buildings with structures they excavated elsewhere, that they had found the main rooms of the palace of an ancient chief. Working with Höfler that spring, they made precise measurements of walls, houses and temples, finding many pieces of pottery, gold, silver and other metals. No one object was spectacular, but the finds helped to fit together the great puzzle of the Homeric Troy and other Trojan cities, a jig-saw not completed until many years after Schliemann's death. The study and exploration was one of Schliemann's most important, but it did not provide the dramatic story hoped for by journalists at the Dardanelles, close enough to be on the scene if another great find was made at Hissarlik. Every few days, perspiring reporters made the trip from the Dardanelles to observe what was being done at Troy and to get a progress report from Schliemann. Their assignment was not an easy one: they suffered from boredom and the intense heat. Even Heinrich said that the heat was worse than any yet experienced at the mound. He hired an extra laborer and a small boy as water crew; the man filled kegs with spring water, and the boy poured it into smaller barrels that were taken to the trenches where men with parched throats quenched their thirst. The reporters of world-wide press services splashed water over their heads before starting back to the Dardanelles, usually without a line of notes for an article.

One morning the correspondents were gathered for a press conference when Yannakis handed Schliemann a telegram from Athens:

> CHAMBER OF DEPUTIES BURNED LAST NIGHT. THE ONLY DEPUTY NOT SAVED WAS VALASSOPOULOS.
>
> SOPHIA

Heinrich, at first shocked, suddenly smiled, and seemed to be patently pleased. Dörpfeld, Höfler, and the reporters were amazed at Heinrich's reaction to the death of Valassopoulos, even though he had been the eagle who daily tore at Schliemann's vitals, the adversary who had thwarted Schliemann's every attempt to begin excavations in Greece. Reporters, provided with a story at last, rushed for the Dardanelles to add their own anecdote to the fire story, which they assumed their press services already had in Athens. One story was much like another, commenting on Dr. Schliemann's reactions to the reported death of Valassopoulos as seeming quite immoral, unfeeling and inhuman.

The next morning the full complement of journalists head-quartered at the Dardanelles descended on Hissarlik, loudly demanding to know why Schliemann had tricked them with the story of a fire that had not happened. Schliemann, amazed, said that he knew no more than they; then suddenly he asked, "What date is today?" When told, he excused himself, and rushing into his house, snatched up the telegram and dashed back to the waiting newsmen. He flourished the telegram, shouting, "Look! Look! My too-smart Sophaki has beaten me again. Yesterday was the Day of the Fools, the first day of April." The disgruntled correspondents had to accept his explanation that he and they had fallen for an April Fools' joke. But knowing him as serious and testy, they found it difficult to credit him with a sense of fun. His pixy sense of humor and his gay pranks were rarely revealed to any but intimates.

The behind-the-scenes trickery of Beder Eddin, the Turkish overseer, and the elusory tactics to which Schliemann, Dörpfeld and Höfler resorted had cloak-and-dagger overtones. Deviously, Beder Eddin won the allegiance of the ten gendarmes and the top sergeant, secretly meeting first with one, then having an open conference with two more, and at last holding a nighttime conclave with all eleven in a deep trench. In mutiny after that clandestine meeting, members of the detachment told Schliemann that thereafter they would take orders only from Beder Eddin. He finally succeeded in cowing two of Schliemann's overseers and subverting even Jocasta in her kitchen.

Heinrich had not even suggested that Sophia go with him to Troy for that season, and she took the children to Paris, then to Germany and Italy before returning to their home in Athens.

Heinrich missed Sophia's soothing presence but understood that her place was with the children. Had she been with Heinrich in Asia Minor, she might have spared him some of the harassment by Beder Eddin, who was by nature a troublemaker. As official delegate of the Turkish government, Beder Eddin had the telegraph facilities at his disposal, and sent off wires denouncing Schliemann, Dörpfeld, Höfler and Battus. When Dörpfeld imported a surveying instrument, Beder Eddin reported directly to Djemal Pasha, military governor of the Dardanelles, that Dörpfeld and Schliemann were using the excavations at Hissarlik as reconnaissance site for drawing plans of the military fort at Koum-Kale. Djemal Pasha, accepting the lie, passed it on as truth to Said Pasha, the Grand Master of the Artillery at Constantinople. He, also gullible, sent word to Hissarlik that Schliemann must neither use the surveying instrument nor draw any kind of plans on paper. He and Dörpfeld and Höfler were confounded when the smirking Beder Eddin relayed to them the message that threatened the success of their archaeological investigation.

The situation became insupportable. Not only did Eddin order guards to watch the three scholars every minute, but since he could not tell the difference between sketches of Troy and detailed designs of fortifications, he also secured permission to restrain the investigators from writing anything on paper. At first challenged by the restriction, Schliemann, Dörpfeld, and Höfler clandestinely made notes and sketches, outwitting the wily Turks right in the digs; and at night, safe inside their house, they drew from memory the plans of walls, houses, temples and streets.

The delaying action irked Schliemann, who applied for redress to the German Embassy at Constantinople, setting off another ridiculous chain of events, which would have been hilarious had the consequences not been so serious. Ambassador Baron von Hirschfeld and his aide, Baron von Testa, sought surcease from the Grand Vizier, who refused to listen to the German diplomats because his Grand Master of Artillery had not seen fit to inform him about the situation at Hissarlik. The Grand Master of Artillery, considering himself to be ultimate authority, refused to discuss the matter with the Grand Vizier.

The stalemate strengthened the position of Beder Eddin, and the vexations at the digs continued until work was stopped at the end of July. Schliemann arranged with Dörpfeld to return in the fall for the resumption of operations, particularly for the continuance of his vital drawings of the various levels of Trojan cities.

By late August, Schliemann had assurance that he would be free to work as he pleased when the digs were reopened. Bismarck again had been in touch with Turkish ministers who had agreed to a relaxation of the rules on the drawing of plans. Then the German diplomat von Radowitz, a devoted friend to Schliemann, was made Ambassador to Turkey. Going over the heads of Turkish officials in Constantinople, Ambassador von Radowitz went directly to His Majesty the Sultan to ask that Schliemann be accorded the consideration that was his due. The Ambassador and the Sultan were both men of intelligence and cultivation, and their meeting resulted in brief dispatches to Hissarlik that peremptorily removed the offensive Beder Eddin Effendi from his post, and gave the archaeologists permission to proceed with the operations without restrictions.

Throughout the harassments of the spring and early summer of 1882, Heinrich had written daily letters to Sophia, keeping her informed about the work and the persecution by the Turkish delegate. She laughed about Heinrich's predicament but, aware that it was humorous only to her, far from the scene of physical suffering and mental torture, she felt pity for her husband. Atlhough he did not need food packages, she sent him fruits and little delicacies she knew he particularly enjoyed. That year her letters to him were filled with the bright and funny doings of their children; Heinrich's letters to her were often gloomy and weighty tomes, but for a change he did not berate her or write a single sharp or unpleasant personal comment.

Schliemann wrote letters to editors of periodicals and journals, presenting new evidence about the excavations resulting from the season's study. After spending long hours in discussions with Dörpfeld about the Trojan cities, Schliemann came to the realistic conclusion that many of his previous interpretations had been quite wrong. He admitted his mistakes in letters for publication and in the 1883 manuscript of *Troja,* the book written about his work at Troy with Dörpfeld. Schliemann's detractors, who pointed to his corrections as signs of his ignorance and instability, might instead have conceded that only a great man publicly acknowledges his errors.

TWENTY-SEVEN

On a June morning in 1883, Heinrich and Sophia sat in a carriage that pulled up in front of a rambling old house in the village of Ankershagen in Mecklenburg. Without waiting for Sophia to help their two children out of the carriage, Schliemann stepped down and walked rapidly toward the entrance, hardly pausing to greet those gathered to welcome him. With his eyes searching out every detail of the garden and building, he strode up to the door and entered the parsonage where his early childhood was spent. The elderly romantic was making a pilgrimage to the scene where his lively imagination had first envisioned the wonders of archaeological exploration.

Having achieved the goal set in childhood, Schliemann increasingly felt the urge to return to the place where his dream had taken shape. Whatever the reason that had so long delayed the sentimental journey of reunion, extensive correspondence had preceded its realization. In advance, he had made known what people from his past he wished to have call on him when he was established with his family at the parsonage.

The four of them were welcomed by the incumbent clergyman, who had willingly accepted a generous rental fee for the parsonage. The pastor and his wife, housed with parishioners for the month of the Schliemanns' stay, made certain that Sophia and Heinrich were comfortable in their quarters, while neighborhood children shyly gathered outside to take the measure of the dark-haired girl and fair-haired boy from the distant land of Greece. Andromache and Agamemnon spoke such fluent German that they were soon friends with the local youngsters, and laughter rang out as the group played happily in the garden. Curious grownups of Ankershagen, including some who had never known Schliemann, called at the parsonage to pay their respects to the distinguished visitor and the elegant wife so many years his junior.

Sophia, relaxed and gracious, charmed the German relatives

and friends about whom she had heard throughout her married life. She ambled with her husband through the woodland surrounding the village, and strolled with her children in deep pastures where cows grazed. It pleased her to see her husband happy with old friends, reminiscing around a dining table bountifully piled with rich food, much of it strange to her. If the vacation was not her ideal, she dissembled well, and seemed neither bored nor restless.

From the moment of arrival, Schliemann was in high spirits, vigorously directing activities at the parsonage. He was courteous to the casual visitors, and enthusiastic in his reception to those who had for so long enriched his memories. One of these was Neiderhöffer, from whom the young Heinrich had heard his first words of Greek, a thrill that had vividly remained with Schliemann from a time of teen-age trial to his adult triumphs.

In the nearly five decades from that evening until the visit at Ankershagen, Schliemann had sporadically written to Niederhöffer, and knew that he was reformed through a happy marriage. At a brief meeting of the two men during a trip to Germany, Schliemann discovered that Niederhöffer has "forgotten neither his Homer nor his Virgil, and still declaims them with the same warm enthusiasm as he did forty-three years ago in the shop at Fürstenberg." In the parlor of the parsonage at Ankershagen, it must have been Schliemann's recitation of Homer that thrilled Niederhöffer, the septuagenarian. He may have been overcome by Schliemann's erudition, because by 1883 Heinrich was using almost exclusively his own form of Homeric Greek. It was a complex adaptation and intrepretation that, when spoken, was hard for purists to understand.

An even older friend from the past was Carl Andres, librarian of the Grand-ducal library and keeper of the Museum of Neu Strelitz, who paid Schliemann a visit. At the age of ten, Heinrich "had the good fortune of having candidate Carl Andres from Neu Strelitz as teacher; and the progress I made under this excellent philologist was so great that, at Christmas 1832, I was able to present my father with a badly written Latin essay upon the principal events of the Trojan War and the adventures of Ulysses and Agamemnon." Through the years, Andres and Schliemann also had been correspondents, with Andres contributing his knowledge of languages to classical interpretations and inscriptions about which Schliemann inquired, after he began his excavations.

Numerous doddering old men, gay blades at the time of Schliemann's childhood, tentatively approached the great personage returned to their community. Encouraged by his friendliness, one of these invited Schliemann for a walk to see something that he might have forgotten. They followed the country road, rutted by the wheels of oxcarts, and at the edge of a woods, the older man beckoned for Schliemann to follow him across rough ground. Stopping a few feet inside the grove, the man pointed to a beech tree on which Schliemann saw the carved initials H.S.

While he may or may not have remembered the location of his personal graffito, it was hardly surprising to find it in the woodland that he frequented as a small boy searching for proof of the legends of the area.

Heinrich had suffered a sad separation from his childhood sweetheart, Minna Meincke, when his father's indiscretions created a scandal in Ankershagen. They met briefly five years later when both were fourteen, and Schliemann's account of that emotional event concluded with the dramatic sentence, "I only implored God that she might not marry before I attained an independent position."

But Minna Meincke married a farmer Richers of Friedland in Mecklenburg in 1846, at the very time when Schliemann, having gained a sufficient fortune to afford a wife, was making overtures to her family through a mutual friend.

In his diary and again in his autobiography, Schliemann recorded the unbearable shock of learning that Minna was married to another. He was so sickened that he had to take to his bed, and was unable to carry on his work for some while. He long mourned for Minna, and only time "which heals all wounds, healed mine." But the passage of years did not dim his memory of his childhood sweetheart, or of their shared dreams and plans, and her visit to Ankershagen, in 1883, was eagerly anticipated.

Only a man with Schliemann's capacity for sustaining romance could have survived the reunion without disillusionment. Minna, remembered from their last meeting as a fourteen-year-old of fascinating beauty, had become a typical *hausfrau,* solid of build and stolid of mien. Schliemann, apparently oblivious to the physical changes wrought by forty-eight years, led her from her carriage into the garden, playground of their childhood. With his curious rolling gait, he moved along the pathways over which he had toddled and skipped as a boy, leading an almost reluctant old lady who walked heavily in his wake. He proudly introduced Minna to Sophia and their children, and insisted on a tour of the inside of the parsonage, where he carried on a lively reminiscence.

It was clear to all but Heinrich that Minna did not share his enthusiastic remembrance of their young days at Ankershagen. His imagination, vivid enough to project the tales of Homer onto excavations of the 19th century, was more than adequate for recapturing memories of just over half a century. With the assurance so typical of him, he seemed not to notice that the meeting with Minna was not mutually rewarding. He willed the realization to be as high as his expectations.

TWENTY-EIGHT

Schliemann and Dörpfeld fortunately encountered no red-tape restrictions when, late in 1883, they applied for a permit to dig at Tiryns, not far from Mycenae in the Peloponnesus. Schliemann had briefly explored the citadel of an ancient fortress at Tiryns in 1876, and was impatient to start a major excavation at the site with Dörpfeld. A newly appointed Greek Minister of Education, M. Boulpiotes, promptly granted official permission for the project, and Dörpfeld realistically scheduled work to begin in March 1884. Eager to start excavation and loath to sit idle for the intervening weeks, Heinrich planned a series of day trips with Sophia.

One, in February, was to Marathon, which they had visited not long before the ill-fated party that had lost four members in the Dilessi affair. Sophia and Heinrich wandered around the Soros, the *tumulus,* popularly called the Mound of the Dead. Turning away from the breathtaking view of the sandy plain below and the Aegean beyond, Sophia looked questioningly at a coin that Heinrich was absent-mindedly flipping. Seeing her interest, Heinrich gave her the ancient coin, struck after the Battle of Marathon as a reminder to Athenians that the Spartans had refused to march to their aid because it was not yet the time of the full moon. A large owl, symbolic of Athena, dominated the coin's design; to the left of the owl there was a half-moon representing the perfidy of the Spartans, and above the moon was an olive twig signifying the Athenian victory. Thousands of Persians lay dead on the plain after the battle in which only 192 men of Athens were killed.

Sophia and Heinrich wondered whether those 192 heroes of Marathon were buried in the Mound of the Dead, as legend had it. After his return to Athens, Heinrich kept talking about the Soros, and, finally, after a few weeks of cogitation decided that he must find out what was beneath the soil of the mound. He and

Sophia went back to Marathon with work crews and dug into the Mound of the Dead. Although they uncovered no bones or skeletal remains of any kind, the story of the mass burial persisted.

Sophia's work at Marathon was her last major and active participation at a dig with Heinrich. It was important for the family that she be attentive mother. Agamemnon, at six, was an energetic and extremely bright little boy who needed maternal supervision. Andromache, at thirteen, was involved with her studies at school and the parties and diversions enjoyed by Athenian girls of her social group. Sophia remained in Athens with her children. During school holidays she traveled with them, often to European watering places where she took cures for her recurring abdominal upsets.

The pattern of their life did not please either of the Schliemanns, who had no choice but to adjust to it. They kept in constant touch through detailed letters about their respective activities. Heinrich spent sporadic periods at Iliou Mélathron, and Sophia made infrequent visits to his excavations. She went with him to survey the ancient site at Crete, returned to Troy, and inspected the digs at Tiryns.

Schliemann and Dörpfeld began their excavations at Tiryns on March 17, 1884, and soon after uncovered a portion of a magnificent mosaiclike floor of crushed limestone and colored pebbles that paved the entire high plateau of the Acropolis. The debris yielded various kinds of objects. One of the many animal-shaped items was a dog standing on a disk of clay. A piece of clay in the form of an ear with a pierced lobe was so large and so obviously masculine that Schliemann wondered if men of that ancient civilization might not have worn earrings.

A number of objects found at Tiryns had a relationship or distinct similarity to others already unearthed at Troy and Mycenae. But a wheel-shaped disk from the Tiryns debris was unique: it had jagged edges pointing counterclockwise with one off-center hole. Similar objects were later excavated at other sites, and proved to be similar to the *ex votos* found at Troy and Mycenae.

Wall paintings, some depicting acrobats leaping over the backs of bulls, lined the passageway through rough-hewn rocks at Tiryns; the same motifs were subsequently excavated at Crete.

Other wall decorations at Tiryns resembled some from Troy and Orchomenus, and still others could be linked to Mycenae. Painted idols and vases were decorated like many found in Asia Minor and on the Boeotian Plain. Painstakingly, Schliemann and Dörpfeld amassed evidence of exchange and relationship between ancient Mycenaean cities; and Dörpfeld proved a close connection by comparing the plans of the city of Tiryns, its individual houses and their rooms, with maps and plans of other Mycenaean sites.

Members of the press corps that trailed Schliemann, bored with the slow progress at Tiryns and by the meticulous comparative studies, one by one left the Argolid. The *New York Times* correspondent wrote: "Schliemann's luck has run out. He has found no more gold, nor things of any value." That reporter was just as wrong as other journalists who popularized Schliemann's gold finds, while minimizing his contributions that far outshone the glittering treasure. The newspaper reporters who forsook Schliemann at Tiryns missed the big story: The ground plan of the palace at Tiryns was found almost intact, and its long central hall, the vestibule, and large circular hearth were exactly the same as those uncovered in the great palaces at Troy and Mycenae. It was well established by the time Schliemann and Dörpfeld excavated at Tiryns that such a building was not a temple, as Schliemann had first thought, but the palace of the king. The discovery of the third identical palace established Schliemann as the guide to the Mycenaean civilization, a prehistoric period that in many ways was more powerful than the better known and less ancient classical age.

As participant with Dörpfeld in resurrecting the past at Tiryns, Schliemann was "bothered constantly and heightened emotionally each hour of every day. The bit-bumps on my entire body give evidence of my soul's reaction to our work here." A new Schliemann continued to emerge from the written page. He had seldom previously used the term *our work,* except occasionally to include Sophia; but increasingly from Troy in 1882, he included not only Dörpfeld but also others to whom he gave credit, admitting that he could not have accomplished certain objectives without their "physical assistance, mental agility and incisive scientific approach to our work at Troy and Tiryns."

Early in his book on Tiryns, Schliemann expressed his regrets that for the first time in more than twenty years, he was starting an excavation without the assistance of Nicholas Saphiros Yannakis, faithful friend, comptroller of the household and cashier at the digs. In the summer of 1883 Yannakis and his family broke a wild horse that was so fractious it snapped its rope three days in a row and was caught only after strenuous chases. Finally the horse let Yannakis mount him; and after the horse had been quiet for two days, Yannakis, with his son Hector behind him, rode across the Plain of Troy. At a crossing of the Scamander River, a wind-blown tree limb whipped across the horse's face, and he reared, throwing father and son into the river. Neither could swim, but the son, light in weight, managed to hold onto the reins and pull himself to the bank. Yannakis, wearing the pantaloons of his native Tsamak Kale, sank in the deep water and drowned. When peasants pulled his lifeless body to shore, his pants were ballooned with water. Sophia sent for Yannakis' family, and his wife remained in Athens with the Schliemanns for years after.

Schliemann did not, as previously, rush into print with the results of the excavations at Tiryns, but waited until Dörpfeld had completed his detailed architectural studies. In *Tiryns,* published in 1885, Schliemann highly praised Dörpfeld, who contributed chapters on architecture to the book.

Restless again after the work at Tiryns was completed, Schliemann went to Crete with Dörpfeld, tramping near Knossos where partial ruins of an ancient palace were exposed. Having visited the site several times over a period of years, Schliemann was thoroughly convinced that the ruins were of the palace of the famous King Minos whose island empire had once controlled the seas and the Greek mainland.

Certain that the excavator at Knossos would uncover another center of Mycenaean civilization, Schliemann negotiated with a peasant who owned the land. They reached an agreement on a price that included 2,500 olive trees in the man's grove; Schliemann, somehow suspicious, counted the trees that numbered only 889. Unfortunately, his business sense for once overruled his archaeological judgment, and he left Crete. Sir Arthur Evans later acquired the land and, like Schliemann, using his own fortune for excavation, uncovered the palace that did link Knossos with the prehistoric cities of the mainland.

After Schliemann gave up his plans for excavation at Crete, he turned his attention to Egypt, making two trips to that country—one by himself in 1887, another with Virchow in 1888. Schliemann visited Flinders Petrie, the famed British archaeologist who helped reveal the life, history and art of ancient Egypt. Sailing in regal luxury along the Nile, Schliemann viewed the famous sites then known, and wrote to Sophia that he wished he might remain long enough to see the total emergence of the giant Sphinx "which raises itself from the sands."

On the 1888 trip with Virchow, Schliemann told his old friend in strictest confidence about a bizarre pilgrimage that began when Schliemann committed the Koran to memory in one month. He had long been curious about the Muslim religion and the ceremony of purification, and decided to experience a pilgrimage to Mecca. In Arabia, he was secretly circumcised, a precaution taken in case he was suspected of being an infidel and made to strip. After circumcision, he went to a secluded spot where he bathed nude three times a day, firm in his conviction that sea water possessed all curative minerals; his phallic surgery healed in five days.

His face was already bronzed by wind and sun, but he lay naked under the Arabian sun to darken his body and balding head. When he decided that he could deceive the faithful and the priests of Mohammed, Schliemann donned the white robe of a penitent and proceeded to Mecca.

Sun poured down on the bazaar as throngs of natives and pilgrims mingled outside Mohammed's holy mosque *Haram.* As a simple, unpretentious suppliant, Schliemann passed unnoticed in the stream of people. Nothing in his appearance, manner or movement distinguished him from the faithful.

Carried along with the crowd, he entered the Kaaba, the holiest of holies, with the black stone of Mohammed in the center. After receiving the supreme blessing for priests, he moved to each of the four corners for silent prayer. Concluding his prayers, he moved back to the black stone and pledged his allegiance to the Muslim faith. While priests again chanted, Schliemann's eyes darted from side to side, seeing all, missing nothing.

He lingered, stood back to let others be the first at the *Zamzam* Well and to be anointed there with its holy water that would cleanse the soul and cure the body. Head bowed, he too bent for his anointing. As the last tones of the Mussulman chant for the pilgrims echoed into silence, Schliemann moved out of the mosque and on into the glaring sun of the bazaar. Inconspicuous in the mass of humanity, he disappeared.

Schliemann did not write of his exploit, either privately or publicly, for fear of retaliation against him and perhaps against members of his family. That Schliemann could on rare occasions be discreet was evidenced by the fact that he never told how the Trojan collection was spirited out of Turkey, or confirmed the date on which the great treasure was excavated at Hissarlik, or wrote about what Muslims would consider his sacrilegious pilgrimage to Mecca.

(COURTESY: ALEX L. MÉLAS)

Illustrirte
Frauen-Zeitung.
Ausgabe der „Modenwelt" mit Unterhaltungsblatt.
Nr. 18. Zweites Blatt.
Berlin, 13. September 1880.
VII. Jahrgang.
Sophie Schliemann

(FREE UNIVERSITY, WEST BERLIN)

Sophia graced the cover of the illustrated Frauen Zeitung *of September 1880.*

In the fall of 1877 Sophia and Andromache lived alone in Paris. Heinrich, visiting museums throughout Europe, frequently forgot to send them money for living expenses.

(GERMAN ARCHAEOLOGICAL INSTITUTE, ATHENS)

At Orchomenus Sophia and her crew discovered one room in the Treasury of the Minyas on November 23, 1880.

Treasury's ceiling decoration of rosettes and spirals was revealed after Schliemanns had the broken ceiling slabs pieced together.

(CHARLES WEBER)

Coin commemorating Battle of Marathon was indirectly responsible for Heinrich exploding Greek legend. He excavated Mound of the Dead in February 1884 and found no skeletons of the 192 Athenian warriors supposedly buried there.

(GENNADIUS LIBRARY, ATHENS)

The great arched-vault passageway at Tiryns was uncovered by Dörpfeld and Schliemann in March 1884.

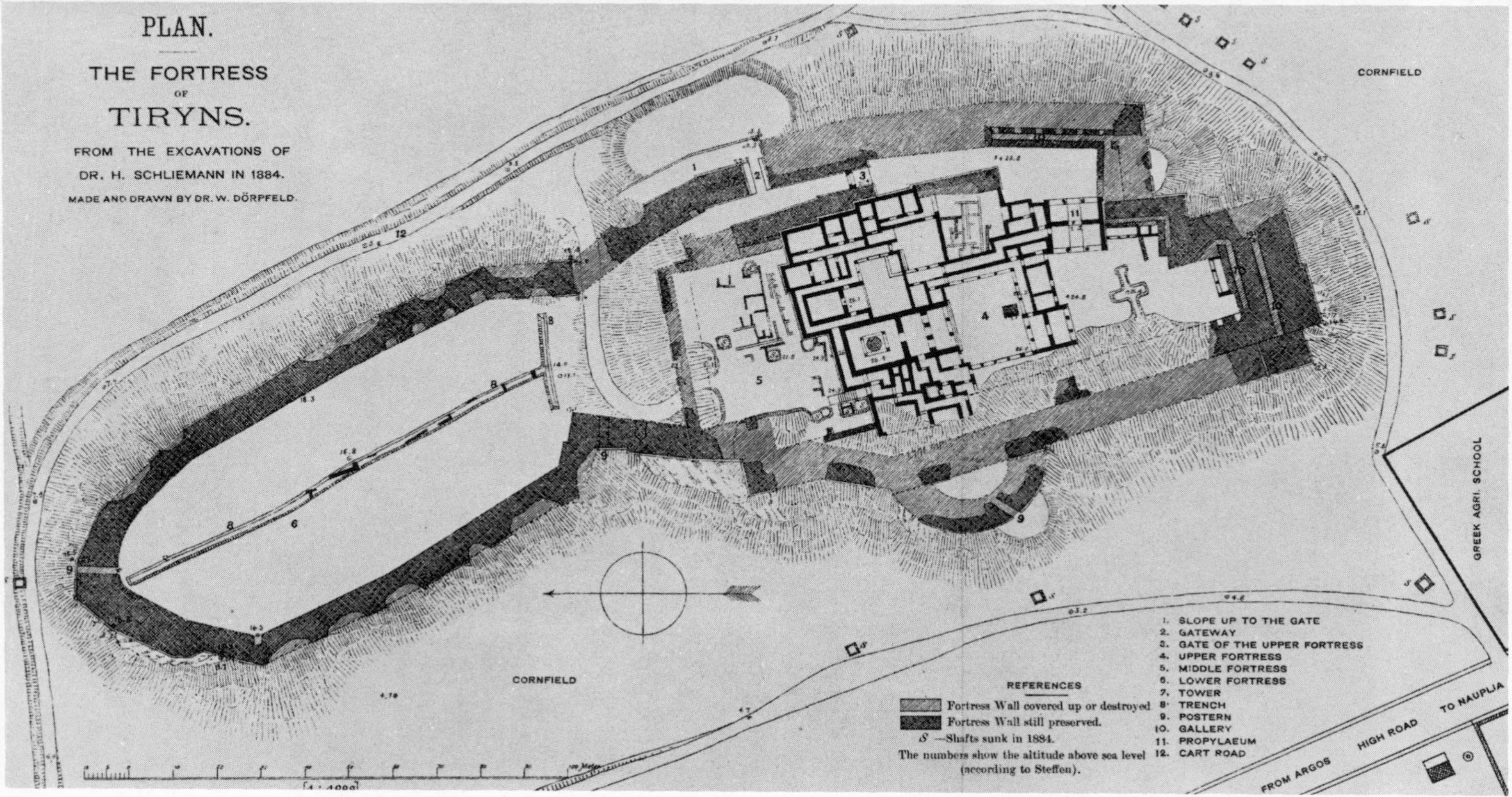

(GENNADIUS LIBRARY, ATHENS)

Plan of the Fortress of Tiryns drawn by Dr. Wilhelm Dörpfeld. Light-shaded sections are parts of Fortress wall that are covered up or destroyed; dark-shaded sections are the parts that are still preserved.

(ILLUSTRATED LONDON NEWS)

Exterior of Schliemanns' Athens home Iliou Mélathron. When Greek officials objected to naked statues on roof, Heinrich mocked them by clothing the statues in garish costumes.

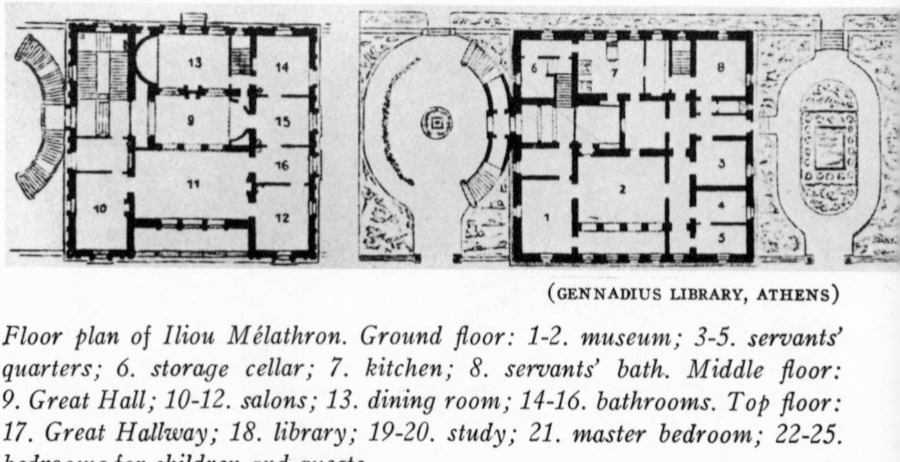

(GENNADIUS LIBRARY, ATHENS)

Floor plan of Iliou Mélathron. Ground floor: 1-2. museum; 3-5. servants' quarters; 6. storage cellar; 7. kitchen; 8. servants' bath. Middle floor: 9. Great Hall; 10-12. salons; 13. dining room; 14-16. bathrooms. Top floor: 17. Great Hallway; 18. library; 19-20. study; 21. master bedroom; 22-25. bedrooms for children and guests.

(NIKOS KONTOS, ATHENS)

A passage from the comic poet Eubulus was painted on the wall of Iliou Mélathron's bathroom. It can be translated in the bawdy language loved by the earthy comic playwrights and poets of Greece. A toned-down translation follows:

Next, Thebes I came to, where they dine all night
And day as well, and every house in sight
Boasts its own privy—to full a man a boon
As great as any known beneath the moon;
For he that wants to and has far to run
Biting his lipps and groaning—he's some fun.

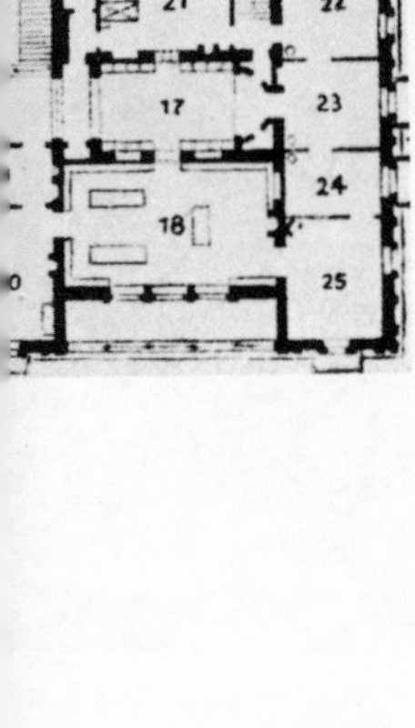

On staircase landing leading to roof is inscription from Hesiod's Works and Days: *"But they who give straight judgments to strangers and to the men of the land, and go not aside from what is just, their city flourishes, and the people prosper in it: Peace, the nurse of children, is abroad in their land, and all-seeing Zeus never decrees cruel war against them. Neither famine nor disaster ever haunts men who do true justice; but lightheartedly they tend the fields which are all their care."*

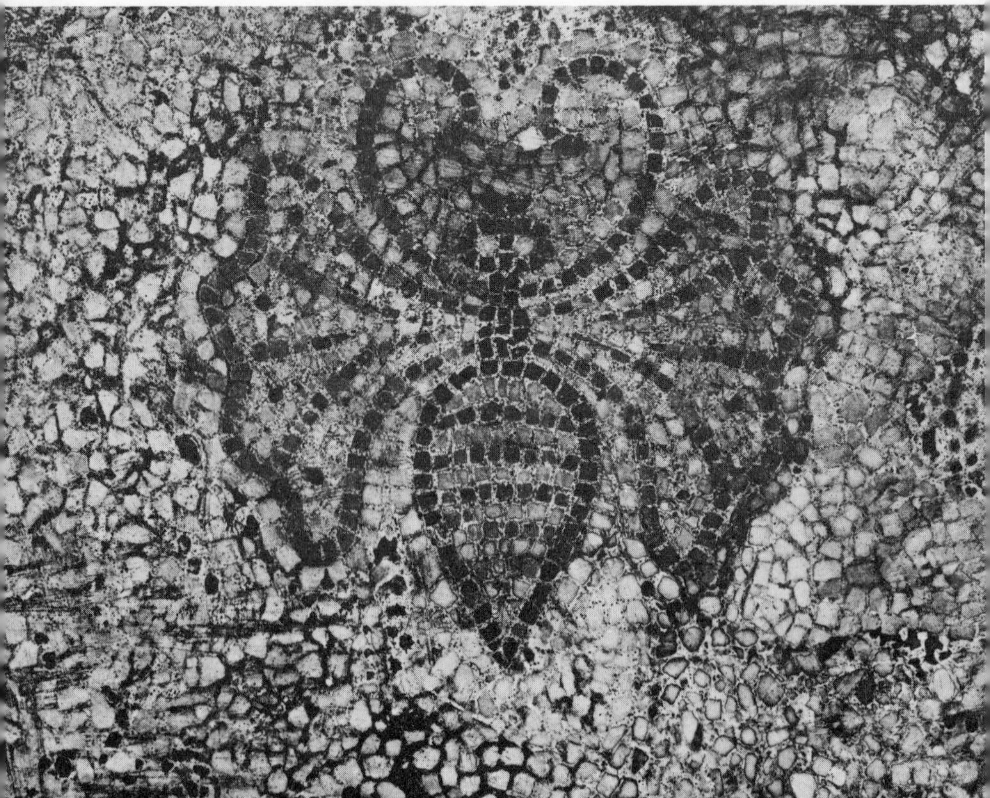

(NIKOS KONTOS & IASON ANTONIADES, ATHENS)

Sample of intricate mosaic floors throughout Iliou Mélathron, which took Italian artisans more than a year to complete.

ΟΙ ΔΕ ΔΙΚΑΣ ΞΕΙΝΟΙΣΙ ΚΑΙ ΕΝΔΗΜΟΙΣΙ ΔΙΔΟΥΣΙΝ
ΙΘΕΙΑΣ ΚΑΙ ΜΗ ΤΙ ΠΑΡΕΚΒΑΙΝΟΥΣΙ ΔΙΚΑΙΟΥ
ΤΟΙΣΙ ΤΕΘΗΛΕ ΠΟΛΙΣ ΛΑΟΙ Δ ΑΝΘΕΥΣΙΝ ΕΝ ΑΥΤΗ
ΕΙΡΗΝΗ Δ ΑΝΑ ΓΗΝ ΚΟΥΡΟΤΡΟΦΟΣ ΟΥΔΕ ΠΟΤ ΑΥΤΟΙΣ
ΑΡΓΑΛΕΟΝ ΠΟΛΕΜΟΝ ΤΕΚΜΑΙΡΕΤΑΙ ΕΥΡΥΟΠΑ ΖΕΥΣ
ΟΥΔΕ ΠΟΤ ΙΘΥΔΙΚΗΙΣΙ ΜΕΤ ΑΝΔΡΑΣΙ ΛΙΜΟΣ ΟΠΗΔΕΙ
ΟΥΔ ΑΤΗ ΘΑΛΙΗΙΣ ΔΕ ΜΕΜΗΛΟΤΑ ΕΡΓΑ ΝΕΜΟΝΤΑΙ

(NIKOS KONTOS & IASON ANTONIADES, ATHENS)

At Dörpfeld's suggestion, Schliemann invited four men who doubted his discoveries to a conference at Troy. From left: Unknown workman; Professor Niemann, head of Academy of Fine Arts, Vienna; Ernst Boetticher, an especially vehement critic; Schliemann (seated); Dörpfeld; Major Steffen, famous for his maps and plans of Mycenae; O. Hamby Bey, director of Imperial Museum at Constantinople.

Double bronze gates leading to garden were decorated with winged figures and the svastika *(left side) and* sauvastika *(right side), symbols found on Trojan antiquities.*

(LYNN POOLE)

(COURTESY: ALEX L. MÉLAS)

Steffen, in deerstalker cap, discusses excavations with Heinrich. Three of the four guests at 1889 conference were convinced of the veracity of Schliemann's finds at Hissarlik. Only Ernst Boetticher refused to capitulate.

(GERMAN ARCHAEOLOGICAL INSTITUTE, ATHENS)

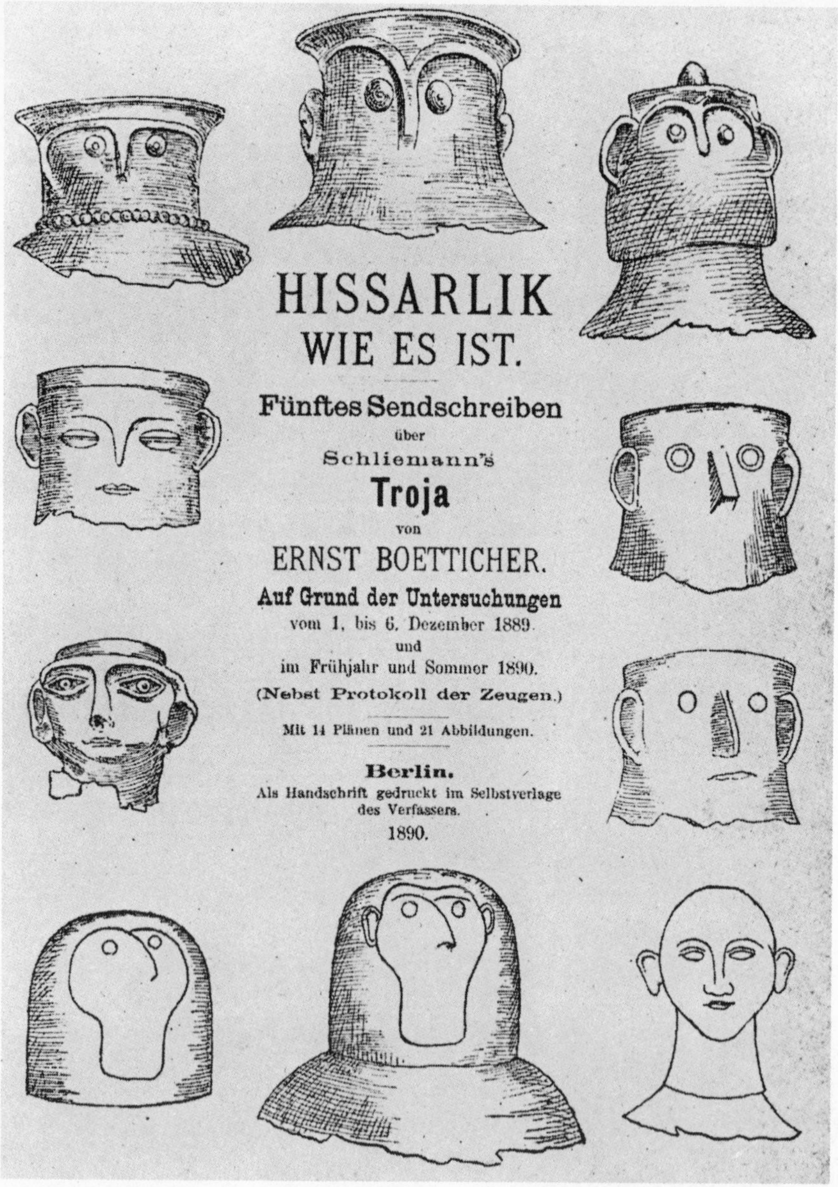

HISSARLIK
WIE ES IST.

Fünftes Sendschreiben
über
Schliemann's
Troja
von
ERNST BOETTICHER.
Auf Grund der Untersuchungen
vom 1. bis 6. Dezember 1889
und
im Frühjahr und Sommer 1890.
(Nebst Protokoll der Zeugen.)

Mit 14 Plänen und 21 Abbildungen.

Berlin.
Als Handschrift gedruckt im Selbstverlage
des Verfassers.
1890.

(LIBRARY OF CONGRESS)

Back in Berlin, Boetticher published Hissarlik Wie Es Ist *(title page shown here) attacking Schliemann's personal honesty and professional integrity.*

(GERMAN ARCHAEOLOGICAL INSTITUTE, ATHENS)

Further digging went on at Troy in 1890, with special tracks for trundle cars to haul away debris. By mid-May Schliemann, suffering from severe ear pains, was forced to leave Troy to see a doctor in Constantinople.

(GERMAN ARCHAEOLOGICAL INSTITUTE, ATHENS)

View of excavations at Hissarlik looking out across Trojan Plain. In center, standing to right of surveying instrument, is Wilhelm Dörpfeld.

(COURTESY: ALEX L. MÉLAS)

Last photo of ailing Schliemann was taken at Troy in 1890. The always dapper Heinrich sported white helmet, new white vest, and walking stick.

TWENTY-NINE

After Heinrich's travels without Sophia, during 1887 and 1888, he hoped to spend more time at Iliou Mélathron, living a quiet family life while writing and studying. The peaceful existence to which he looked forward was not realized because a few detractors continued to harass him and Sophia. A less dynamic and determined man and a less devoted and dominant wife would have been crushed by the bitter attacks. Those issued especially from German pedants, and particularly Ernst Boetticher, the former German Army captain, who still contended that Bunarbashi was the site of ancient Troy and accused the Schliemanns of deceit at every excavation.

Boetticher accelerated his headline-seeking attacks on Heinrich's purpose, methods, interpretations, even on his personal honesty and professional integrity. In one of many vicious pronouncements, Boetticher accused Schliemann of forging finds by burying objects and then digging them up as new discoveries. That offensive charge so angered Dörpfeld that he suggested to Schliemann that Boetticher be invited to Troy. Dörpfeld reasoned that if Boetticher, as principal guest at a scholarly conference, saw the remains of the Trojan civilization he might ". . . have the decency to admit his errors and withdraw his daily attacks."

Approving Dörpfeld's idea, Schliemann reluctantly prepared to leave Athens where he had wanted to stay. He arranged for the conference and paid the expenses of those who were invited: Professor Niemann, head of the Academy of Fine Arts in Vienna; Major Steffen, famous for his maps and plans of Mycenae; O. Hamby Bey, director of the Imperial Museum at Constantinople; and Boetticher. After studying the entire excavation at Troy, all were convinced of the veracity and fidelity of Schliemann—except Boetticher. He refused to do more than withdraw his imputation of bad faith.

Boetticher rushed off to Berlin and renewed his attacks on

Schliemann, even implying that Curtius, Müller and other reputable scholars had been paid in gold for defending Schliemann. Boetticher made it known he was going to publish a book that would negate everything that Schliemann, Dörpfeld, Virchow, and their colleagues had said they had achieved. The former army captain said that what he saw at Troy convinced him more than ever that Hissarlik had only been an ancient funeral pyre and that, as he had always held, Bunarbashi was the site of *Novum Ilium*. He made no defense for never having dug there to try to substantiate his conviction.

Before the publication of Boetticher's book, an article about his libelous attacks on Schliemann was printed in Berlin's *Vossiche Zeitung*. The author, Richard Engelmann, proved how Boetticher twisted and deliberately misinterpreted facts to use against Schliemann. Boetticher again and again accused Schliemann of having buried his finds. An amateur archaeologist of no professional standing, Boetticher attracted attention to himself by repeated public condemnations of Schliemann, a man of world renown. Engelmann stressed the change of Schliemann's procedure, stabilized by his association with Dörpfeld, and the willingness of Schliemann to admit early mistakes, attributable in part to lack of precise methods of investigation. Pointing out that gratitude was due Schliemann, Engelmann continued: "If it is possible nowadays to give an account of the art which existed during Homer's time and even before that in Greece, if we can clearly visualize the rooms in which Homer's heroes lived and acted, to whom do we owe this but Schliemann? . . . Who else dared to devote his entire life and fortune so fully to an ideal? No one. Cannot a mortal be allowed mistakes, especially one of high genius so wrapped in an ideal? The Bible provides the positive answer."

Schliemann has as faithful adherents: Dörpfeld, Virchow, Mahaffy, Gladstone and Burnouf; and as converts: Ernst Curtius of Germany and A. L. Simpson, the British archaeologist. The latter had been one of the few opponents to Schliemann in England. Curtius, in his opposition, had at least been a gentleman. When he wholeheartedly accepted Schliemann's major theories, he called on Sophia at Iliou Mélathron, leaving a letter of genuine apology for the absent Heinrich.

Simpson made a statement that might have been written by

any of a number of scholars: "Dr. Schliemann and his faithful wife have without doubt created a new approach to the study of archaeology and have fired students to face facts never before encountered. Never again will the world of archaeology be as it has been. For this the world must always recognize this intrepid pair as the founders of a new science. We may disagree with them in various details, but we cannot in good faith disagree with the principle of what they have so unselfishly presented to future generations."

Although buoyed by the support of his peers, Schliemann, in 1890, at the age of 68, was increasingly weary and ill. He did zestfully record new finds, and proudly stated that his visitors' book was bulging with names of eminent travelers who passed through Troy to see for themselves what Schliemann had accomplished, and was then doing. But his diary of that spring season contained many pitiful passages in shaky handwriting. He complained of fatigue, heat, and thirst, and expressed a fear of venturing far from the digs that prevented him from going to the Hellespont to swim. On May 5 he wrote: "I am deaf, according to the doctors." Four times a day he took water through his nose, a treatment that seemed to clear his ears a little. On the advice of a doctor, he also put cotton dipped in sea water into his ears.

In mid-May Schliemann was forced by intolerable pain to go to Constantinople, where a Dr. von Mellinger said there were four loose bones in Schliemann's left ear, two in his right. The doctor advised immediate surgery, but Schliemann explained that he was too busy at Hissarlik to take the time for an operation. After a second visit to von Mellinger, Schliemann returned to Hissarlik and continued to dig, finding on May 22 a finely carved head that he identified as a portrait of the Roman Emperor Caligula.

Throughout the trying spring Sophia wrote love letters to Heinrich, expressing her concern for him, and frequently suggesting that she travel to Troy with Andro and Memeko. Heinrich answered that he did not want the family there because of the terrible heat and the blowing sand that almost obscured the sun. Sophia could not bear the separation, and arrived at Hissarlik with the children on June 10. Although weak from her usual abdominal trouble, she worked with Heinrich at the digs every day. At night, the Schliemanns made plans to return for further explorations later that year. Dörpfeld, who was to stay on at Troy until August, frequently joined Sophia and Heinrich for coffee, and contributed to the future planning. Dörpfeld and Sophia both realized that Schliemann was a sick man, and she diplomatically induced Heinrich himself to suggest a return to Athens. They reached there the end of June.

Heinrich, working feverishly throughout the summer of 1890, supervised the editing of new publications, planned for future excavations, and answered mail carried by a postman who literally staggered under its weight. In October, Schliemann was forced to curtail his activities because of increasing deafness and agonizing pain in both ears.

Reluctantly, he at last agreed to take Virchow's advice, and prepared to go to the Schwartz Clinic at Halle, Germany, for surgery. Assuring the distraught Sophia that the ear operation would be minor, Heinrich refused to allow her to accompany him. In the days before his departure in November, the dichotomy and prescience of his nature surfaced. He insisted that his cure would be quick and complete. But he made a new will, spent days going over his investments with Dentopoulos, and wrote numerous letters about financial holdings in eleven countries. While packing, he surveyed his extensive wardrobe and wondered aloud to Sophia who would wear the clothes after he was gone. His actions and attitude were not those of a man sanguine about the outcome of medical treatment.

From Halle, Heinrich wrote to Sophia that on November 4 he had been examined by Dr. Wagner, assistant to Professor Schwartz, who was away. On November 12, Schliemann, lying on a rough wooden operating table, inhaled chloroform and went quietly to sleep. When he came to, three hours later, the floating bones in each ear had been removed. Ignoring postoperative pain, Heinrich reread the *Arabian Nights* in Arabic, and wrote about forthcoming books to his Leipzig publisher, Brockhaus. Yet Schliemann, because of almost unbearable pain, refused to see Virchow, who had traveled from Berlin to Halle for the specific purpose of seeing Heinrich. Dörpfeld and Virchow called at the hospital on November 19 and were turned away; Schliemann sent word by the nurse that Dörpfeld should go to Leipzig to confer with Brockhaus.

When Schliemann's doctors said he must be hospitalized for at least a month, his temper rose like blood pressure; quieted by strong sedatives, he relaxed, sleeping long and reading little. His waking hours were spent writing long letters to Sophia, sending tender expressions of love for her and their two children, and always raging against his confinement, and the stultifying life in the hospital.

Sophia's daily letters to him expressed her deepest love, her concern for his welfare, and the constant reiteration of her wish to be with him. That wish he would not grant. In each letter Sophia told of new praise printed about Heinrich, related some amusing anecdote about the children, and reported on plans for his homecoming. She anticipated the time when ". . . you will be restored to health and enjoy the gaiety of the household during the holidays."

Virchow and Dörpfeld carried out Schliemann's request to supervise the printing of an article he had written while at Halle, awaiting the operation. In a letter assuring Heinrich that publication was arranged, Virchow wrote: "Max Mueller writes me that he has returned from a meeting of archaeologists and philologists in London . . . and your joy will soar when I report the great honor paid you. My dear friend, you have done that which you swore to do as a boy in Ankershagen, and today the greater percentage of scholars pay tribute to you."

By December 10 pain in one of Schliemann's ears had subsided; in the other it prodded him with continuous severity. But unable to stand "this hospital which is a jail," he left against his doctor's orders. Free at last, Heinrich went directly to Leipzig to see Brockhaus and two scholarly friends, Kraft and Wachsmuth. After a joyous reunion in Berlin with Virchow, Dörpfeld, and Hans Müller, on winter holiday from Oxford, Schliemann visited his collection at the Museum and sent to Greece for additional objects. Elated by the visits and emotionally stimulated, he later wrote to Virchow, "Long live Pallas Athena!" and assured him that their next journey together should be to the Canary Islands. By letter he made plans with Dörpfeld for new excavations, drawing up lists of equipment needed, and advising about what permits should be secured.

Schliemann arrived in Paris on a December morning when the temperature was below freezing, the sky ominously gray, and the atmosphere damp. From his hotel, he took a cab directly to Place St. Michel and aimlessly wandered there. Five times he started to enter the house at Number 6, and five times he turned away, writing later to Sophia that he could not stand to go alone into the house "where we began our marriage, endured stormy times and found the bliss of emotional and physical love." As he had so frequently in the past, he assured Sophia that he would be at home for the Christmas holidays, and reminded her to send invitations to the annual New Year's Ball at Iliou Mélathron.

In spite of Schliemann's physical and emotional pain, his internal and external conflict, he attended to business matters, called on friends, and visited museums and libraries, searching for fresh approaches to archaeological problems yet unsolved.

Paris and Parisians were in holiday spirits. No one in the jostling crowds noticed the mustached elderly man, shrunken in his expensive clothes, who swung a walking stick without verve or assurance as, lonely, he ambled from place to place. Alone and carrying one small valise, Heinrich took his place in a drafty compartment on a train headed for Naples. Tense and tortured, he sat with his greatcoat pulled up around his neck. Stabs of pain from his ear shot through his body, and he did not know whether he shook from cold or pain. With the wheels clicking and clattering below him, he wondered if he had been wrong to refuse Sophia's pleas to return directly to Athens.

Wrong? How could he have been wrong when in Naples he would see ancient objects he had never studied; would learn facts that might prove of great value in the next excavations. Naples, with its sun and warm air and ebullient atmosphere, beckoned. Things would be better when he reached the South.

But Schliemann was mistaken. Naples was wrapped in the mantle of an unusually gloomy winter. Heinrich stepped from his railroad car, gave orders to porters in flawless Italian and, shivering, walked down the platform to a carriage. After checking into a luxurious but chilly suite at the Grande Hotel, Schliemann went for a walk, confident that the exercise would stimulate his system and relieve his pain. The pain, however, instead of subsiding, increased; and he returned to the hotel and summoned a doctor who, unfortunately for Schliemann, had a great interest in antiquities. The man listened briefly to Schliemann's account of his operations at Halle, and then switched to a more fascinating subject: Schliemann's archaeological investigations. The doctor suggested that together they go out to Pompeii to look at recent excavations and, excited by the conversation, Schliemann agreed, joining the physician in a foolhardy jaunt.

On his return from Pompeii, Schliemann sank into a deep sleep from which he awakened in torture, pain wracking his ear and his whole upper body. He knew that he dared not leave for Greece, and at 11:15 A.M. on December 22 he wired Sophia that he could not leave Italy then, but would arrive in Athens on Saturday afternoon. At 10:30 A.M. on the 23rd he sent another message, informing Sophia that he was still unable to travel but would be in Athens by Tuesday.

With Heinrich ill and absent, Christmas at Iliou Mélathron was a dismal day that Sophia did her best to make jolly for Andro and Memeko. In Naples, shortly before noon, Heinrich dressed for a walk to the home of his doctor, a destination he was never to reach.

Schliemann was destined to play out a scene as tragic as any written by Sophocles and Euripides. Tired and trembling, pain-wracked and afraid, Heinrich started to cross the Piazza Santa Carita, and collapsed. Passers-by stopped. Policemen were called. An ambulance took the unconscious Schliemann to a hospital, which refused admittance to a penniless man, whose pockets contained neither money nor identification. Without pity for one so seriously ill, the hospital authorities sent him to a police station. Revived, but unable to speak, Schliemann rolled his head from side to side in agony. Finally a policeman found in Heinrich's pocket a slip of paper on which was scribbled the address of his doctor. From him, Neapolitan police officials were amazed to learn the identity of the illustrious man. Schliemann was immediately returned to his hotel suite.

Under sedatives, Heinrich passed Christmas night in semi-consciousness, paralyzed and speechless. Dawn broke through scattered clouds on December 26. Heinrich Schliemann, the parson's son whose birth was attended by a village midwife, was surrounded by eight famous Italian doctors. After examining the patient, the doctors withdrew for a consultation about the advisability of surgery.

When they returned to the suite, Heinrich Schliemann was dead.

The tragic tidings stunned Sophia. For a moment she was incapable of thought or action. Then calling on her inner reserves of strength, she sent word to Naples that Schliemann's body should be placed in a lead casket. Dörpfeld and Sophia's brother Yiango were dispatched to Naples to accompany the body back to Athens.

The ship bearing Heinrich's corpse put into the Piraeus, and Sophia, alone, met the small boat that brought the casket ashore. She willed it that way, refusing King George's offer to send an honor guard to the port. The lead coffin was lifted onto a carriage, and Sophia stepped into another in which she followed the coffin of her husband. As the two carriages halted in front of Iliou Mélathron, members of the family, servants, government officials, and friends surged forward. The casket, borne on the shoulders of men who cried unashamedly, was carried through the two bronze gates bearing the signs of the *sauvastika* and the *svastika*. With measured tread, the bearers ascended the sweeping outer stairway, went through the wide doors, passing under the mural of Phoebus Apollo, the rising sun god ready to bring light to a new day, and on into the Great Hall of Iliou Mélathron. There the coffin was placed on a prepared bier; a Greek flag was draped over the coffin and a pedestal topped by a bust of Homer was placed at its head.

Telegrams of condolence, sent by royalty, scholars and friends, poured in from around the world. One of the first was from Kaiser Wilhelm II.

MY SINCEREST CONDOLENCES FOR YOUR HEAVY LOSS MAY THE GENERAL PARTICIPATION TO YOUR GRIEF, AS WELL AS THE ADMIRATION AND VENERATION WHICH YOUR DECEASED HUSBAND HAD SECURED FOR HIMSELF AS RESEARCHER AND ALSO AS A MAN FOR THE WORLD OF OUR AGE AND FOR POSTERITY, BE SOMEWHAT OF A CONSOLATION

Signed: WILHELM
KAISER WILHELM OF GERMANY
BERLIN SCHLOSS

The casket in the Great Hall was guarded by Evzones, the King's guards, and people streamed past it to pay their last respects to Heinrich Schliemann. Among the first to call at the house of mourning were King George I of Greece and Crown Prince Constantine.

A simple notice written by Sophia and published in Athenian

newspapers announced Schliemann's death and the plans for his funeral on Sunday, January 4, 1891. As night fell on January 3, King George and Prince Constantine returned to Iliou Mélathron and there stood silent watch throughout the night. Early on January 4, Sophia joined the King and the Crown Prince at the bier. Recollection of the joys and sorrows shared with her beloved husband crowded her mind as she reviewed the turbulent twenty-one years of their marriage.

The King had decreed that Schliemann should be given the full honors of a state burial. The funeral, held at Iliou Mélathron, began midmorning when the Protestant Chaplain to the Royal Household arrived with the aging Archbishop Vimbos. The Great Hall, the salons and stairways were filled with mourners as the Chaplain intoned the short service. The coffin could hardly be seen for flowers, and on top was Heinrich's copy of the *Iliad,* torn and frayed from his repeated readings of Homer's epic. Sophia stood throughout the service, tightly gripping the hands of Andromache and Agamemnon.

As the last words of the service died away, the sobs of mourners crescendoed. The casket was carried down to a gun carriage waiting in front of Iliou Mélathron. Queen Olga, a devout Greek Orthodox communicant, did not attend the funeral; but after Sophia and the children were handed into a black carriage, King George and Prince Constantine fell in behind the Evzone honor guard that surrounded the caisson drawn by eight black horses. The funeral procession, moving down University Street, passed the Royal Palace where a lone figure stood on the balcony. Queen Olga, looking over the heads of the thousands crowding the dirgeful route, mingled her tears with those of others gathered to pay belated homage to the man who had brought such fame to Greece.

At the cemetery, Sophia and her two children accompanied the casket into the templed mausoleum, which Heinrich had placed on the high spot with the unobstructed view of the blue Aegean. Sophia stood in the shadowy mausoleum while the casket was put in place; then everyone retired, leaving her alone. Ten minutes later she emerged into the sunshine and watched the closing of the giant bronze doors.

She looked up at the tomb's pediment and at the lower frieze which, encircling the mausoleum, depicted Heinrich and her with

Yannakis and workmen, digging at Troy. The weeping of others ceased when they heard her clear voice speak:

"Helen rose third leading the lament:
Oh Hector, most dear of all my stalwart brothers, and most close to my heart! Truly my husband is the royal Alexandros who fled me to Honored Troy, yet would I had died before this. Twenty years have come and gone since I left mine homeland for Troy, yet while here none among you has said an unkind and cruel word to me. If others spoke harshly of me, a sister or brother among you, or even a brother's wife, or your mother; fair indeed was your father to me as though my own; you challenged them, silenced them, with your loving spirit and loving words. For this I weep for you all and we together weep for my sorrowing self. Throughout all Troy there is no one good and kind; instead they revile me. Dawn on the following day showed her rosy fingers through the clouds, and Trojans circled round the funeral pyre of great Hector. At first they quenched the flame with their wine where flames still burned. Next, Hector's brothers and dearest friends brushed together his white-ash bones, while tears of sorrow wet their cheeks. Placing his remains in a golden casket, wrapping it in fine purple cloth, they put the casket in a grave and piled heavy stones atop the grave. Swiftly they formed the marked-place as guards stood alert lest the Achaeans attack without warning. This accomplished, mourners returned to the city . . . the Palace of their King, Priam. That was the funeral of Hector."

Full twenty years had passed since the young Sophia had recited those lines for Dr. Heinrich Schliemann, the stranger who had visited the Arsakeion School to observe her. On the day of the funeral, Sophia omitted only "and all in family and of friends partook of a great feast in" the second from the last line of the passage.

The whole funeral assemblage did return to Heinrich's palace, where Sophia, stepping from her carriage, looked down the street toward The Arsakeion. Then, thanking the King and the Crown Prince, and others who stood silently by, she took Andromache and Agamemnon by the hand. The three mounted the sweeping stairs and passed through the open doors, disappearing into Iliou Mélathron.

(GERMAN ARCHAEOLOGICAL INSTITUTE, ATHENS)

In 1894 Sophia (seated) and daughter, Andromache S. Mélas, visited theater at Troy. Wilhelm Dörpfeld (left) continued excavations, which were financed by Sophia.

Left: Sophia with nine-year-old Andromache and two-year-old Agamemnon in 1880. Above: Andromache Schliemann (standing), now grown up, with a friend. Below: Leon Mélas, Andromache's husband, with their three sons: left, Alex; center, Michel, the oldest; right, Leandros, the youngest.

(COURTESY: ALEX L. MÉLAS)

(LYNN POOLE)

Mausoleum planned by Schliemann to house Sophia and himself after death. Sophia commissioned portrait bust of Heinrich (left). Above: Frieze, which encircles building, shows Schliemanns, Yannakis, and workmen digging at Troy.

(LYNN POOLE)

(COURTESY: ALEX L. MÉLAS)

Agamemnon Schliemann, who became a successful businessman and financier, lived in the house at 6, Place St. Michel, Paris. Here he visits his mother at Phaleron, where she spent her later years.

(COURTESY: ALEX L. MÉLAS)

Sophia Schliemann as she looked in 1900, age forty-eight, wearing the pearls bought for her in 1880 by her husband. She was active until a few days before her death in 1932.

EPILOGUE

When Heinrich died, Sophia was thirty-eight years old. She was an experienced archaeologist; an executive of considerable ability; a gracious woman of intelligence, charm and wit. After her husband's death, she alone supported the work of Wilhelm Dörpfeld at Troy for four years, until the German government arranged to share the financial burden.

Traveling widely, Sophia kept in touch with old friends on the Continent and made new ones. When she was in residence at Iliou Mélathron, she received scholars, notable private citizens, and statesmen. Ideas for many creative projects were fomented in her salon. She personally originated plans for Greek orphanages, and initiated the establishment of tubercular sanatoriums, directing the building and operation of those institutions. Her generous donations, made possible by the fortune left her by Heinrich, helped to build and support Soteria, a hospital and research center for the treatment and study of tuberculosis; and Sophia was frequently there, visiting patients and consulting with staff members.

Sophia was a devoted mother to Andromache and Agamemnon. He was reared in Athens and capitals in Europe, and resided in Paris for most of his adult life at 6, Place St. Michel. Like his father, he had an unfortunate first marriage that ended in divorce. His second marriage was happy but childless. Having inherited his father's business acumen, Agamemnon amassed a fortune, and died wealthy in Paris, where he was buried in the cemetery Père Lachaise.

In October 1892, Andromache married Leon Mélas, namesake and young relative of the man who had taken Heinrich to see Sophia at The Arsakeion. Their wedding was the most fashionable social event of the season. Andromache's handsome and eminent husband followed his family's tradition as devoted patriot to Hellas through years of stormy internal and external strife.

Widowed at an early age, Andromache Mélas raised three sons, Michel, Alex and Leandros, distinguished men who served Greece as foreign diplomats, military officers and government officials. The only living grandson of Heinrich and Sophia Schliemann is General Alex Mélas, who sat in the Chamber of Deputies as elected representative, and fought with gallantry in five wars, giving of himself and his fortune to his country.

One of Sophia's devoted friends and a supporter of many of her charitable projects was Eleutherios Venizelos, the modern Pericles of Greece, champion of democracy who was many times Premier. Venizelos Street is the second name of University Street on which Iliou Mélathron, now a law court, faces. Sophia Schliemann lived at Iliou Mélathron until 1927 when she moved into a small house that she built for herself near the sea at Phaleron.

As Sophia grew older, she suffered from heart trouble, and in vain her doctors tried to make her curtail activities; she would promise that some journey for charity would be her last, and then, soon after, would go on another. Dr. Sakkorafos, a professor of medicine with whom Sophia had consulted about various hospitals and orphanages, had her assurance that a 1932 trip to the Peloponnesus would be her final one. And it was.

She set out to find a suitable location for a new sanatorium, and returned home full of enthusiasm for the ideal site that she had discovered high in the mountains of the Peloponnesus. Only a night or two after, she wakened in distress, sharp pains shooting through her chest. Dr. Sakkorafos, called at three o'clock on a bitter cold morning, drove from Athens to Phaleron, and without even examining Sophia, told Andromache that her mother could not live long.

The indomitable Sophia battled for life for thirteen days. While she lay ill, prominent Greeks asked for hourly bulletins on her condition; telegrams from around the world expressed concern and consolation. Poor people, who had known Sophia's charity and love, gathered at Phaleron and stood outside the home of the great lady for whom they prayed.

Sophia Engastromenos Schliemann, like her husband Heinrich, had a state funeral. Thousands of people, rich and poor, unknown and famous, filed past her coffin that was covered with the white-and-blue flag of Greece. Many of those who paid their last respects to Sophia placed sheaves of flowers beside her coffin and knelt at the church altar, their tears flowing unchecked.

Premier Venizelos, on foot, followed Sophia Schliemann's bier from the Metropolitan Cathedral in Athens to the cemetery, where her coffin was placed in the mausoleum beside that of Henry, her husband, friend, colleague and lover.

> Sing through me, O Muse, and through me relate the story
> of that man skilled in methods of contending,
> the wanderer, plagued over the years,
> after he plunged through the fastness
> on the proud Hill of Troy.
>
> *Odyssey,* Book I, lines 1–5

APPENDIX A

The address given by Madame Schliemann for a special meeting held in her honor by The Royal Archaeological Institute of Great Britain and Ireland, June 8, 1877, and printed in Volume XXXIV of the *Archaeological Journal* of 1877.

A very large and brilliant company assembled this day, under the presidency of Lord Talbot de Malahide, to receive Mrs. Schliemann. Among those present were the Duke of Argyle, Lord Houghton, the Right Hon. W. E. Gladstone, M.P., the Very Rev. Dr. Hieronymus Myriantheus (Archimandrite of the Greek Community), M. Gennadius (Greek *Chargé d'Affaires*), Dr. Schliemann, Lady Alcock, the Hon. M. Mostyn, C. T. Newton, Esq., C.B., Robert Browning, Esq., Sir J. D. Scott, Bart., J. Bonomi, Esq., Sir W. H. Drake, K.C.B., Professor Donaldson, M. Karl Blind, Baron Julius Reuter, Rear-Admiral Spratt, Dr. Birch, E. Oldfield, Esq., the Rev. J. Fuller Russell, C.D.E. Fortnum, Esq., M. Ralli, E. J. Reed, Esq., M.P., S. Tucker, Esq., *Rouge Croix,* M. Lascaridi, Dr. L. Schmidt, J. Murray, Esq., A. H. Grant, Esq., Miss Amelia B. Edwards, the Rev. H. J. Bigge, J. Thorne, Esq., &c. His Excellency the Turkish Ambassador was prevented from being present by a previous engagement.

The noble CHAIRMAN introduced Mrs. Schliemann to the meeting in a few happy words of welcome, and presented her with a bouquet of flowers, representing the Greek national colours.

Mrs. SCHLIEMANN then read the following paper:—"On the High culture of the Ancient Greeks; the Long Series of Agents which contributed to it; the reason of its Decay; of the Advantages of the Language of Plato; and further, of the Share she had taken in the Discoveries at Troy and Mycenæ,"

"At a time when the rest of the world was still living in barbarism's dark night, my ancestors, the ancient Greeks, had in science and arts reached such a pitch of perfection as can never be surpassed by man.

Of the hundred thousands of master-pieces of sculpture which once ornamented the public edifices, the Agoras, and the streets of our ancient cities, only a few have escaped the pious zeal of the early Christians, or the ignorance of the barbarians, who turned them into lime, and those few now adorn the modern museums as precious relics of Greece's past glory, and as mournful monuments of the fragility of human things.

Our political institutions, our statesmen, our orators, our philosophers, and our poets have in all posterior ages been objects of wonder and admiration to the world at large; they have for thousands of years been the ideals of perfection to all those who aspired to a high culture; in fact, so much so, that even at the present day no one is considered to have a high education unless he be thoroughly acquainted with them. But, alas! Greek books have had a like fate as Greek works of art, and I make bold to say that not even one-thousandth part of our ancient classics has escaped destruction. But I must not forget that my ancestors have also distinguished themselves by their heroism and military skill, and that our Greek history is full of names such as Agamemnon, Achilles, Diomedes, Ulysses, Aristodemos, Miltiades, Themistocles, Phocion, Pericles, Epaminondas, Philip II, Alexander the Great, whom the mightiest of the mighty and the proudest of the proud warriors of posterior ages took as ideals of military virtue. But with their superior wisdom and all their other great qualities, my ancestors had a great vice, without which they would probably have subjugated the world by their arms, in the same way as they in later ages subjugated it by their genius. That vice was 'envy.' The decay of Greece dates from that unfortunate day, in 413 B.C., when some Athenians, who were envious of Alcibiades' past and coming glory, succeeded in persuading the people to send out a ship to Sicily to fetch him back as prisoner, in order that he might be judged for his irreverence to the gods. Had this not happened, Sicily would in a few weeks have fallen into our hands, because Alcibiades' genius had already captured Catania, and was on the very eve of capturing Messina; and, when once in possession of Sicily, the Athenians would have had no trouble in conquering the whole of Italy, because Rome was at that time still weak and powerless. But it was our ill fate that it should be so. The fragile fingers of men cannot arrest the rotation of destiny's wheel.

The question now arises how it came that, in the midst of nations which lingered in barbarism, Greek genius could lift its head to the heavens. I think that this could only be produced by the combination of a whole series of fortunate circumstances, of which I must first mention our beautiful, sonorous language, the mere sound of which filled my husband with wild enthusiasm at a time when he did not know yet a word of Greek. Further, the quickness and vivacity of the Greek mind, the beautiful sky of Greece, from which the sun shines nearly always the whole day in full brilliancy; in fact, there is no day in the year on which we do not see the sun, there is seldom a night in which the starry heavens cannot be seen in all their splendour. Further the indescribable beauty of the outlines and colours of the Greek mountains; then the marvellous beauty of the sea, studded as it is with magnificent islands, which, by the reverberation of the sun-light, present the appearance as if they were floating; hence the myth of the floating Greek islands. I further mention the infinite number of gods and the firm faith people had in them. But this world of gods could only be engendered in the minds of Greeks and in an atmosphere like that of Greece. Thus the natural enthusiasm of my ancestor for the sublime was stimulated by their beautiful language, by the splendour of the sky by day and night, by the magnificence of the mountains, the sea, the seemingly floating islands, and by the firm belief in the supernatural power and beauty of their gods. But, in spite of all these stimulants, Greek genius could never have reached such a lofty height as can never again be attained by man had it not been for divine Homer, from whom orators and sculptors, statesmen and painters, wise men and poets, freely borrowed their grandest ideas. So, for instance, Phidias, when asked whence he had taken the idea for his Olympian Jupiter, answered with the verses of the "Iliad:"—(I, 528—530.)

"Ἦ, καὶ κυανέῃσιν ἐπ' ὀφρυσι νευσε Κρονὶων'
'Αμβρίσιαι δ' ἄρα χαῖται ἐπερρώσαντο ἄναχτος
Κρατὸς ἀπ' ἀθανάτοιο μέγαν δ' ἐλέλιξεν Ὄλυμπον."

"He said, and nodded with his shadowy brows,
Waved on the immortal head the ambrosial locks,
And all Olympus trembled at his nod."

Alexander the Great never slept without having under his pillow a copy of "Homer," which he called "the store of military virtue." To Dr. Schliemann's and my admiration for Homer are we indebted for the discoveries of Troy and the five royal tombs of Mycenæ with their treasures. The part I have taken in the discoveries is but small, in Troy as well as in Mycenæ. I have only superintended thirty workmen. One of my explorations at Troy was the excavation of the large heroic tomb which, according to Homer, was attributed by the immortal gods to the Amazon Myrine and by men to Baticia, the Queen of Dardanus. In Mycenæ I excavated the large treasury close to the Lions' Gate. This excavation, one of the most difficult works we ever accomplished, lasted four months, and though I found no treasures there, yet this exploration has been of some importance to science, because, besides a number of sculptures, I found there a mass of most interesting pottery, which shows us the remote antiquity in which the treasury was shut up.

I have further taken an active part in the excavation of the five royal tombs in the Acropolis; all of them were rock-cut, and at a depth of from twenty-five to thirty-three feet below the surface of the ground. The flat bottom of these tombs was covered with a layer of pebble stones, which can have had no other intention than that of giving ventilation to the funeral pyres, which were put on it, and on which the dead bodies overladen with jewels were laid. There were in all fifteen bodies in the tombs, and each of them had been burnt on a separate pyre. The fire of the pyres was not yet extinct when the whole of the sepulchres were covered with a thick layer of white clay, and then with another layer of pebble stones, upon which earth was thrown. Above these tombs were erected sepulchral slabs, and, when these had been covered up by, and disappeared in, the dust of ages, other tombstones were erected three or four feet above them. Until the upper layer of pebble stones the excavation was easy, because we had only to direct our workmen to dig here or there; but from thence it was exceedingly difficult, because, on our knees in the mud, my husband and I had to cut out the pebbles, to cut away the layer of clay, and to take out one by one the precious jewels. But the joy we felt in seeing our efforts crowned with such marvellous success made us forget our hardships, and our enthusiasm was so great that we often thought we had breakfasted and dined when we had not got anything at all for the whole day.

We Greeks owe to England an everlasting gratitude, because without the generous assistance of this great country Greece could never have attained her independence. Only lately, again, England has with generous liberality ceded to us the beautiful Ionian Islands. But it is said that gratitude is a lively anticipation of future favours, and so I venture to hope that England will not desert the cause of Greece in the present eventful crisis.

I conclude with an appeal to the English ladies to teach their children the sonorous language of my ancestors, so that they may be enabled to read "Homer" and our other immortal classics in the original. The immense difficulties of our ancient language could be easily overcome by the highly intelligent English children if they first thoroughly learnt our modern Greek language, and afterwards the ancient tongue. Instead of ten years, the children would in this way acquire in less than one year a thorough knowledge of ancient Greek, and they would have the immense advantage of our modern language, which, as a spoken tongue, would make it totally impossible for them ever to forget the language of Plato and Homer. I, therefore, with intense enthusiasm advocate and advise you to get from Greece teachers for all your schools.

I terminate in warmly thanking you for the indulgence with which you have listened to an enthusiast for Homer.

APPENDIX B

When Heinrich Schliemann presented the Treasure of Troy to the German people in 1881, the collection was housed in one of the many buildings comprising the Staatliche Museum. At the ceremony of acceptance, officials, dignitaries, and scholars, in varying phrases, pledged that the Schliemann Collection, well guarded, would remain on view for all time. Unfortunately for posterity, the pledges, made in good faith, were not to be realized. Most of the magnificent Trojan Treasure is missing today.

During World War II, the bulk of the pottery objects was removed for safekeeping to Lebus Castle on the Oder River. Many metal objects and gems were stored under a Berlin museum. Some precious objects, Mycenaean as well as Trojan, were secreted in a German mine. Gold treasures in packing cases were placed in a bunker beneath the Zoological Station in Berlin.

In a late offensive of the war, the Russian army launched an attack in the Oder River region, and Lebus Castle was demolished. Most of the Trojan pottery in the castle was destroyed by military action. Some pieces, salvaged and returned to Berlin, were lost in subsequent bombardment there.

American armed forces gave to the Allied Art Treasure Commission the objects stored in the German mine. Those objects, transported to the central point of collection of German art, are now catalogued and preserved in West Berlin.

When Russian forces took over the East Sector of Berlin, the irreplaceable gold treasure was discovered in the bunker under the Zoological Station. Written instructions ordered that the gold be taken under heavy guard to Moscow, not to the collection center of the Allied Art Treasure Commission.

Here fact ends and supposition must begin. Our research findings lead us to postulate (1) that the gold treasure remains hidden by Russian authorities; (2) that the gold of Troy en route to Moscow was sidetracked by those charged with its safe conduct.

Unknown persons, realizing the monetary worth of the shipment headed for Moscow, may have hidden the gold for future recovery, or may have melted the objects for sale on the profitable postwar black market. Each of the two suppositions has its champions among scholars and government officials of various countries. Which one is true is anybody's guess. If the second conjecture is correct, the mystery probably will be forever unsolved. If the first is right, the Russians may one day place the Trojan gold on exhibition.

On October 11, 1965, we saw twenty-eight minor objects from the Schliemann Collection at the Staatliche Museum in East Berlin. It is expected by the world's art experts that other insignificant objects will turn up one by one because of the expiration of Germany's twenty-year statute of limitations on pilfering of art objects in wartime. Art objects returned to any German museum today are accepted and paid for with no questions asked.

Some optimistic experts entertain the vain hope that important pieces from the Schliemann Collection will be recovered within the next few years. Certainly a substantial return is impossible because great numbers of stored objects were destroyed by bombardment, not only at Lebus Castle but elsewhere.

INDEX

B
Schliemann
Poole
One passion, two loves